MVFOL

Macroeconomics of Self-fulfilling Prophecies

Macroeconomics of Self-fulfilling Prophecies
second edition

Roger E. A. Farmer

The MIT Press
Cambridge, Massachusetts
London, England

This book was set in Times New Roman by Asco Typesetters, Hong Kong.
Printed and bound in the United States of America.

Library of Congress Cataloging-in-Publication Data

Farmer, Roger E. A.
  Macroeconomics of self-fulfilling prophecies / Roger E. A. Farmer. — 2nd ed.
    p.   cm.
  Includes bibliographical references and index.
  ISBN 978-0-262-06203-9 (hc. : alk. paper)
  1. Macroeconomics—Mathematical models. 2. Equilibrium
(Economics)—Mathematical models. I. Title.
HB172.5.F37   1999
339—dc21   98-48432
                                                                      CIP

10 9 8 7 6 5

for Edward Arthur Farmer
1920–1987

No one so much as you
  Loves this my clay
Or would lament as you
    Its dying day
(Edward Thomas, 1917)

Contents

Preface to Second Edition

The first edition of this book was published in 1993. Since that time the research agenda of self-fulfilling prophecies has grown rapidly, and there is now a blossoming literature that studies multiple equilibria and sunspots in calibrated general equilibrium models. The book was written with two ends in mind. First, I wanted to persuade my colleagues that they should treat indeterminacy more seriously as an explanation of macroeconomic phenomena. Second, I wanted to interest graduate students in the topic and to persuade a new generation of students to pursue research in the area. In both respects it was successful, and self-fulfilling prophecies has now become a major competing paradigm to the real business cycle view of economic fluctuations.

The second edition has been updated in three ways.

1. Many of my colleagues urged me to supplement the book with exercises that would enhance its usefulness as a teaching tool. In response, the new edition has been expanded to include problems at the end of every chapter, most of which have appeared as questions on exams in the core graduate macroeconomics course I have taught at UCLA over the past five years. Answers to the problems are available by visiting http://mitpress.mit.edu and searching for "Farmer."

2. Chapter 8 of this new edition ("Some Recent Developments") is an entirely new chapter devoted to the discussion of research that has appeared over the past five years. This new work asks if business fluctuations can be driven by self-fulfilling prophecies in economic models chosen to have realistic parameter values. An emphasis is given to models in which the production function has "small" increasing returns to scale in line with recent empirical estimates from U.S. data.

3. I have added an appendix to chapter 5 on representative agent growth models that explains the transversality condition.

I was gratified by the enthusiastic response that greeted the first edition of the *Macroeconomics of Self-fulfilling Prophecies* both as a research monograph and as a teaching tool. The additions to the second edition will make the book an even more accessible teaching tool for graduate macroeconomics courses where it has already become popular in graduate programs around the world.

Many people have helped me with the ideas in this book. Thanks especially to the coauthors of joint research papers, Jess Benhabib,

Rosalind L. Bennett, and Jang-Ting Guo for their permission to quote from our work. Thanks to my colleagues and students at UCLA who gave me suggestions and help with this and with earlier editions. Thanks to Terry Vaughn and the team at The MIT Press for their efforts in producing the final book. I would like to thank Yulei Luo, of Princeton University, and Steven Jordan, of Yale University, for pointing out a number of typographical errors in the first printing. Finally, thanks to my wife Roxanne and my son Leland for their love and support throughout the project.

Roger E. A. Farmer
Los Angeles, 1998.

Macroeconomics of Self-fulfilling Prophecies

1 Introduction

1.1 Equilibrium Theory as an Approach to Macroeconomics

In the last few decades there has been a big change in the way that economists think about macroeconomics. For many years it was fashionable to treat macroeconomics and microeconomics as separate subjects without inquiring too deeply into the relationship between them. But in the 1970s a developing consensus, that had promised to unite different schools of macroeconomic thought, was shattered by the occurrence of an episode of high inflation and high unemployment that was inconsistent with orthodox theory. As a consequence of this clash, of theory with fact, macroeconomists began to pay much greater attention to the microfoundations of their subject. Since macroeconomics deals with the behavior of the economy as a whole the natural foundation for macroeconomics lies in the microeconomic theory of general equilibrium. In this book I am going to take a point of view that is becoming less controversial but that is by no means universally accepted. I will argue that the future of macroeconomics *is* as a branch of applied general equilibrium theory.

In the book I am going to introduce a number of dynamic general equilibrium models, each of which maintains the assumption that agents have *rational expectations* of future prices. I will argue that much of the resistance to this approach, from economists who think of themselves as so-called Keynesians, can be attributed to the unfortunate fact that much of the debate on rational expectations in macroeconomics has taken place in context of very simple general equilibrium models in which the competitive mechanism functions smoothly. The use of overly simple environments to convey the central messages of the rational expectations research agenda has led to widespread misunderstanding of the implications of rational expectations. My main message is contained in the idea that one can think about macroeconomics as the study of equilibrium environments in which the welfare theorems, which equate competitive equilibria with Pareto optimal allocations of resources, may break down. Once one accepts this idea it becomes possible to discuss the role of government policies in a context in which policy may serve some purpose.

All of the models in this book begin with a version of the general equilibrium economy described by Debreu in *Theory of Value* [37], but most of the interesting features of macroeconomies require departures from the assumption that markets are perfect.[1] I will argue that departures that seem relatively minor can have major consequences for both the positive and normative implications of the theory. These consequences suggest that general equilibrium models may have a much greater potential for helping us to organize our observations of the data than one might believe from observing early attempts to implement the approach. The book focuses on two important departures from the general equilibrium model of Arrow-Debreu [5].[2] These departures both exploit the idea that macroeconomic equilibria need not be uniquely determined by the *fundamentals* of the economy. The apparently irrelevant beliefs of actors may become self-fulfilling. Hence the title of this book.

As an example of one of the apparent failures of the positive implications of general equilibrium theory take the observation that prices are sticky. This feature of the data has led many observers to abandon equilibrium theory and to search for non-market-clearing explanations as a means of understanding the co-movements of real and monetary variables.[3] I will argue that the observation that prices do not move one for one with nominal magnitudes does not imply that one must abandon the equilibrium approach. Rather, the implication that prices should be highly sensitive to nominal disturbances is an implication of models in which equilibria are *determinate*. I will make this concept more precise in the following chapters, but roughly speaking, it means that equilibria are (at least locally) uniquely determined by preferences and technologies. An important focus will be economic structures that lead to equilibria and do not have this property.

As a consequence of studying economies that do not preserve the normative features of the Arrow-Debreu model, we will be able to discuss environments in which all agents are fully rational and in which all markets clear, though the competitive mechanism may not deliver a socially desirable outcome. More important, the models that we will study will frequently contain different equilibria associated with alternative policy options that may be pursued by the central government. Often it will be the case that one policy regime will be unanimously preferred to another. A key feature of general equilibrium economies with perfect markets is the normative implication that equilibria are *Pareto optimal*. Arguably it is this feature of equilibrium theory that has led to the strongest resistance from Keynesian economists to the idea that one may model unemployment as an equilibrium phenomenon. But, in the applications we will study, it will often be the case that the welfare theorems no longer hold, and in these economies employment may fluctuate over the business cycle in a way that resembles the movements that are observed in advanced industrial economies. Models of this kind, in which equilibria may be suboptimal, are natural structures within which to ask questions of relevance to economic policy-makers.

1.2   Preview of the Argument

Equilibrium macroeconomic models are described by systems of difference equations. These equations involve a number of dynamic relationships between a set of endogenous variables $Y_t \in R^n$ and a set of exogenous variables $X_t \in R^m$. Although the equations that describe economies look a lot like the equations that describe physical systems, they are different in one important respect. The behavior of economies depends on the expectations of thinking human beings.

Typically one models the dependence of actions on beliefs by introducing the subjective probability distributions of agents as explanatory variables in an economic model. The following equations might be generated by such a model:

$$Y_t = E_t[f(Y_{t+1}, X_t, u_t)], \tag{1.1}$$

$$X_t = g(X_{t-1}, v_t), \tag{1.2}$$

where the symbol E_t represents the expectation of the random variable Y_{t+1} evaluated with respect to a subjective probability distribution that is supposed to summarize the so-called beliefs of the actors in the model. Equation 1.1 summarizes the content of economic theory. It links the current value of a set of endogenous variables to the probability distribution of future values of these variables and to current values of some exogenous variables X_t and some disturbances u_t. The function f maps $R^{m+2n} \mapsto R^n$. X has dimension m; u and Y have dimension n. The second equation, which describes how the exogenous variables X_t are related to their own past values and to a set of disturbances v_t, is often referred to as a policy rule. It represents the behavior of the government and in most macroeconomic models the interaction of the policy rule with the economic structure is taken to be outside the scope of inquiry. The disturbances u_t and v_t are random variables which are assumed to have probability distributions known by the agents in the model, and ex post they may or not be observable to the agents or to the econometrician.

The above equations are already quite special because they represent the beliefs of all of the agents in the economy in terms of a single probability distribution. In general, if one did not impose the *rational expectations assumption*, one might expect that the beliefs of agents would be diverse and that different agents could condition their expectations on very different subjective probabilities. But, if agents operate in a stationary environment, then they will each build up a picture of the actual frequency distribution of endogenous variables through repeated observations over time. It is this idea that drives the rational expectations assumption, which asserts that one should evaluate the expectations operator in equation 1.1 and replace the subjective probabilities of agents by the true probability distribution of Y_{t+1} conditional on the information available to agents at date t.

Notice that equation 1.1 is a *functional* equation. This is a more complicated object than a simple difference equation, since the entire probability distribution of Y_{t+1} can affect Y_t. The solution to a functional equation of this type is a sequence of probability distributions that describes the evolution of the random variable $\{Y_t\}_{t=1}^{\infty}$. One way of generating a sequence of probability distributions is by writing down a stochastic difference equation that satisfies equation 1.1, which describes the evolution of Y_t as a function of X_t and u_t. This is the route that is usually taken in analyzing models like the one described above.

1.3 Example

The main ideas that I wish to convey can be understood by comparing two cases of a nonstochastic version of 1.1. To keep things simple, we assume that the content of economic theory is represented by a model with a single state variable and that the policy rule is to set X_t equal to a constant for all time. In this special case equation 1.1 may be reduced to a first-order equation of the form

$$y_t = E_t f(y_{t+1}). \tag{1.3}$$

The expectations operator on the right-hand side of equation 1.3 is conditional on the agents' subjective belief, and the rational expectations assumption lets us replace this distribution with the actual distribution of

y_{t+1} conditional on time t information. Since nothing in the model is stochastic, one might conclude that the actual probability distribution is degenerate with point mass at a single value, and one might be tempted to replace the functional equation 1.3 with a simple nonstochastic difference equation. We will resist this temptation for reasons that will become apparent shortly.

Since econometricians usually deal with linear equations, we will make one further assumption. This assumption is that the equation

$$\bar{y} = f(\bar{y})$$

has a unique solution and that the equation

$$dy_t = E_t b \, dy_{t+1}, \tag{1.4}$$

where $b = \partial f / \partial y |_{y=\bar{y}}$ and $dy \equiv y - \bar{y}$, is a good approximation to 1.3. An approximation of this nature is good when the support of the probability distribution of y_{t+1} is small and when $\bar{y}$ is hyperbolic.[4] An economic equilibrium is a sequence of probability distributions for the endogenous variable y that satisfies the difference equation 1.4, *plus* some associated boundary conditions. Let us dispense with an uninteresting possibility first. Some economic models that generate first-order systems may be represented by difference equations in which there is an initial condition. For example, y_t may represent the stock of capital, with the initial stock of capital as a precondition of the model. In *first-order* systems of this kind the difference equation that describes equilibrium has a representation of the form:

$$dy_t = b \, dy_{t-1}, \tag{1.5}$$

$$y_0 = \bar{y}_0. \tag{1.6}$$

Notice that this differs from equation 1.4 in that the current value of y depends on an actual past value and not on an expected future value. This case is analogous to simple physical models, and there is not much that economics has to add. If the initial stock of capital is in the neighborhood of the steady state $\bar{y}$ and if b is less than one in absolute value, then the sequence $\{y_t\}_{t=1}^{\infty}$ converges to the steady state $\bar{y}$. If b is greater than one, then the steady state is unstable and sequences diverge.

A more interesting situation arises when the variable y_t represents a price or some other variable for which there is no initial condition and when the difference equation that describes equilibrium is of the form given in equation 1.4. Models in this class arise frequently in simple monetary environments in which the demand for real balances depends on expected future values of the price level. They do not generate an initial condition like equation 1.6. They are associated with a different type of boundary condition; this is the condition that the value of the variable y_t must remain finite for all t,[5]

$$\lim_{t \to \infty} |y_t| < \infty. \tag{1.7}$$

1.3.1   Regular Case

In discussing models in which expectations matter I will distinguish two cases. The *regular* case that has been studied most closely in the literature delivers a parameter restriction from economic theory which implies that the absolute value of b in equation 1.4 is less than one. Recall that an equilibrium is a sequence of probability distributions that satisfies equation 1.3. One way that one might generate such a sequence is to pick an arbitrary initial value of y_1 close to $\bar{y}$ and to generate values of y_t by iterating the equation

$$dy_t = \frac{1}{b} dy_{t-1} + \eta_t, \tag{1.8}$$

where η_t is an arbitrary random variable with small bounded support and with a conditional mean equal to zero. Equation 1.8 defines a Markov process. It may be used to define a sequence of probability distributions for the random variable $\{y_t\}_{t=1}^{\infty}$ that satisfies 1.4 for finite periods of time. However, this process cannot succeed for all time. Since the process is unstable, sequences of probability distributions that are generated in this way will generate sequences of values of y_t that eventually violate the condition 1.7, and the probability that $|y_t - \bar{y}|$ is arbitrarily large will converge to one.

There is, however, one case in which the above procedure will be successful. This is the case where y_1 is set equal to $\bar{y}$ and the influence of the extraneous random variable η_t is removed entirely. Since sequences that begin at the steady state stay at the steady state and since the constant sequence $\{y_t = \bar{y}\}_{t=1}^{\infty}$ satisfies equation 1.3, we have identified one possible rational expectations equilibrium. It is not hard to show that this is the only rational expectations equilibrium, since the fixed point $\bar{y}$ is assumed to be unique and all nonstationary sequences that obey 1.4 eventually violate the boundedness condition. Notice that we have used the fact that the steady state is unstable to show that there exists a unique rational expectations equilibrium.

I want to draw attention to an important implication of the above argument which may not be immediately apparent. In economic models with thinking beings, beliefs may influence actions. This dependency was modeled by including agents' subjective beliefs of future values of endogenous variables in the equations that determine economic equilibria. But (at least in our special example with no uncertainty) we have added rational expectations and arrived at the proposition that beliefs must themselves be functions of the fundamental economic parameters of the model. This proposition has often been associated with *all* models in which markets clear and in which agents form rational expectations. It is a central theme of my argument that the proposition that *all* such models imply that beliefs cannot independently influence allocations is false and that the way in which it is false has something important to say about economics.

1.3.2   Irregular Case

Some of the economic models we will study will generate equations that characterize equilibria of the same form as 1.4, with the polar opposite restriction on the value of the parameter b. This can happen in the case of overlapping generations models, and it also occurs in economies in which externalities are important. If b is greater than one in absolute value, then the procedure for generating an equilibrium, that is, beginning with a value of y_1 close to $\bar{y}$ and iterating the equation

$$dy_t = \frac{1}{b} dy_{t-1} + \eta_t \tag{1.9}$$

will be successful for any value of y_1 in the neighborhood of $\bar{y}$. The difference equation 1.9 defines a Markov process. Associated with this Markov process is a sequence of probability distributions, from which the random variables y_t are drawn, which satisfies equation 1.4 by construction. If the support of η_t is small and bounded, all sequences that begin in the neighborhood of y_1 will be associated with sequences of probability distributions that converge to a stationary distribution with a bounded support that contains the fixed point $\bar{y}$. Since these distributions converge

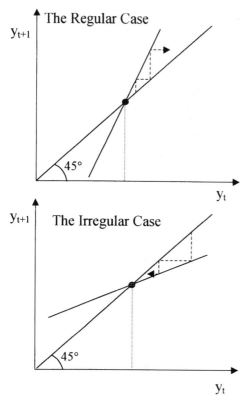

Figure 1.1
Regular and irregular equilibria

to a stationary distribution with bounded support, they will all generate sequences of random variables y_t that satisfy the boundedness condition 1.7 with probability one. One is led to the conclusion that economic environments in which $|b|$ is greater than one are consistent with the existence of multiple rational expectations equilibria.

How is one to interpret an equilibrium that is constructed by iterating equation 1.9 for an arbitrary initial value y_1 and an arbitrary sequence of stochastic shocks $\{\eta_t\}$? One interpretation that has been pursued in the literature is that η_t represents the belief of agents that some variable η, observed by the agents but not by the econometrician, influences the evolution of y_t. In an irregular economic environment it is possible for a belief of this nature to be self-fulfilling. The idea that self-fulfilling beliefs may play an important role in the business cycle has a long history. It is the basis for Keynes's explanation of the Great Depression. What is novel about the above argument is that self-fulfilling beliefs may be consistent with a rational expectations equilibrium.

1.4   Concluding Remarks

In the course of the book we will investigate a number of economic environments that give rise to equilibria that are Markov processes, of the type discussed above, and I will show how these equilibria can be supported by rules that agents use to forecast the future. I will argue that our economic models lead to multiple equilibria because we have failed to fully specify the economic environment. What is missing is a description of the agents' forecast rule which should itself be treated as an economic fundamental. Since different specifications of beliefs will have different implications for the time-series properties of the data, there is no reason to treat the parameters that index beliefs any differently from the parameters that index preferences and technologies.

1.5   Problems

Solutions to all of the problems in the book will be made available in an electronic solutions manual by Shankha Chakraborty and Roger E. A. Farmer. The manual can be found on the internet by pointing your web browser to *http://mitpress.mit.edu* and searching for "Farmer."

1. What do economists mean by an equilibrium? How does this differ from the concept of equilibrium typically used in the physical sciences?

2. Consider an economic model represented by the difference equation

$$y_t = 0.5 y_{t+1}, \qquad y_1 = 1.$$

Show that if y_t must remain bounded as part of the equilibrium concept, then there are no sequences $\{y_t\}_{t=1}^{\infty}$ that are consistent with equilibrium. Now suppose that the model is instead represented by the difference equation

$$y_t = 0.5 y_{t+1}$$

with no initial condition. Find the unique bounded sequence that satisfies this equation.

3. Consider the model in which

$$p_t = a p_{t+1}^E,$$

where a is a parameter and p_{t+1}^E is the agents' common expectation of the price at date $t + 1$. Suppose that expectations are determined by the equation

$$p_{t+1}^E = \lambda p_t^E + (1 - \lambda) p_t, \qquad p_1^E = 1.$$

Find conditions on the parameters a and λ that lead to the existence of multiple bounded sequences $\{p_t, p_{t+1}^E\}_{t=1}^{\infty}$ that satisfy these equations. How do the restrictions on a change as λ converges to 1 or 0? Can you interpret these special cases in terms of the way agents learn?

4. Give a brief synopsis of the main differences between a *regular* and an *irregular* economic model.

2 Linear Difference Equations: Part 1

2.1 Introduction

In chapters 2 and 3 we are going to study some of the tools that are needed to understand the evolution of economies through time. There are two reasons why time enters into decisions in nontrivial ways. The first reason leads to a study of dynamic models that are closely related to the kinds of systems that are studied in the natural sciences. It involves a dependence of the present on the past that arises from the accumulation of capital. The second reason that the study of dynamics is important in economics has no counterpart in the natural sciences. It arises from the dependence of current actions on beliefs about the future.

In this chapter we are going to study dynamics of the first kind, and we are going to examine the idea that linear economic models are, under some circumstances, good approximations to nonlinear economic models. In chapter 3 we will extend this idea to the study of economies in which stocks from the past and beliefs about the future are both important in influencing the way agents behave in the present.

2.2 Linearizing Nonlinear Models

2.2.1 Nonlinear Models to Represent Economies

It would be absurd to believe that all of the relationships that describe variables that we are interested in as economists are linear. But linear models are much easier to study than nonlinear models, and under some circumstances the behavior of nonlinear systems can be approximated by the behavior of a linear model. Suppose that we believe that some variable, in which we are interested, is described by the following equation:

$$y_t = f(y_{t-1}; x_t, t). \tag{2.1}$$

The variable y_t is an *endogenous* variable which is determined by the economic behavior of agents. For example, it might represent the gross national product (GNP) of the United States. The variable x_t is an *exogenous* variable determined by factors that are outside of the domain of inquiry. For example, x_t might represent the weather, or it might be some aspect of the political process. Equation 2.1 summarizes the content of economic theory. It is a description of our belief about the way that y_t depends on its own past history and on the exogenous variable x_t.

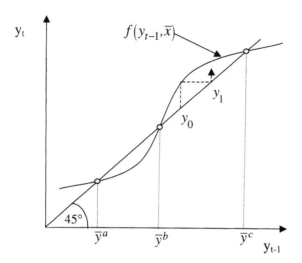

Figure 2.1
Solving a nonlinear difference equation

Although equation 2.1 looks disarmingly simple, equations of this kind can describe exceedingly complicated dynamics.[1]

2.2.2 Linearizing Autonomous Equations

Figure 2.1 provides an example of a nonlinear model in which the policy sequence $\{x_t\}$ is assumed to be constant at the value $\bar{x}$. Equations of this kind, in which the function $f(\cdot)$ does not depend explicitly on time, are called *autonomous*. Notice that as I have drawn it, the function $f(\cdot)$ has three fixed points each of which is a solution to the equation:

$$\bar{y} = f(\bar{y}, \bar{x}). \tag{2.2}$$

These fixed points are represented in the picture by the intersections of the function $f(\cdot)$ with the line

$$y_t = y_{t-1},$$

which slopes up from the origin at 45 degrees to the x axis. I have labeled the fixed points of $f(\cdot)$ as $\bar{y}^a$, $\bar{y}^b$, and $\bar{y}^c$, respectively. The behavior of the time series $\{y_t\}$ for any initial condition y_0 is found by tracing out sequences in figure 2.1 that move back and forth between the function $f(\cdot)$ and the 45-degree line. For example, if the initial value of y, is set at

y_0 when $t = 0$, then y will move to point y_1 at $t = 1$. Successive values of the sequence $\{y_t\}_{t=0}^{\infty}$ are found the same way.

Inspection of 2.1 reveals an important distinction between the fixed point $\bar{y}^b$ and the fixed points $\bar{y}^a$ and $\bar{y}^c$. Notice that the sequence that begins at point y_0 moves away from the fixed point $\bar{y}^b$ and toward the fixed point $\bar{y}^c$. A little thought will reveal that all sequences obeying 2.1 which begin in the interval $(\bar{y}^b, \bar{y}^c)$ will behave in the same way. Similarly all sequences which begin in the interval $(\bar{y}^a, \bar{y}^b)$ will converge to the fixed point $\bar{y}^a$. The fixed point $\bar{y}^b$ is said to be unstable, and the fixed points $\bar{y}^a$ and $\bar{y}^c$ are stable.[2] Stable fixed points are important in the study of economic models, since they are useful points around which to *linearize* a nonlinear model.

The idea of linearization is to recognize that the function $f(\cdot)$ can be approximated by a Taylor series expansion around any point that we care to pick. The stable fixed points of a nonlinear model are good candidates around which to linearize, since sequences that begin close to such points will remain close to them. The continued proximity of y_t to a fixed point ensures that the Taylor series approximation around that fixed point will continue to remain accurate as time progresses.

Suppose that equation 2.1 has a stable fixed point $\bar{y}$. In the neighborhood of $\bar{y}$, it will be approximately true that

$$y_t = b + a y_{t-1}, \tag{2.3}$$

where $a \equiv f_y(\bar{y}, \bar{x})$ is the slope of the function $f(\cdot)$ evaluated at the fixed point $\bar{y}$ and $b \equiv \bar{y} - a\bar{y}$ is a constant. In figure 2.2 I have depicted the idea of linearization graphically. The sequence $\{y_0, y_1, \ldots\}$ represents the solution to the linear equation 2.3 for initial condition $y = y_0$. Notice that as the sequence approaches $\bar{y}$, the difference between the nonlinear function $f(\cdot)$ and the approximation 2.3 becomes smaller.

2.2.3   Linearizing Nonautonomous Equations

The idea of linearizing a function extends in a straightforward manner to a class of more useful models; those in which the variable x_t is a nontrivial function of time. I am going to restrict my attention to economic models in which x_t remains in the neighborhood of some point $\bar{x}$. An important class of models that satisfies this assumption[3] treats x_t as a random variable with a small bounded support that contains $\bar{x}$. In this case one defines $\bar{y}$ as in equation 2.2 and approximates the function $f(\cdot)$ with the first-order Taylor series:

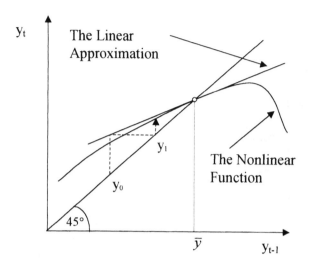

Figure 2.2
Linearizing a nonlinear difference equation

$$y_t = b + a y_t + c x_t,$$

where $c \equiv f_x(\bar{y}; \bar{x})$ is the derivative of $f(\cdot)$ with respect to x and $b \equiv \bar{y} - a\bar{y} - c\bar{x}$. The assumptions that the fixed point $\bar{y}$ is stable and that the support of x is small ensure that the deviation of $\{x_t, y_t\}$ from $\{\bar{x}, \bar{y}\}$ can be kept arbitrarily small at every point in time by picking the bounds on x appropriately.

2.2.4 Example of Linearization: The Solow Model

One of the simplest examples of a dynamic model in economics is Solow's [107] model of economic growth.[4] The Solow model attributes growth in productivity to exogenous improvements in technological progress. It consists of the following equations:

$$Y_t = F(K_t, A_t L_t),   \tag{2.4a}$$

$$K_{t+1} = (1 - \delta)K_t + Y_t - C_t, \quad K_0 = \bar{K}_0,   \tag{2.4b}$$

$$C_t = (1 - s)Y_t,   \tag{2.4c}$$

$$L_t = 1,   \tag{2.4d}$$

$$A_t = \gamma^t A_0, \quad A_0 = \bar{A}_0.   \tag{2.4e}$$

2.4a is a production function: Y_t is output, K_t is the stock of capital, L_t is labor input, C_t is consumption, and A_t represents labor-augmenting technical progress. The function $F(\cdot)$ is assumed to be homogeneous of degree one,[5] monotonically increasing, and twice continuously differentiable in its two arguments. Equation 2.4b is the GNP accounting identity. The term δ is depreciation and $K_t - (1 - \delta)K_{t-1}$ is gross investment. Equation 2.4c is the main behavioral equation of the model. It postulates the assumption of a constant savings rate, s. Equations 2.4d and 2.4e model the assumptions that labor supply is constant (and equal to one) and technological progress grows exogenously[6] with growth factor γ.

The assumption that $F(\cdot)$ is homogeneous of degree one implies that the Solow model has the following representation as a first-order non-linear difference equation:

$$\gamma\tilde{k}_{t+1} = (1 - \delta)\tilde{k}_t + sf(\tilde{k}_t), \tag{2.5}$$

where

$$\tilde{k}_t \equiv \frac{K_t}{L_t A_t} \equiv \frac{K_t}{A_t},$$

is the ratio of capital to labor measured in efficiency units. This means that labor hours are weighted by the productivity of labor A_t where productivity is assumed to be growing through time. The production function also has a representation in ratio form:

$$\tilde{y}_t = f(\tilde{k}_t),$$

where

$$\tilde{y}_t \equiv \frac{Y_t}{L_t A_t} \equiv \frac{Y_t}{A_t},$$

is output per efficiency unit of labor input and the function $f(\cdot)$ is defined as

$$F\left(\frac{K_t}{A_t}, 1\right) = \frac{1}{A_t}F(K_t, A_t).$$

In figure 2.3 I have drawn a picture of equation 2.5. The assumption that $F(\cdot)$ is monotonically increasing in K_t implies that the model has at most one strictly positive steady state that obeys the goods market clearing

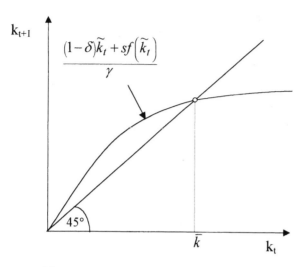

Figure 2.3
Solow growth model

equation:[7]

$$(\gamma + \delta - 1)\bar{k} = sf(\bar{k}).$$

To linearize around the steady state, one would take a first-order approximation to $f(\cdot)$ evaluated at $\bar{k}$. Using the definition

$$\hat{k}_t \equiv \left(\frac{\tilde{k}_t - \bar{k}}{\bar{k}}\right),$$

it follows that

$$\hat{k}_{t+1} \simeq a\hat{k}_t, \qquad (2.6)$$

where

$$a \equiv \frac{(1-\delta) + sf_k(\bar{k})}{\gamma}.$$

The Solow model predicts that $\tilde{k}_t$ will converge to a constant, $\bar{k}$. Since $\tilde{k}_t$ is the ratio of the stock of capital to a growing productivity trend, it follows that the stock of capital is predicted to converge to a constant trend growth path. The model also predicts that all of the variables that are functions of the stock of capital will converge to trend growth paths.

For example, the steady state output per efficiency unit of labor, $\tilde{y}$, is a function of the steady state capital labor ratio, $\tilde{k}$, also measured in efficiency units of labor. Since the effective units of labor are growing by a factor of γ, the Solow model predicts that capital and output will grow by this same factor:

$$\frac{K_t}{A_0\gamma^t} = \bar{k} \Rightarrow K_t = A_0\gamma^t\bar{k},$$

and

$$\frac{Y_t}{A_0\gamma^t} = f(\bar{k}) \Rightarrow Y_t = f(\bar{k})A_0\gamma^t.$$

In the United States capital and output grow through time, but they do not grow at a steady rate. A much better statistical model of the data is one that predicts that GNP and capital fluctuate around a growing trend and that the fluctuations are random variables. To understand how one might construct a theoretical model that has these properties, we are going to introduce the idea of a stochastic difference equation. The tools for understanding the dynamics of simple difference equations that are excited by random variables are discussed below.

2.3 Solving First-Order Linear Models

In this section I am going to review solution techniques for first-order difference equations of the form:

$$y_t = b + ay_{t-1} + cx_t, \tag{2.7}$$

where a, b, and c are parameters. In general, I will assume that x_t is a random variable, but before tackling this case, I am going to review the study of nonstochastic difference equations.

Since we are confining our attention to linear models, one may wonder why the *dynamics* of a nonstochastic difference equation are interesting. A linear model has a unique steady state,[8] and as long as this steady state is stable, our model predicts that after the transitional dynamics have run their course, the economy will be at the steady state.

If nonstochastic models were good representations of the data, then this argument would make some sense. However, most of the economic models that interest us can be represented by a stable linear difference equation whose steady state value is being continuously buffeted by a random disturbance. In some sense a variable described by a stochastic difference equation settles down over time, but the object that it settles down *to* is more complicated than a simple point. It is a stationary probability distribution. To understand how a stochastic linear model generates a *stationary* probability distribution, one must first know something about the *nonstationary* behavior of the nonstochastic model.

2.3.1 First-Order Deterministic Equations

The key feature that determines the stability of a linear equation is its slope. Consider the special case of equation 2.7 in which $c = 0$. In this case the system is deterministic, and the stability of the fixed point $\bar{y}$ is determined by the sign of $|a| - 1$. If $|a| < 1$, the system is stable, and y_t converges to the fixed point $b/(1 - a)$ as $t \to \infty$ for all initial values y_0. If $|a| > 1$, the system is unstable, and y_t diverges to infinity for all y_0 except for the special case in which the system starts off at the unstable fixed point $\bar{y} = b/(1 - a)$.

In figure 2.4, I have drawn a picture of equation 2.7 for the case where the slope is positive. The case when a is negative is similar although in this case y_t flips back and forth each period from one side of the fixed point to the other. These oscillations are convergent[9] if a is between 0 and -1, and they are divergent if a is less than -1.

2.3.2 First-Order Stochastic Equations

In a probabilistic model one describes the movements of the variable y_t with a linear stochastic equation of the form:

$$y_t = b + ay_{t-1} + cx_t, \tag{2.8}$$

where x_t is a random variable. In order to be able to make inferences about the values of the parameters of models in this class, it is important to assume that one observes repeated observations from the same probability distribution. For this reason one typically assumes that the disturbance to the equation, x_t, is drawn from a probability distribution that is invariant through time and the parameter a is less than one in absolute value. If either of these assumptions is violated, then the model will not generate a stationary distribution for the values of the endogenous variables, although there may be some transformation of y_t that *is* stationary.

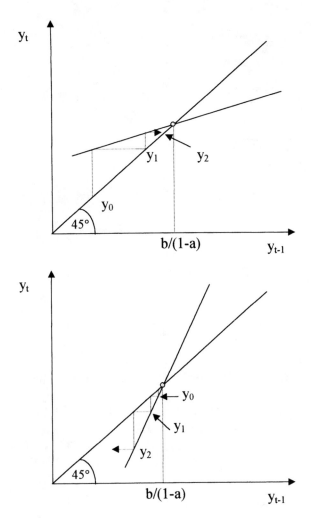

Figure 2.4
First-order nonstochastic difference equations

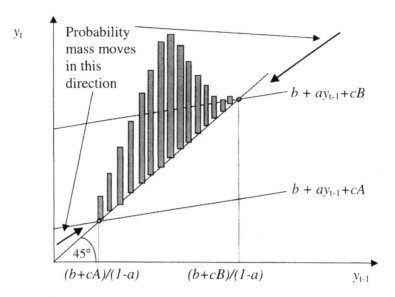

Figure 2.5
First-order stochastic difference equation

The sequence $\{y_t\}$ that is generated by equation 2.8 is an example of a *Markov process*[10] on some closed interval $[A, B]$. In figure 2.5 I have depicted this case. The picture shows the two linear functions $b + ay_{t-1} + cA$ and $b + ay_{t-1} + cB$, which represent the extreme values that could be taken by y_t for any given value of y_{t-1}. I have drawn the figure on the assumption that a is between zero and one. In any given period the value that is taken by y_t is a random variable which is determined by one of the possible linear functions

$$b + ay_{t-1} + cx_t.$$

The particular function that applies in any given period is determined by selecting a draw from the probability distribution of x_t.

Suppose that the initial value of y_0 is outside the interval $[(b + cA)/(1 - a), (b + cB)/(1 - a)]$. Notice that as long as $0 < a < 1$, the sequence $\{y_t\}$ will get closer to the interval $[(b + cA)/(1 - a), (b + cB)/(1 - a)]$ in every successive period, and if y_t ever enters this interval, it will never leave it. In fact, under relatively mild conditions on the random variable x_t, one can show that the probability distribution of y_t converges to an invariant probability distribution with support on the interval $[(b + cA)/(1 - a), (b + cB)/(1 - a)]$. This probability distribution is represented heuristically in figure 2.5 by the vertical bars.

2.3.3 Sequences of Probability Distributions

The solution to a nonstochastic difference equation is a sequence of numbers that obeys the recursive relationship defined by the equation itself and which also satisfies a given boundary condition. Usually this boundary condition is the initial value of the sequence. The solution to the stochastic model 2.8 is a more complicated object. It is a sequence of probability distributions $\{G_t(\cdot \mid y_0)\}_{t=1}^{\infty}$, where the term $G_t(S \mid y_0)$ represents the probability that y_t will lie in the set S at date t given the information that y is equal to y_0 at date 0. To construct this sequence, observe that each value y_t is a weighted sum of the past values taken by x_t. For example, in period 1, y_1 is given by

$$y_1 = b + x_1 + ay_0;$$

in period 2,

$$y_2 = b + x_2 + a(b + x_1 + ay_0);$$

and in period t,

$$y_t = \sum_{s=0}^{t-1} a^s(b + x_s) + a^t y_0.$$

Using these equations, the sequence of probability distributions of $\{y_t\}$,

$$\{G_t(\cdot \mid y_0)\}_{t=1}^{\infty}, \tag{2.9}$$

can be constructed recursively from the known distributions of $\{x_t\}$. In the case where $|a| < 1$ this sequence of probability distributions converges[11] to an invariant distribution

$$\lim_{t \to \infty} G_t(\cdot \mid y_0) = G(\cdot) \qquad \text{for all } y_0. \tag{2.10}$$

The distributions described in 2.9 are conditional on the initial condition y_0. Sometimes, however, the conditioning information may involve more than just the knowledge of the initial condition of the system. Suppose, for example, that one is interested in the probability that y_{t+T} lies in any given interval for some forecast horizon T, but instead of analyzing this probability at date zero, one has observed the history of realizations of x_s for values of s up to and including some date t, where $0 < t < T$. In this case the best information about y_{t+T} is contained in the conditional distribution

$$G_t(y_{t+T} \mid \{y_s\}_{s=0}^{t}). \tag{2.11}$$

As the horizon T gets larger, the information about the value of y_t becomes less useful, and in the limit the conditional distribution 2.11 will converge to the invariant distribution 2.10.

2.3.4   The Solow Model Revisited

In this section I am going to illustrate how linear stochastic difference equations are used in economics by looking at a stochastic version of the Solow model.

$$Y_t = v_t F(K_t, A_t L_t), \tag{2.12a}$$

$$K_{t+1} = (1 - \delta)K_t + Y_t - C_t, \quad K_0 = \bar{K}_0, \tag{2.12b}$$

$$C_t = (1 - s)Y_t, \tag{2.12c}$$

$$L_t = 1, \tag{2.12d}$$

$$A_t = \gamma^t A_0, \quad A_0 = \bar{A}_0, \tag{2.12e}$$

$$v_t \sim D[A, B]. \tag{2.12f}$$

Equations 2.12 duplicate the nonstochastic Solow model with the exception that the production function is assumed to be continuously hit by the productivity disturbance, v_t, which is a random variable with support $[A, B]$. The probability distribution of v_t is represented as $D[A, B]$ and its mean is given by

$$\bar{v} \equiv E[v_t]. \tag{2.13}$$

I will assume that the expectation $\bar{v}$ is evaluated using the unconditional distribution of v_t. If v_t is independently and identically distributed through time, then the conditional expectation:

$$E_{t-1}[v_t \mid v_{t-1}],$$

will be the same as the unconditional expectation 2.13. In general, however, I will allow for the possibility that the disturbance term v_t is auto-correlated. This assumption will turn out to be important when one is interested in fitting the simple Solow model to time series data.

The stochastic model can be transformed to a first-order stochastic difference equation by dividing each equation by $A_t L_t$. The transformed model is described by

$$\gamma \tilde{k}_{t+1} = (1 - \delta)\tilde{k}_t + v_t s f(\tilde{k}_t), \tag{2.14}$$

where

$$\tilde{k}_t \equiv \frac{K_t}{L_t A_t} \equiv \frac{K_t}{A_t}.$$

Now linearize equation 2.14 around the point $\{\bar{k}, \bar{v}\}$, where $\bar{k}$ is defined as the solution to:[12]

$$(\gamma + \delta - 1)\bar{k} = \bar{v} s f(\bar{k}). \tag{2.15}$$

The linear model takes the form

$$\hat{k}_{t+1} \simeq a_1 \hat{k}_t + c_1 \hat{v}_t, \tag{2.16}$$

where $\hat{k}_t$ is the proportional deviation of $\tilde{k}_t$ from $\bar{k}$, $\hat{v}_t$ is the proportional deviation of v_t from $\bar{v}$,

$$\hat{k}_t \equiv \frac{(\tilde{k}_t - \bar{k})}{\bar{k}}, \quad \hat{v}_t \equiv \frac{(v_t - \bar{v})}{\bar{v}},$$

and a_1 and c_1 are found by evaluating the derivatives of 2.14 at $\{\bar{k}, \bar{v}\}$.

Since GNP is a function of the capital stock and of the productivity shock, the model has an alternative representation as a first-order linear stochastic equation using output, measured in efficiency units, as the state variable. From the definition of technology it follows that

$$\tilde{y}_t = v_t f(\tilde{k}_t), \tag{2.17}$$

where

$$\tilde{y}_t \equiv \frac{Y_t}{A_t}. \tag{2.18}$$

One may define $\bar{y}$ as

$$\bar{y} \equiv \bar{v} f(\bar{k})$$

and linearize equation 2.17 around the point $\{\bar{y}, \bar{v}, \bar{k}\}$. This procedure leads to the approximation

$$\hat{k}_t \simeq b_2 \hat{y}_t - b_2 \hat{v}_t, \tag{2.19}$$

where

$$b_2 \equiv \frac{f(\bar{k})}{\bar{k} f_k(\bar{k})}$$

and

$$\hat{y}_t \equiv \frac{(\tilde{y}_t - \bar{y})}{\bar{y}}.$$

Equation 2.19 may be substituted back into 2.16 to generate the first-order difference equation:

$$\hat{y}_t \simeq a_3 \hat{y}_{t-1} + \varepsilon_t,$$

where

$$\varepsilon = \hat{v}_t + c_3 \hat{v}_{t-1},$$

and the parameters a_3, and c_3, are functions of a_1, c_1, and b_2.

To match the Solow model with data, one may make use of 2.18 to rewrite the definition of $\hat{y}_t$:

$$\hat{y}_t \equiv \left(\frac{Y_t}{\bar{y} A_0 \gamma^t} \right) - 1.$$

The usefulness of defining the approximation in terms of *proportional* deviations from the steady state follows from the fact that

$$\log(1 + x) \simeq x$$

for small x. This approximation implies that

$$\hat{y}_t \simeq \log(Y_t) - t \log(\gamma) - \log(\bar{y} A_0).$$

Using this approximation one arrives at a representation of the linearized stochastic Solow model:

$$y_t = b + a y_{t-1} + ct + d\varepsilon_t, \tag{2.20}$$

where y_t is the logarithm of GNP and the parameters of equation 2.20 are functions of the underlying parameters of the nonlinear model.

In figure 2.6 I have graphed the behavior of the logarithm of GNP in U.S. data together with its deviations from a linear trend. The top panel

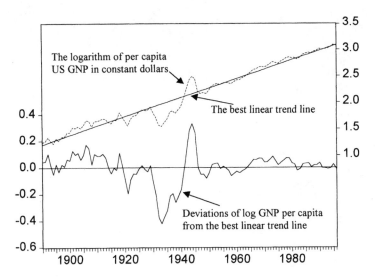

Figure 2.6
Logarithm of U.S. GNP and its deviations from a linear trend

of figure 2.7 depicts a scatter of the deviations of log. GNP from trend (labeled y_t in the figure) against its own lagged value. This panel also contains the least squares regression line of y_t on y_{t-1}. The bottom panel of the same figure represents the empirical frequency distribution of y_t for the same data set.

2.4   Solving Higher-Order Linear Models

Although the first-order model is an interesting special case, most economic models are described by difference equations in which two or more variables are related to each other and to their own past histories. The natural generalization of the first order equation 2.8 is a stochastic vector difference equation:

$$Y_t = b + A Y_{t-1} + C X_t, \tag{2.21}$$

where Y_t is an $n \times 1$ vector of endogenous variables, X_t is an $m \times 1$ vector of exogenous random variables, b is an $n \times 1$ vector of constants, and A and C are conformable matrices of coefficients. Higher-order vector systems, such as the model

$$Z_t = b_1 + A_1 Z_{t-1} + A_2 Z_{t-2} + C_1 V_t,$$

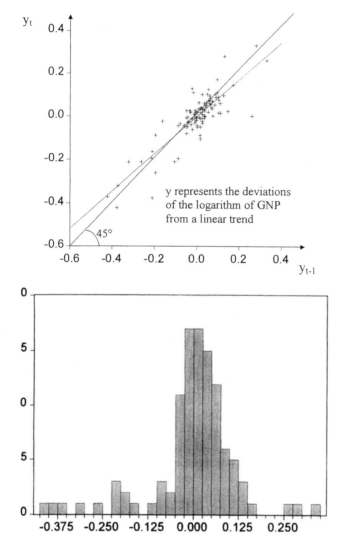

Figure 2.7
Empirical behavior of deviations of log: GNP from trend

are easily handled as first-order vector systems by increasing the dimension of the state vector and redefining variables in the following way:

$$Y_t \equiv \begin{bmatrix} Z_t \\ Z_{t-1} \end{bmatrix}, \quad X_t \equiv \begin{bmatrix} V_t \\ 0 \end{bmatrix},$$

$$b \equiv \begin{bmatrix} b_1 \\ 0 \end{bmatrix}, \quad A \equiv \begin{bmatrix} A_1 & A_2 \\ I & 0 \end{bmatrix}, \quad C \equiv \begin{bmatrix} C_1 \\ 0 \end{bmatrix}.$$

2.4.1 Eigenvalues and Eigenvectors

The behavior of first-order vector models such as equation 2.21 is found by decomposing the matrix system into a set of first-order equations which are *uncoupled* in the sense that each equation describes the evolution of a single variable that does not depend on the other variables in the set. Each of these equations is of the same form as 2.8, and each equation is associated with a parameter that plays the role of the parameter a in the first-order scalar model. The parameters that govern the stability of the system of equations are called the *roots* or *eigenvalues* of the system, and in this section I am going to provide an informal introduction to the matrix algebra that one requires to compute *eigenvalues*.

To provide some intuition into eigenvalues, it is helpful to think of a geometric interpretation of a matrix as a transformation of space. As an example, consider the 2×2 matrix A as a map $R^2 \mapsto R^2$ given by the linear equation $Y \mapsto AY$. The roots of A are the two solutions λ^a and λ^b to the equation $AY = \lambda Y$, where λ is a scalar and Y is an *eigenvector*. There will (generically) be exactly two (different) roots of a 2×2 matrix, three roots of a 3×3 matrix, and n roots of an $n \times n$ matrix. Similarly there will be exactly two different eigenvectors, Y^a and Y^b. The case of multiple identical eigenvalues must be handled differently, and since it almost never happens in the applications that we will be concerned with, we will not get into that case here.

The matrix A moves every point in the plane to a different point by the transformation $Y \mapsto AY$. Points that lie on the eigenvectors are moved in a special way. They are scaled up or down by the amount λ. Figure 2.8 illustrates the case in which one eigenvalue of A is positive and less than one and one eigenvalue is positive and greater than one. The two eigenvectors of the matrix A are represented in the figure as Y^a and Y^b. The two points a and b lie on the eigenvector Y^b. This eigenvector is

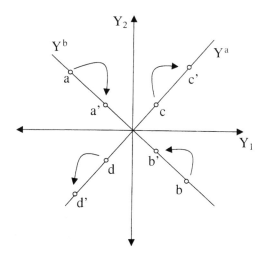

Figure 2.8
One stable and one unstable eigenvalue

associated with an eigenvalue, λ^b, which is positive and less than one. The transformation $Y \mapsto AY$ moves a and b closer to the origin to a' and b'. Similarly the two points c and d lie on the eigenvector Y^a, which is associated with an eigenvalue, λ^a, and is positive and greater than one. The matrix A moves c and d further away from the origin to c' and d'.

Since the roots of A solve

$$AY = \lambda Y \tag{2.22}$$

for scalar λ, it follows that the matrix

$$A - \lambda I$$

must be singular. To calculate the eigenvalues of A, one must solve the polynomial

$$\left| \begin{bmatrix} a_{11} & a_{12} \\ a_{21} & a_{22} \end{bmatrix} - \begin{bmatrix} \lambda & 0 \\ 0 & \lambda \end{bmatrix} \right| = 0, \tag{2.23}$$

where the notation $|A|$ means "compute the determinant of the matrix A." In the 2×2 case this restriction on the determinant of $A - \lambda I$ generates the quadratic equation:

$$\lambda^2 - \lambda(a_{11} + a_{22}) + (a_{11}a_{22} - a_{12}a_{21}) = 0.$$

The eigenvalues of A are the roots of this quadratic, and the eigenvectors Y^a and Y^b are computed by substituting each of the roots back into the equation,

$$A Y^i = \lambda^i Y^i, \qquad i = \{a, b\}.$$

For each root λ^i this expression generates two linearly dependent equations in the elements of Y^i. These equations determine the direction of the vector Y^i, but in view of the linear dependence of the equations, they do not pick a particular point on that vector.

2.4.2 Higher-Order Deterministic Equations

The above analysis of the properties of the linear transformation $Y \mapsto A Y$ has an obvious application to the properties of linear difference equations in higher dimensions. This connection is explored below. Before proceeding on this front, however, I state some properties of square matrices and their application to difference equations in an informal way. The reader who requires a more complete analysis should consult a text on difference equations.

1. If A is symmetric, then the roots of A are real; otherwise, they may be complex.

2. If the roots are complex, then they may be inside or outside the unit circle. If they are real, then this reduces to the statement that they may be bigger than or less than one in absolute value.

3. If the roots are complex, then they come in complex pairs, and both roots of a pair are either inside or outside the unit circle.

4. If all roots of the system are inside the unit circle, then the steady state is stable for all initial conditions.

5. If the roots are outside the unit circle, then the steady state is unstable for all initial conditions.

6. If the system has at least one root that is outside the unit circle, then for most initial conditions the system will diverge from the steady state.

In a second-order system, if both roots are positive and less than one, then the system converges monotonically to the steady state. If the roots are complex and inside the unit circle, then the system spirals into the steady state. If at least one root is negative, but both roots are less than

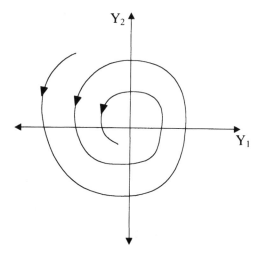

Figure 2.9
A sink: This example has a pair of complex roots that lie inside the unit circle

one in absolute value, then the system will flip from one side of the steady state to the other as it converges. In all of these cases the steady state is called a *sink*.

If both roots are positive and greater than one, then the system diverges monotonically to plus or minus infinity. If the roots are complex and outside the unit circle, then the system spirals out away from the steady state. If at least one root is negative, but both roots are greater than one in absolute value, then the system will flip from one side of the steady state to the other as it diverges to infinity. In each of these cases the steady state is called a *source*.

If one root is greater than one and the other root is less than one in absolute value, then the steady state is called a *saddle point*. In this case the system is unstable for almost all initial conditions. The exception is the set of initial conditions that begin on the eigenvector associated with the stable eigenvalue.

Three examples of the dynamics of equation (2.24) are presented in figures 2.9, 2.10, and 2.11. Figures 2.10 and 2.11 are examples in which both roots of the system are real and in these cases the eigenvectors are represented as Y^a and Y^b. Figure 2.9 represents a case in which the eigenvalues and the eigenvectors are complex.

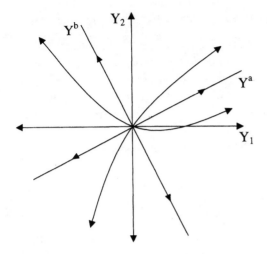

Figure 2.10
A source: This example has a pair of real positive roots with modulus greater than one

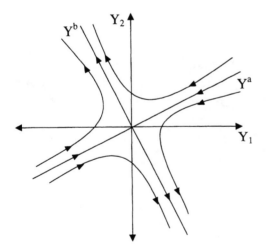

Figure 2.11
A saddle point: This example has two positive roots, one with modulus greater than one and
one with modulus less than one

2.4.3 Diagonalizing Systems of Nonstochastic Equations

The roots of a matrix are useful because they allow one to construct solutions to linear vector difference equations by combining the solutions to simpler first order systems that are independent of each other. These first order systems are found by computing the eigenvectors of the matrix A. The method of computing solutions by finding linear combinations of transformed variables is achieved by *diagonalizing A*.

I will begin, as in the first-order case, with the nonstochastic example:

$$Y_t = b + A Y_{t-1}. \tag{2.24}$$

Diagonalization is achieved by stacking the two eigenvalue equations:

$$A[Y^a, Y^b] = [Y^a, Y^b]\begin{bmatrix} \lambda^a & 0 \\ 0 & \lambda^a \end{bmatrix}. \tag{2.25}$$

The matrix of stacked eigenvectors, $Q \equiv [Y^a, Y^b]$, is square and in general invertible. Using this fact, we can postmultiply 2.25 by Q^{-1} and express the matrix A in the form

$$A = Q\Lambda Q^{-1}, \tag{2.26}$$

where Λ is the diagonal matrix of eigenvalues.[13] Now premultiply equation 2.24 by the inverse matrix of eigenvectors, Q^{-1}, and define a new vector of transformed variables, Z_t, and a transformed vector of coefficients, β:

$$Z_t = \Lambda Z_{t-1} + \beta, \tag{2.27}$$

where

$$Z_t \equiv Q^{-1} Y_t$$

and

$$\beta \equiv Q^{-1} b.$$

The usefulness of this transformation lies in the fact that since Λ is diagonal, each of the equations (2.27) is independent of the others:

$$Z_t^i = \lambda^i Z_{t-1}^i + \beta^i. \tag{2.28}$$

The equations described by 2.28 are *scalar* difference equation of exactly the same form that we studied in the first part of this chapter. Each variable Z_t^i is a linear combination of Y_t where the weights of the combination are the elements of one of the rows of the inverse of the matrix of eigenvectors of A and the constant in each equation, β^i, is the ith row of $Q^{-1}b$.

2.4.4   Stochastic Vector Difference Equations

The behavior of the stochastic system

$$Y_t = b + A Y_{t-1} + CX_t \tag{2.29}$$

can be handled in exactly the same way as the nonstochastic system by decomposing the matrix equation (2.29) into n independent first-order equations. The time path of the original variables Y_t can then be reconstructed by combining the solutions of the independent first-order systems.

The following analysis achieves the solution for Y_t by construction. Iterating equation (2.29) into the past, it follows that one can write the behavior of Y_t in terms of all past values of the random variables X_t. For example, in period 1,

$$Y_1 = b + A Y_0 + CX_1;$$

in period 2,

$$Y_2 = b + CX_2 + A(b + CX_1 + A Y_0);$$

and in period t,

$$Y_t = \sum_{s=0}^{t-1} A^s(b + CX_{t-s}) + A^t Y_0. \tag{2.30}$$

To understand how this equation behaves as $t \to \infty$, one can write the powers of A in the following way:

$$A^s = (Q\Lambda Q^{-1})^s = Q\Lambda^s Q^{-1}.$$

The importance of this way of writing the powers of A follows from the fact that the matrix Λ is diagonal with elements that are equal to the eigenvalues of A. As long as every one of these eigenvalues is less than one in absolute value, each element of Λ^s will converge to zero as $s \to \infty$. But if any eigenvalue is outside the unit circle (greater than one in absolute value), then the matrix Λ will contain a diagonal element that grows without bound. The stability condition for a vector-valued equation therefore requires that all of the eigenvalues of A should be inside the unit circle. If this condition holds, then equation 2.30 can be written as

$$Y_t = (I - A)^{-1}b + C\sum_{s=0}^{\infty} A^s X_{t-s}. \tag{2.31}$$

This way of representing a time series is sometimes called the *moving average representation*, since the value of Y_t is described as a moving average of all past realizations of the disturbance terms X_t.

2.4.5 Example of a Vector System—The Behavior of the Solow Residual

To close this chapter I am going to return to the example of the Solow model to show how a very simple generalization of the first order system can provide a more accurate representation of the data. Recall that the first-order model that we used to describe U.S. GNP took the form

$$y_t = b + ay_{t-1} + ct + d\varepsilon_t, \tag{2.32}$$

$$\varepsilon_t = v_t + c_3 v_{t-1}, \tag{2.33}$$

where the productivity disturbance, v_t was assumed to be drawn from a distribution $D[A, B]$. If the productivity shock v_t is independently distributed through time, then the error term ε_t is predicted to be a *moving average* of the independent shocks, v_t. In the U.S. data the model described by 2.32 and 2.33 does not do a very good job of describing the data. Even if one allows for the possibility that the disturbance to the regression equation 2.32 may be composed of a moving average of independent shocks, the residual of the regression of y_t on y_{t-1} and t still shows substantial autocorrelation. Most applications of simple growth theory account for this fact by modeling v_t as an *autocorrelated* process. In this section I will show how a linear vector difference equation can be used to model the properties of the disturbance to the production technology in a way that provides a plausible representation of the time series properties of the data.

One of the concepts that has been used extensively in recent macroeconomic articles that deal with business fluctuations is that of the *Solow residual*. The idea of the Solow residual is that if the assumptions of the Solow model are correct, then one can measure the combined effects of technological progress A_t and of the productivity disturbance v_t by subtracting a weighted sum of the growth in inputs from the growth of output. We will deal with a special case of the Solow model in which the function $F(\cdot)$ is described by the Cobb-Douglas functional form:

$$Y_t = v_t(K_t)^{\alpha}(A_t L_t)^{1-\alpha}. \tag{2.34}$$

In this case the compound residual is represented by the term

$$v_t A_t^{1-\alpha} = v_t A_0^{1-\alpha} \gamma^{(1-\alpha)t}.$$

As a first pass at estimating the residuals $\{v_t\}$, one might try to directly estimate the production function 2.34 using ordinary least squares on the logarithms of the equation

$$\log Y_t = a_0 + \alpha \log K_t + (1 - \alpha)\log L_t + a_1 t + a_2 \log v_t.$$

But this approach will not work if labor supply fluctuates over time, since the values for labor inputs $\{L_t\}$ will be correlated with the disturbance term of the equation and the least squares estimates of α and $(1 - \alpha)$ will be biased. High values of v_t might be expected to cause an increase in the demand for labor, which would increase the real wage and elicit a supply response in the form of an increase in hours supplied to the labor market, L_t. In fact an ordinary least squares regression of output on labor input leads to a coefficient on labor that is greater than one and a coefficient on capital that is very imprecisely estimated. The large coefficient on labor is associated with the fact that in the data, output is proportionately more volatile than labor input.

  As a way around this problem, Solow pointed out that there is indirect evidence on the magnitude of α if one is prepared to assume that factor markets are competitive. For example, in the case where the production function is Cobb-Douglas, the assumption of competitive factor markets leads to the first-order condition:

$$\frac{(1 - \alpha) Y_t}{L_t} \equiv \omega_t,$$

where ω_t is the wage rate in units of commodities. This can be rewritten to yield the implication that

$$1 - \alpha = \frac{\omega_t L_t}{Y_t},$$

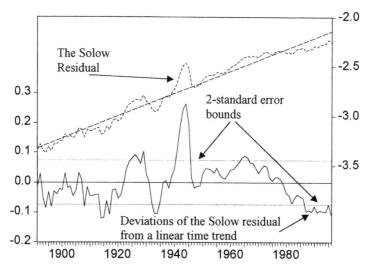

Figure 2.12
Solow residual

where the parameter $1 - \alpha$ is equal to labor's share of the national income. In the postwar U.S. data labor's share has remained relatively stable at around 0.64. Using this indirect evidence, the *Solow residual* is defined by the identity

$$sr_t \equiv \log Y_t - 0.64 \log L_t - 0.36 \log K_t.$$

In figure 2.12 I have graphed the Solow residual computed from U.S. data together with the best linear trend and the deviations from trend. Notice how the deviations from trend are highly persistent—the residual takes very long swings away from trend. Under the maintained assumptions of the model, the time series on the Solow residual represents observations on the productivity disturbance $\{v_t\}$. The observation that the Solow residual is highly persistent suggests that the productivity disturbance v_t is not independently distributed through time. A better way of representing the behavior of v_t is by the statistical model

$$v_t = a_4 v_{t-1} + c_4 t + e_t,$$

where c_4 measures the trend in productivity, a_4 measures the persistence of deviations from trend, and e_t is an i.i.d. shock. Combining this model of v_t with the equations 2.32 and 2.33 leads to the vector difference equation:

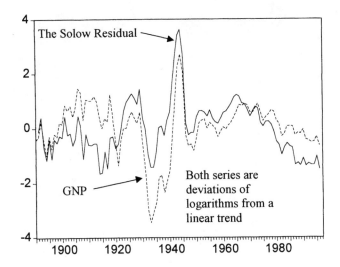

Figure 2.13
Deviations from trend of GNP and the Solow residual

$$\begin{bmatrix} 1 & -d \\ 0 & 1 \end{bmatrix}\begin{bmatrix} y_t \\ sr_t \end{bmatrix} = \begin{bmatrix} a & dc_3 \\ 0 & a_4 \end{bmatrix}\begin{bmatrix} y_{t-1} \\ sr_{t-1} \end{bmatrix} + \begin{bmatrix} b & c \\ 0 & c_4 \end{bmatrix}\begin{bmatrix} 1 \\ t \end{bmatrix} + \begin{bmatrix} 0 \\ e_t \end{bmatrix}, \tag{2.35}$$

where y_t is the logarithm of GNP and the series on the Solow residual is assumed to represent a direct observation of the series of productivity shocks $\{v_t\}$. Premultiplying 2.35 by

$$\begin{bmatrix} 1 & -d \\ 0 & 1 \end{bmatrix}^{-1}$$

leads to a first-order vector model for $\{y_t, sr_t\}$:

$$\begin{bmatrix} y_t \\ sr_t \end{bmatrix} = \begin{bmatrix} a & d(c_3 + a_4) \\ 0 & a_4 \end{bmatrix}\begin{bmatrix} y_{t-1} \\ sr_{t-1} \end{bmatrix} + \begin{bmatrix} b & c + dc_4 \\ 0 & c_4 \end{bmatrix}\begin{bmatrix} 1 \\ t \end{bmatrix} + \begin{bmatrix} d \\ 1 \end{bmatrix}e_t. \tag{2.36}$$

In figure 2.13, I have graphed the deviations from trend of GNP and the Solow residual, and in figure 2.14, I have graphed the residuals from the ordinary least squares regression suggested by equation 2.36. The GNP residual is from the regression of $\hat{y}_t$ on $\hat{y}_{t-1}$ and $\widehat{sr}_{t-1}$, where the hat denotes deviation from trend, and the SR residual is from a regression of $\widehat{sr}_t$ on $\widehat{sr}_{t-1}$. These residuals should be identical under the maintained hypothesis of the model which is driven by a single shock, e_t. Although the hypothesis that these residuals are identical is false, the residual series

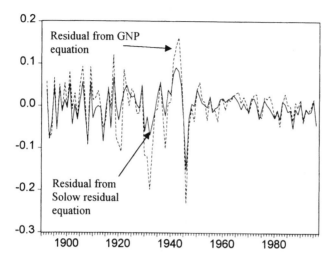

Figure 2.14
Residuals from the statistical model of GNP and Solow residual

are remarkably similar. Notice also that the residual series in figure 2.14 are far less persistent than the Solow residual itself. Although the vector model is not perfect, it provides a better fit of the time series evidence than the simple scalar equation.

2.5 Concluding Remarks

Most macroeconomic models can be represented as linear difference equations that are being continuously disturbed by random variables. In this chapter we have studied the relationship of linear models to nonlinear models, and we have argued that linear models can be thought of as approximations around stable steady states.

We have introduced an important example of a stochastic linear model which was first introduced by Solow in 1956, and we showed how the Solow model can be linearized to provide a statistical model of postwar data that provides a reasonably good fit to the time series on U.S. GNP.

In the later part of the chapter we provided a review of the matrix algebra that one needs to study vector-valued difference equations and showed how a stochastic vector model can be used to improve the fit of the Solow model to U.S. data.

2.6 Problems

1. Consider an abstract economic model of the form:

$$y_t = E_t[f(y_{t+1}, x_{t+1}, u_t)],$$

$$x_t = g(x_{t-1}, y_{t-1}), \qquad t = 1, 2 \ldots, \tag{2.37}$$

$$x_0 = \bar{x}_0, \quad y_0 = \bar{y}_0,$$

where y and x are scalar economic variables, E_t is the conditional expectations operator and u_t is an i.i.d. random variable.

a. What do you need to assume about the functions f and g, and about the density function of the random variable u, in order for a linearized version of this model to be a good local approximation to the nonlinear model.

b. What would be a good point around which to linearize this model? Why?

c. Explain how to derive a log-linear model using a first-order Taylor series approximation.

d. Under what conditions on the functions f and g does the log-linear model deliver a locally determinate steady state?

2. Log linearize each of the following equations. In each case define a point $\{\bar{y}, \bar{x}, \bar{z}\}$ such that $\bar{y} = f(\bar{x}, \bar{z})$, and compute the linear function

$$\tilde{y}_t = \varepsilon_{fx}\tilde{x}_t + \varepsilon_{fz}\tilde{z}_t.$$

a. $y_t = (ax_t^\theta + (1-a)z_t^\theta)^{1/\theta}$

b. $y_t = (ax_t^\theta + (1-a)z_t^\theta)^{\gamma/\theta}$

c. $y_t = (ax_t + bz_t)$

d. $y_t = x_t^\alpha z_t^\beta$

e. $y_t = z_t^\alpha x_t^\beta + 1$

3. Express each of the following two matrices in the form $Q\Lambda Q'$ where Λ is a diagonal matrix of eigenvalues, Q is a symmetric matrix of eigenvectors, and $Q' = Q^{-1}$:

$$\begin{bmatrix} 4 & 3^{1/2} \\ 3^{1/2} & 2 \end{bmatrix}, \quad \begin{bmatrix} 3 & 2^{1/2} \\ 2^{1/2} & 2 \end{bmatrix}$$

4. Consider the linear economic model described by the equations

$$\begin{bmatrix} y_t \\ x_t \end{bmatrix} = A \begin{bmatrix} y_{t-1} \\ x_{t-1} \end{bmatrix} + \begin{bmatrix} u_t \\ v_t \end{bmatrix}, \quad \begin{bmatrix} y_0 \\ x_0 \end{bmatrix} = \begin{bmatrix} 0 \\ 0 \end{bmatrix},$$

where y_t and x_t are endogenous economic variables and u_t and v_t are i.i.d. white noise error terms. The matrix A is given by

$$\begin{bmatrix} \frac{1}{2} & 1 \\ \frac{1}{16} & \frac{1}{2} \end{bmatrix}.$$

a. Find a pair of univariate stochastic difference equations in transformed variables that completely characterizes the behavior of this system.

b. Suppose that u and v are each uniformly distributed on the interval $[-1, 1]$. Find values for the support of the invariant distribution of y and x.

5. Consider the following linear model:

$$y_t = \alpha y_{t+1}^e + \beta x_t + u_t, \tag{2.38}$$

$$x_t = \gamma x_{t-1} + \delta + v_t, \tag{2.39}$$

where equation 2.38 describes the evolution of an endogenous variable and equation 2.39 represents a policy rule. The parameters α, β, γ, and δ are all positive, and α and γ are both less than 1.

a. The terms u_t and v_t are independent, serially uncorrelated error terms with zero mean. Under the assumption that the subjective expectation, y_{t+1}^e is determined adaptively by the rule

$$y_{t+1}^e = \lambda y_t^e + (1 - \lambda) y_t, \qquad 0 < \lambda < 1, \tag{2.40}$$

find a stochastic difference equation involving only the observable variables y_t and x_t (y^e is *not* observable), lags of y_t and x_t, and (lags of) the error term u_t that describes the behavior of y_t through time.

b. Assume that the support of v_t is the interval $[-a, a]$ where a is finite. Find the support of the distribution of x_t as $t \to \infty$.

3 Linear Difference Equations: Part 2

3.1 Introduction

This chapter has two parts that deal with related but distinct topics. In the first part of the chapter I am going to return to an idea that was introduced in chapter 1. This concerns the fact that most economic models differ from models of physical systems since they represent the behavior of thinking human beings who form beliefs about the future. In chapter 1 I discussed first-order systems in which the *only* dynamics arise from the influence of beliefs on current actions, but most economic models combine expectations of this kind with the class of dynamics that we studied in chapter 2. The way that these two types of dynamics are combined in linear rational expectations models is the subject of section 3.3.3.

In the second part of the chapter I am going to discuss an implication of the fact that rational agents make forecasts of the future when they decide how to behave in the present. This implication is widely known as the *Lucas critique of econometric policy evaluation*, following an important 1976 article by Robert Lucas [75]. Lucas observed that the use of econometric models to forecast the effects of policy changes is not likely to succeed if agents form their expectations rationally. The reason for this breakdown of conventional forecasting techniques arises from the fact that the estimated parameters of an econometric model will incorporate the beliefs of the individuals that are conditional on the particular policy that was followed *at the time the model was estimated*. If government policy is subsequently altered, the parameters of the model would be expected to change to reflect the new regime.

The theme of this book is that under some circumstances, beliefs about the future can themselves influence what happens. The connection of this idea to rational expectations hinges on the way that one solves rational expectations models. To understand when beliefs matter, and when they do not, in this chapter I will show how the idea of *regular* and *irregular* models can be extended to systems with higher dimensions than the simple first order example that we studied in chapter 1. But although I will define what I mean by an irregular model, the examples that I focus on in this chapter are confined to the regular case. Later in the book I will introduce examples that violate the conditions of the regular case, and I will talk about the implications of these models for the conventional wisdoms of rational expectations.

3.2 Linear Rational Expectations Models

Most economic models consist of equations that combine the dynamics induced by beliefs about the future with the dynamics induced by the effects of accumulating stocks from the past. These equations are derived by linearizing nonlinear economies around stationary states using the technique that we studied in chapter 2. In equation 3.1, I have laid out a class of linear models that is general enough to cover most of the cases that one meets in practical macroeconomic examples:

$$\begin{bmatrix} y_t^1 \\ y_t^2 \end{bmatrix} = A \begin{bmatrix} y_{t+1}^1 \\ y_{t+1}^2 \end{bmatrix} + B \begin{bmatrix} v_{t+1} \\ w_{t+1} \end{bmatrix}, \quad y_0^1 = \bar{y}_0^1, \tag{3.1}$$

$$w_{t+1} = E_t[y_{t+1}] - y_{t+1}.$$

In these equations I have used the terminology $y_t \in R^n$ to refer to an n vector of variables, and I have partitioned these variables into two sets:

$$y_t = \begin{bmatrix} y_t^1 \\ y_t^2 \end{bmatrix}, \quad y_t^1 \in R^{n_1}, \quad y_t^2 \in R^{n_2}, \quad n_1 + n_2 = n.$$

The variables y_t are referred to as *state variables*, and they are assumed to include exogenous and endogenous variables as well as variables that are unobservable to the economist. The idea is that y_t is a complete description of all of the factors that influence economic behavior at date t. There may be other variables not part of the state vector that are of interest to the economist, but all such variables are assumed to be *functions* of the state. For example, in the version of the optimal growth model that we will study in this chapter, one may choose either the capital stock or GNP to be a state variable. If one chooses the capital stock, then GNP can be calculated as a function of the capital stock and of the shock to productivity. Similarly, if one chooses GNP, then the capital stock can be found as a function of GNP and of the productivity shock. This is an example of a model in which the state vector is two dimensional and all other economic variables are functions of this two-dimensional state.

In equation 3.1, I have partitioned the state vector into those variables that are *predetermined* and those variables that are *free*. A predetermined variable is a variable that is associated with an initial condition.[1] The number of predetermined variables is an important component of an economic model, since it is closely linked to the possibility that beliefs may have an independent influence on economic activity. An example of a predetermined variable would be the stock of capital which is chosen one period in advance. An example of a free variable would be the real value of the money supply, which is free to move around in every period as the prices of commodities adjust to clear markets. One of the main ideas that we will develop below, is that beliefs can independently influence activity when there are too few predetermined variables. "Too few" is made precise by comparing the number of free variables with the number of eigenvalues of the matrix A that lie inside the unit circle.

The disturbance terms in equation 3.1 are of two types. First, I have included a set of *fundamental* disturbances $v_t \in R^m$ that are independently and identically distributed through time (i.i.d.). I will also assume that

$$E[v_t] = \bar{v}.$$

Fundamental disturbances are factors that affect the preferences, the endowments, or the technology of the economic environment. The assumption that these fundamental shocks are i.i.d. is general enough to cover the case of autocorrelated shocks, since I will allow for the possibility that some of the variables, y_t, may be unobservable. The matrix A is assumed to contain all of the intertemporal linkages of the model. This point is relevant to the leading application of the techniques that I will describe, the stochastic optimal growth model, which assumes that business cycles are generated by an autocorrelated productivity shock. In the framework of equation 3.1 the productivity shock becomes one of the state variables and the disturbance, v_t, is modeled as the innovation to this disturbance.

The second set of disturbances in equation 3.1 consists of deviations of the vector of state variables, y_t, from their one-step-ahead expected values. By constructing the matrices A and B appropriately, equation 3.1 can include equations in which the value of a state variable at date t is influenced by the expected value of the state variables at date $t+1$ but not by their realizations. It can also include equations in which the realizations of y_{t+1} enter the equation but the expectations of these variables are absent; for example, the capital accumulation equation in the optimal growth model is of this type. The best way to understand these points is to go through an example.

3.2.1 Optimal Growth as an Illustration of a Rational Expectations Model

In this section I am going to introduce a model that forms the basis for the theory of *real business cycles,* one of the major current research agendas in theoretical and applied macroeconomics. Although, for historical reasons, I refer to the model as one of optimal growth, I am going to concentrate on its implications for short-run fluctuations, and I will introduce a version that abstracts from growth entirely. The idea is to explain the co-movements of capital, investment, output, consumption, and labor hours *as if* they were chosen by a single infinitely lived household. The approach, in its simplest form, sidesteps the determination of market prices and asks directly how Robinson Crusoe would allocate his resources through time. Since society is assumed to consist of a single agent, one can safely ignore any complications that might arise from the difficulties of coordinating economic activity.

The assumption of a single representative agent is very strong, although the approach is quite a bit more general than it at first appears. In chapter 5 I will examine a set of conditions under which multiple agents may interact through markets and achieve the same allocation that would be achieved by a single central planner.

The representative agent's problem is set out below:

$$\max_{\{c_t\}_{t=1}^{\infty}} E_t \left[\sum_{t=1}^{\infty} \beta^{t-1} \log(c_t) \right],$$

$$c_t + k_{t+1} \leq (1 - \delta)k_t + s_t k_t^{\alpha},$$

$$s_t = s_{t-1}^{\rho} v_t, \quad 0 \leq \rho < 1,$$

$$k_0 = \bar{k}_0, \quad s_0 = \bar{s}_0.$$

The variable c_t represents consumption, and k_t is capital that depreciates at rate δ. I assume that the consumer has logarithmic preferences and that he discounts the future at rate $\beta \in [0, 1)$. The term s_t represents a technological disturbance to the production technology which is modeled as an autocorrelated process driven by an innovation v_t which I take to be a random variable with bounded support:

$$v_t \in V = [v_1, v_2], \quad t = 1, \ldots.$$

I will make two assumptions about v_t that are needed to justify the technique of taking a linear approximation to the model. The first assumption is that

$$0 < v_1 < v_2 < \infty,$$

where the support of the distribution is small; namely v_1 is close enough to v_2 for linear approximations to the nonlinear first-order conditions to remain approximately valid. The second assumption is that v_t is independent of v_{t+s}, for all s and that the distribution of v_t is identical at each point in time.

For the purpose of this chapter I will represent technology by a Cobb-Douglas production function with a factor, labor, that is in fixed supply. The assumption of fixed labor supply is made to simplify the algebra, and it must be relaxed if one wishes to describe a model of business cycles in which employment fluctuations play an important role. I have also abstracted from growth in this chapter, although the same technique of a disturbance that fluctuates around a growing trend applies to this model as well as to the Solow model discussed in chapter 2. All of the above assumptions have been generalized in the literature to allow, for example, variable labor supply, technological progress, and more general preferences and technologies.

The first-order conditions to the consumer's problem are given by a set of equations:

$$\frac{1}{c_t} = \beta E_t \left[\frac{1}{c_{t+1}} \{ (1 - \delta) + F_k^{t+1} \} \right], \tag{3.2}$$

$$k_{t+1} = (1 - \delta)k_t + s_t k_t^\alpha - c_t, \tag{3.3}$$

$$s_{t+1} = s_t^\rho v_{t+1}, \tag{3.4}$$

where

$$F_k^{t+1} = \alpha s_{t+1} k_{t+1}^{\alpha - 1},$$

is the marginal product of capital in period $t + 1$, state s_{t+1}.

Equations 3.2, 3.3, and 3.4 are nonlinear analogues of 3.1. There are a number of ways of handling nonlinear equations directly and much recent effort has gone into a study of solution techniques that can be applied to the kinds of nonlinear functional equations that arise in economics. One of the main conclusions of this research has been that, at least for the problems that have been studied so far, exact nonlinear solutions do not differ greatly from linear approximations within the bounds of the fluctuations that have been experienced in the U.S. economy.

The approach that I will take in this book is to explore the implications of taking a linear approximation. The first step is to choose a point around which to linearize. For this purpose I am going to define

$$\bar{s} = \bar{v}^{1/(1-\rho)}, \tag{3.5}$$

where $\bar{v}$ is the expected value of v_t. Now define $\bar{c}$ and $\bar{k}$ as the implicit solutions to the following equations:

$$\frac{1}{\bar{c}} = \frac{\beta}{\bar{c}}(1 - \delta + \alpha\bar{s}\bar{k}^{\alpha-1}),$$

$$\bar{k} = (1 - \delta)\bar{k} + \bar{s}\bar{k}^{\alpha} - \bar{c};$$

that is, $\bar{c}$ and $\bar{k}$ are defined as the steady state values of consumption and capital that would occur in an economy in which the value of the productivity shock was equal to its unconditional mean in every period. Taking a first-order Taylor series approximation to 3.2–3.4 around the vector

$$x \equiv \{\bar{c}, \bar{k}, \bar{s}\},$$

leads to the following linear equations:[2]

$$-\hat{c}_t = E_t[-\hat{c}_{t+1} + a_1\hat{k}_{t+1} + a_2\hat{s}_{t+1} + O(x^2)],$$

$$\hat{k}_{t+1} = b_1\hat{k}_t + b_2\hat{s}_t + b_3\hat{c}_t + O(x^2), \tag{3.6}$$

$$\hat{s}_{t+1} = \rho\hat{s}_t + \hat{v}_{t+1} + O(x^2),$$

where the parameters a_i, and b_i are given by the expressions

$$a_1 = \beta\alpha(\alpha - 1)\bar{s}\bar{k}^{\alpha-1}, \quad a_2 = \beta\alpha\bar{s}\bar{k}^{\alpha-1},$$

$$b_1 = 1 - \delta + \alpha\bar{s}\bar{k}^{\alpha-1}, \quad b_2 = \bar{s}\bar{k}^{\alpha-1}, \quad b_3 = -\frac{\bar{c}}{\bar{k}},$$

and the variables $\hat{c}_t$, $\hat{k}_t$, $\hat{s}_t$ and $\hat{v}_t$ are defined as deviations from the nonstochastic steady state

$$\hat{c}_t \equiv \frac{c_t - \bar{c}}{\bar{c}}, \quad \hat{k}_t \equiv \frac{k_t - \bar{k}}{\bar{k}}, \quad \hat{s}_t \equiv \frac{s_t - \bar{s}}{\bar{s}}, \quad \hat{v}_t \equiv \frac{v_t - \bar{v}}{\bar{v}}.$$

Putting these equations into the form of a first-order vector system and dropping terms of order less than or equal to x^2 leads to the following system:

$$
\begin{bmatrix} -1 & 0 & 0 \\ b_3 & b_1 & b_2 \\ 0 & 0 & p \end{bmatrix}
\begin{bmatrix} \hat{c}_t \\ \hat{k}_t \\ \hat{s}_t \end{bmatrix}
=
\begin{bmatrix} -1 & a_1 & a_2 \\ 0 & 1 & 0 \\ 0 & 0 & 1 \end{bmatrix}
\begin{bmatrix} \hat{c}_{t+1} \\ \hat{k}_{t+1} \\ \hat{s}_{t+1} \end{bmatrix}
$$

$$
+
\begin{bmatrix} 0 & -1 & a_1 & a_2 \\ 0 & 0 & 0 & 0 \\ -1 & 0 & 0 & 0 \end{bmatrix}
\begin{bmatrix} \hat{v}_{t+1} \\ w^c_{t+1} \\ w^k_{t+1} \\ w^s_{t+1} \end{bmatrix},
\tag{3.7}
$$

where

$$
w^x_{t+1} = E_t[x_{t+1}] - x_{t+1} \qquad \text{for } x = c, k, s.
$$

Now premultiply equation 3.7 by the matrix:

$$
\begin{bmatrix} -1 & 0 & 0 \\ b_3 & b_1 & b_2 \\ 0 & 0 & p \end{bmatrix}^{-1}.
\tag{3.8}
$$

What is left is a linear first-order system of the same form as equation 3.1. Writing out the result of this premultiplication explicitly leads to the system

$$
\begin{bmatrix} \hat{c}_t \\ \hat{k}_t \\ \hat{s}_t \end{bmatrix}
= A
\begin{bmatrix} \hat{c}_{t+1} \\ \hat{k}_{t+1} \\ \hat{s}_{t+1} \end{bmatrix}
+ B
\begin{bmatrix} \hat{v}_{t+1} \\ w^c_{t+1} \\ w^k_{t+1} \\ w^s_{t+1} \end{bmatrix},
\qquad \hat{k}_0, \hat{s}_0 \text{ predetermined,}
\tag{3.9}
$$

with matrices A and B that arise from premultiplying equation 3.7 by the matrix 3.8.

3.3 Solving Linear Rational Expectations Models

3.3.1 Different Types of Rational Expectations Models

In the first part of this chapter I alluded to a relationship between the stability of the steady state of a model and the number of predetermined variables. More precisely the relationship between the number of roots of the matrix A that lie within the unit circle and the number of variables that are *free* is important in determining the properties of a rational expectations model. If the number of stable roots is equal to the number of free initial conditions, there will be a *unique* rational expectations equilibrium. When there are too *many* roots inside the unit circle a stationary rational expectations equilibrium will not exist. When there are too *few* roots inside the unit circle there will exist many rational expectations equilibria. This latter possibility forms the basis for the macroeconomics of self-fulfilling prophecies on which the title of this book is based.

In describing how to solve rational expectations models, I am going to separate the types of models that one meets into two classes. To define these two classes, I am first going to partition[3] the roots of A into two sets:

$$i \in S \quad \text{if} \quad |\lambda_i| < 1,$$

and

$$i \in U \quad \text{if} \quad |\lambda_i| > 1,$$

where the roots for which $i \in S$ are *forward stable* and the roots for which $i \in U$ are *forward unstable*. I have used the word *forward* to emphasize that the equations that we will study describe how the combinations of the state variables depend on expectations of the future rather than how they depend on the past as in more familiar examples of dynamical systems in the natural sciences. This reversal of the direction in which the equations are solved also reverses the conditions under which an equation is either stable or unstable.

The idea of stable and unstable roots lets us think about the *dimension* of the set of initial conditions for which convergence to the steady state of the model is guaranteed. In the example of a two-dimensional state vector, and a steady state that has one root that is stable and one root that is unstable, the dimensions of S and U are both equal to one. A steady state of this kind is called a *saddle point*, and if the steady state of a model is a saddle point, there is a linear restriction relating the pairs of initial values of the two variables such that the model will converge to the steady state if and only if this restriction holds. But the number of predetermined variables can also be thought of as a linear restriction on the set of initial conditions. When there are exactly enough restrictions from the stability conditions and from the initial conditions combined, to uniquely pick a path that converges to the steady state, we will say that the model is *regular*.[4] A model is regular if

$$n_s + n_1 = n.$$

The case of a regular model is one that is most frequently encountered in the literature. The optimal growth model that we studied above, for example, always has a regular steady state. It is associated with two initial conditions, s_t and k_t that are predetermined, and it always leads to a steady state with a single eigenvalue that is inside the unit circle for reasons that I will discuss in chapter 5.

Although regular models have been studied more closely than other cases, in this book we will also examine several examples of economic models in which there are not enough restrictions to uniquely pin down the initial conditions; in this case we say that the model is *irregular*. A model is irregular if

$$n_s + n_1 < n.$$

I will show in chapter 7 that externalities in the optimal growth model can lead to an example of an irregular model, and I will provide an example of how this situation can allow beliefs to influence economic activity.

The final possibility that cannot be logically ruled out is one in which

$$n_s + n_1 > n.$$

In this case a stationary rational expectations equilibrium does not exist, although there may still be nonstationary sequences of probability distributions that obey all of the dynamic equations of the model but fail to converge to an invariant distribution.

3.3.2   Case of a Regular Equilibrium

In this section I am going to show how to solve models of the form described by equation 3.1 when there are exactly enough initial conditions to uniquely determine a stationary equilibrium, and I am going to concentrate on the specific example of the optimal growth model, described above.

Since the variables y_t are deviations from stationary values, the equation has no constant term. The first step in constructing a solution is to premultiply 3.1 by Q^{-1} where $A = Q\Lambda Q^{-1}$; here Λ is a diagonal matrix of eigenvalues, and Q contains the eigenvectors of A. The purpose of diagonalization is that it allows us to write the matrix system as a set of first-order equations in the transformed variables z_t^i, where z_t^i is the ith element of $Q^{-1} y_t$:

$$z_t^i = \lambda_i [z_{t+1}^i] + \phi_{t+1}^i, \tag{3.10}$$

and ϕ_{t+1}^i is the ith row of,

$$Q^{-1} B \begin{bmatrix} v_{t+1} \\ w_{t+1} \end{bmatrix}.$$

Now take conditional expectations of 3.10 and make use of the fact that

$$E_t[\phi_{t+1}^i] = 0,$$

since the fundamental disturbances have zero means, and the conditional expectations of the forecast errors, w_t, are by definition equal to zero:

$$z_t^i = \lambda_i E_t[z_{t+1}^i]. \tag{3.11}$$

To solve the above system of independent equations, one must recognize that the roots, λ_i, may be greater than or less than one in absolute value.[5] If $|\lambda_i|$ is less than one, then equation 3.11 can be iterated into the future to find how z_t^i depends on $E[z_{t+s}^i]$ for all s. As we will show below, this process leads to a convergent sequence that sets z_t^i equal to zero. If, on the other hand, $|\lambda_i|$ is greater than one, equation 3.11 determines how $E_t[z_{t+1}^i]$ depends on z_t^i.

3.3.3 Solving a Rational Expectations Model by Iterating into the Future

In the example of the optimal growth model, exactly one of the roots of A is less than one. This means that there is exactly one value of $i \in S$. Taking this value of i, we can iterate 3.11 into the future and write

$$z_t^i = \lambda_i^T E_t[z_{t+T}^i]. \tag{3.12}$$

But since

$$\lim_{T \to \infty} \lambda_i^{t+T} = 0,$$

it follows that

$$z_t^i = 0, \qquad i \in S. \tag{3.13}$$

In the case of more general examples, S may have n_s elements and U may have n_u elements, where $n_s + n_u = n$. In this case equation 3.13 would define n_s linear restrictions on the vector y_t. In the case of the optimal growth model, however, the single stable root places one linear restriction on y_t that relates the value of the free variable, c_t, to the values of the predetermined variables, s_t, and k_t. In the special case in which there is no stochastic term v_t, this function causes the free variable to be placed on the eigenvector associated with the stable branch of the saddle path of the steady state of the system. For this reason the steady state is often said to be *saddle path stable* in two-dimensional systems.

3.3.4 Completing the Solution by Solving Equations That Depend on the Past

To describe the evolution of k_t, s_t, and c_t, one needs to find probability distributions of these variables as functions of time that satisfy the set of equations 3.1. But now that we have described how c_t is determined, the linearized forms of the capital accumulation equation and the evolution of the driving uncertainty imply that

$$\hat{k}_{t+1} = b_1 \hat{k}_t + b_2 \hat{s}_t + b_3 \hat{c}_t,$$
$$\hat{s}_{t+1} = \rho \hat{s}_t + \hat{v}_{t+1}. \tag{3.14}$$

By substituting the solution

$$\hat{c}_t = q^{i1} \hat{k}_t + q^{i2} \hat{s}_t,$$

into equation 3.14, where

$$[q^{i1}, q^{i2}]$$

is the row of Q^{-1} associated with the stable eigenvector of A, one arrives at a first-order vector equation that describes the evolution of the economy as a Markov process with state variables $\tilde{k}_t$ and $\tilde{s}_t$:

$$\begin{bmatrix} \hat{k}_t \\ \hat{s}_t \end{bmatrix} = \bar{A} \begin{bmatrix} \hat{k}_{t-1} \\ \hat{s}_{t-1} \end{bmatrix} + \bar{b} \hat{v}_t. \tag{3.15}$$

The parameter matrix $\bar{A}$ and the vector $\bar{b}$ are combinations of b_1, b_2, b_3, ρ, and the elements of the ith row of Q^{-1}, and v_t is a scalar i.i.d. innovation to the productivity disturbance s_t.

3.3.5   Optimal Growth Model and the Solow Model Compared

In chapter 2 we discussed a model of growth proposed by Solow that began with the assumption that consumption was linearly related to income. In conjunction with a model in which the technology was subject to autocorrelated disturbances the Solow model generated the following two equations:

$$\begin{bmatrix} \hat{y}_t \\ \widehat{sr}_t \end{bmatrix} = A \begin{bmatrix} \hat{y}_{t-1} \\ \widehat{sr}_{t-1} \end{bmatrix} + be_t, \tag{3.16}$$

where $\widehat{sr}_t$ is a technology shock, $\hat{y}_t$ is output, and e_t is a scalar i.i.d. innovation. I have used the tilde to denote deviations from a trend growth path. The matrix A and the vector b consist of combinations of the parameters of the linearized model.

In this chapter I have discussed an example of *optimal* growth in which the behavior of consumption is derived from optimizing behavior by rational individuals. Although I have stated the optimal growth model in the form of 3.15, using capital as the state variable, there is a simple transformation of the model, by the fact that $\hat{y}_t$ is (approximately) a linear function of $\hat{k}_t$ and $\hat{s}_t$, that has the same form as equation 3.16. One is entitled to ask the question: What has been gained from a complicated digression into infinite horizon optimization theory?

The answer to this question is that the optimal growth model is more restrictive than the Solow model because it contains restrictions on the parameters of the matrix $\bar{A}$ that have important implications for the use of the model as a vehicle for evaluating different kinds of policies. Thomas Sargent calls these *cross-equation restrictions* the hallmark of rational expectations models . In the example that we have studied so far, these restrictions mean that the parameters of the process followed by $\hat{y}_t$ are functions of the parameters of the driving process $\hat{s}_t$. If the driving process is unchanged through time, as in the example of optimal growth, these restrictions do not have important consequences for the conduct of economic policy. But in many examples of rational expectations models, the driving process itself is an object of choice by the political authorities. In the following section I am going to discuss a second important example of a rational expectations model, and I am going to use this example to discuss the importance of the cross-equation restrictions in the context of economic policy.

3.4 Cross-equation Restrictions and the Lucas Critique

I now am going to dig a little deeper into the idea of cross-equation restrictions by introducing an example of an economic model in which one of the equations is interpreted as a rule that is followed by the government. This example is drawn from the work of Phillip Cagan [30] who used a simple money demand equation to study the dynamics of hyperinflations. Sargent and Wallace [99] picked up on Cagan's work and added rational expectations. It is the Sargent and Wallace route that we follow here.

3.4.1 Dynamics of a Monetary Model—A Second Example

There are a number of simple theories of behavior that lead to an equation in which the demand for money, measured in units of commodities, depends on a scale variable, usually income, and on the opportunity cost of holding money, usually the rate of interest. Later in this book we will look at two different cases of economic environments that lead to specific interpretations of the demand for money. One of these environments is Samuelson's [97] model of "the social contrivance of money," and the other follows up on Don Patinkin's [89] suggestion that money should be thought of as a productive asset that yields a flow of transactions services. Both of these models lead to an equation of the form:

$$m_t - p_t = a + by_t - ci_t,$$

where m_t is the logarithm of the stock of money, p_t is the logarithm of the price level, y_t is the logarithm of GNP, and i_t is the rate of interest.[6] By defining the *real* rate of interest as

$$r_t = i_t - E_t[p_{t+1}] + p_t, \tag{3.17}$$

where $E_t[p_{t+1}]$ represents the agent's expectation of the logarithm of the future price level, this equation can be rewritten as

$$m_t - p_t = a + by_t - c(r_t + E_t[p_{t+1}] - p_t).$$

Cagan began with an equation this kind, and he pointed out that in periods of hyperinflation, movements in r_t and y_t would be swamped by movements in expected inflation. He assumed that to a first approximation, r_t, and y_t, are constant. Sargent and Wallace added to this argument the assumption that expectations are rational; that is, the expectation in equation 3.17 is evaluated using the true probability distribution of p_{t+1}. Putting these ideas together leads to a first-order functional equation:

$$p_t = \alpha + \beta E_t[p_{t+1}] + \gamma m_t, \tag{3.18}$$

where

$$\alpha = \frac{cr - by - a}{1 + c}, \quad \beta = \frac{c}{1 + c}, \quad \gamma = \frac{1}{1 + c}.$$

Although equation 3.18 would be expected to be a better description of a period of high inflation, rather than a period of stable prices, for the purpose of describing the idea that policy rules matter, I am going to examine the predictions of the model in a period in which the money supply is stationary. Suppose, for example, that the Federal Reserve Board follows a policy that picks m_t, using the rule

$$m_{t+1} = \bar{m} + \lambda m_t + u_{t+1}, \tag{3.19}$$

where $\bar{m}$ and λ are constants, u_t is an i.i.d. random variable with an expected value of zero, and the policy parameter λ is less than one in absolute value. This assumption on λ means that the solution that we are going to study does not apply to inflationary environments. To cover the case of growing or accelerating money growth rates, one must find a transformation of the model, by taking differences, that has a stationary solution.

Letting the tilde over a variable denote deviation from the non-stochastic steady state, the policy equation 3.19 can be combined with the behavioral equation 3.18 to generate the model

$$\begin{bmatrix} 1 & -\gamma \\ 0 & \lambda \end{bmatrix} \begin{bmatrix} \tilde{p}_t \\ \tilde{m}_t \end{bmatrix} = \begin{bmatrix} \beta & 0 \\ 0 & 1 \end{bmatrix} \begin{bmatrix} \tilde{p}_{t+1} \\ \tilde{m}_{t+1} \end{bmatrix} + \begin{bmatrix} 0 & \beta \\ 1 & 0 \end{bmatrix} \begin{bmatrix} u_{t+1} \\ w_{t+1} \end{bmatrix}, \tag{3.20}$$

where

$$w_{t+1} = E_t[\tilde{p}_{t+1}] - \tilde{p}_{t+1}.$$

Premultiplying 3.20 by

$$\begin{bmatrix} 1 & -\gamma \\ 0 & \lambda \end{bmatrix}^{-1} = \begin{bmatrix} 1 & \frac{\gamma}{\lambda} \\ 0 & \frac{1}{\lambda} \end{bmatrix}$$

We arrive at the equation

$$
\begin{bmatrix} \tilde{p}_t \\ \tilde{m}_t \end{bmatrix} = \begin{bmatrix} 1 & \dfrac{\gamma}{\lambda} \\ 0 & \dfrac{1}{\lambda} \end{bmatrix} \begin{bmatrix} \beta & 0 \\ 0 & 1 \end{bmatrix} \begin{bmatrix} \tilde{p}_{t+1} \\ \tilde{m}_{t+1} \end{bmatrix} + \begin{bmatrix} 1 & \dfrac{\gamma}{\lambda} \\ 0 & \dfrac{1}{\lambda} \end{bmatrix} \begin{bmatrix} 0 & \beta \\ 1 & 0 \end{bmatrix} \begin{bmatrix} u_{t+1} \\ w_{t+1} \end{bmatrix},
$$

or

$$
\begin{bmatrix} \tilde{p}_t \\ \tilde{m}_t \end{bmatrix} = \begin{bmatrix} \beta & \dfrac{\gamma}{\lambda} \\ 0 & \dfrac{1}{\lambda} \end{bmatrix} \begin{bmatrix} \tilde{p}_{t+1} \\ \tilde{m}_{t+1} \end{bmatrix} + \begin{bmatrix} \dfrac{\gamma}{\lambda} & \beta \\ \dfrac{1}{\lambda} & 0 \end{bmatrix} \begin{bmatrix} u_{t+1} \\ w_{t+1} \end{bmatrix},
\tag{3.21}
$$

which is the same form as equation 3.1 which we introduced at the beginning of the chapter.

3.4.2   Solving the Example Explicitly

To show how to use the technique that I introduced in section 3.3.3 I am going to go through the example provided by equation 3.21 step by step. Since some of the algebra of the model can get a little tedious, you may wish to skip quickly through this section on first reading.

Recall that the first step in solving the model is to diagonalize the matrix A, which in this example is given by

$$
\begin{bmatrix} \beta & \dfrac{\gamma}{\lambda} \\ 0 & \dfrac{1}{\lambda} \end{bmatrix}.
$$

To find the roots of A, we must solve the equation

$$
\left| \begin{bmatrix} \beta - x & \dfrac{\gamma}{\lambda} \\ 0 & \dfrac{1}{\lambda} - x \end{bmatrix} \right| = 0,
$$

which leads to the quadratic

$$
(\beta - x)\left(\frac{1}{\lambda} - x\right) = 0,
$$

with roots β and $1/\lambda$. Since the money supply process is stationary, one of these roots, $1/\lambda$, is greater than one in absolute value. The second root,

$\beta = c/(1 + c)$, is less than one as long as the demand for money goes down when the opportunity cost of holding money goes up; that is, as long as c is positive.

The eigenvectors of A are found by solving the equations

$$\begin{bmatrix} \beta & \dfrac{\gamma}{\lambda} \\ 0 & \dfrac{1}{\lambda} \end{bmatrix} \begin{bmatrix} 1 \\ q_1 \end{bmatrix} = \beta \begin{bmatrix} 1 \\ q_1 \end{bmatrix}, \quad \begin{bmatrix} \beta & \dfrac{\gamma}{\lambda} \\ 0 & \dfrac{1}{\lambda} \end{bmatrix} \begin{bmatrix} 1 \\ q_2 \end{bmatrix} = \frac{1}{\lambda} \begin{bmatrix} 1 \\ q_2 \end{bmatrix},$$

where I have normalized the first element of each eigenvector to unity. These equations imply that

$$q_1 = 0 \quad \text{and} \quad q_2 = \frac{1 - \lambda\beta}{\gamma}.$$

The matrix A can then be decomposed as $Q \Lambda Q^{-1}$:

$$\begin{bmatrix} \beta & \dfrac{\gamma}{\lambda} \\ 0 & \dfrac{1}{\lambda} \end{bmatrix} = \begin{bmatrix} 1 & 1 \\ 0 & \dfrac{1 - \lambda\beta}{\gamma} \end{bmatrix} \begin{bmatrix} \beta & 0 \\ 0 & \dfrac{1}{\lambda} \end{bmatrix} \begin{bmatrix} 1 & \dfrac{-\gamma}{1 - \lambda\beta} \\ 0 & \dfrac{\gamma}{1 - \lambda\beta} \end{bmatrix}$$

where

$$Q^{-1} = \begin{bmatrix} 1 & 1 \\ 0 & \dfrac{1 - \lambda\beta}{\gamma} \end{bmatrix}^{-1} = \begin{bmatrix} 1 & \dfrac{-\gamma}{1 - \lambda\beta} \\ 0 & \dfrac{\gamma}{1 - \lambda\beta} \end{bmatrix}.$$

To apply the solution technique that we discussed in the first part of this chapter, we can take expectations of equation 3.21 and write the equation as

$$\begin{bmatrix} \tilde{p}_t \\ \tilde{m}_t \end{bmatrix} = A E_t \begin{bmatrix} \tilde{p}_{t+1} \\ \tilde{m}_{t+1} \end{bmatrix}. \tag{3.22}$$

Recall that we must multiply equation 3.22 by Q^{-1}, which leads to the pair of independent scalar equations:

$$\begin{bmatrix} z_t^1 \\ z_t^2 \end{bmatrix} = \begin{bmatrix} \beta & 0 \\ 0 & \dfrac{1}{\lambda} \end{bmatrix} E_t \begin{bmatrix} z_{t+1}^1 \\ z_{t+1}^2 \end{bmatrix}.$$

Since β is less than one in absolute value and $1/\lambda$ is greater than one in absolute value, the first equation can be iterated forward to generate the restriction

$$z_t^1 = \left[1, \frac{-\gamma}{1 - \lambda\beta}\right]\begin{bmatrix} \tilde{p}_t \\ \tilde{m}_t \end{bmatrix} = 0.$$

The rational expectations solution to this example is therefore given by the function

$$\tilde{p}_t = \frac{\gamma}{1 - \lambda\beta}\tilde{m}_t. \tag{3.23}$$

3.4.3   Lucas Critique and Cross-equation Restrictions

The form of the solution represented by equation 3.23 looks a lot like the kind of equation that econometricians estimated in the 1960s when large-scale econometric models were in their prime. An economist might, for example, believe that high prices were caused by a high stock of money. To test his theory, he might estimate an equation of the form

$$p_t = a + bm_t + u_t,$$

believing that his estimated parameter $\hat{b}$ represented a good description of the way that prices would respond to a change in the stock of money. Robert Lucas pointed out in his (1976) paper [75] that this belief may be false if expectations are rational, since the parameter b is not a structural parameter. If our simple model were correct, then the parameter b is in fact given by the relationship

$$b = \frac{\gamma}{1 - \lambda\beta},$$

where λ depends on the action of the policy makers themselves. Lucas's paper had a profound impact on the activity of econometric policy evaluation, and it led to the development of an entirely new approach to estimation in which economists began to pay more attention to the role of economic theory.

3.4.4   Irregular Solutions

The situation in which a second-order system is associated with a saddle point is one that occurs frequently in economic applications. The saddle-point condition is necessary for the existence of a unique rational expectations equilibrium in two-dimensional models where there is a single variable that is predetermined. What would happen if the matrix A did not possess two roots that were respectively less than and greater than one in absolute value? There are two possibilities. It may be the case that *too many* roots of A are inside the unit circle. In this situation there will not exist a *stationary* rational expectations equilibrium. The other possibility that one must consider is that *too few* roots of A are inside the unit circle. This situation generalizes the *irregular* case that was introduced in chapter 1.

In this chapter I am not gong to deal with the irregular case explicitly, since it is important to learn about the research program that has dominated macroeconomics for the last decade, in advance of looking at new or alternative approaches. Before taking up the theme that irregular models may help us to understand the data, I am going to look a little more closely at the economic theory that forms the underpinning for the linear econometric models that we have studied so far.

3.5   Concluding Remarks

Linear rational expectations models are described by functional equations. This chapter has provided a simple introduction to these equations and to the techniques that are used to solve them. The examples that were used are of regular economies in which the rational expectations equilibrium is unique, but this will not be the case for other examples in later chapters.

A second theme introduced in this chapter is that in *regular* rational expectations models, conventional exercises of econometric policy evaluation may be flawed, so econometricians need to rethink the way in which they estimate their models if they are to recover the ability to make conditional forecasts. I have emphasized the word regular because later in the book we will see that the Lucas critique may break down in environments in which beliefs can independently influence outcomes. In chapter 7 I will introduce a simple variant of the optimal growth model in which there may be too few stable roots, and I will show how this model can provide a framework for understanding an idea that is a central part of Keynesian views of business cycles. In chapter 11, I will take up some simple variants of monetary models, and I will show how the irregular case can provide a way of understanding the behavior of prices in U.S. data that is difficult to understand using more conventional equilibrium models.

3.6 Problems

1. The following difference equation characterizes the rational expectations equilibrium of the real business cycle model:

$$\begin{bmatrix} c_t \\ k_t \end{bmatrix} = A \begin{bmatrix} c_{t+1} \\ k_{t+1} \end{bmatrix} + B \begin{bmatrix} u^c_{t+1} \\ e_{t+1} \end{bmatrix}.$$

The variable c_t represents log deviations of consumption from its steady state value. k_t is the log deviation of capital. The matrices A and B are matrices of known constants. e_{t+1} is an i.i.d. fundamental error that represents a shock to technology and the term u^c_{t+1} is defined as

$$u^c_{t+1} = E_t[c_{t+1}] - c_{t+1}.$$

a. You are handed a vector of 100 draws that represent values of realizations of the sequence $\{e_t\}$ for $t = 1 \ldots 100$. Explain how you would calculate the values of the Euler equation errors, $\{u^c_t\}$.

2. Consider the following model of the economy. The demand-for-money is given by the equation

$$\frac{M^D_t}{P_t} = K \left(E_t \left[\frac{P_t}{P_{t+1}} \right] \right)^c,$$

and the money supply is generated by the rule

$$M^S_t = M^S_{t-1} + P_t g_t$$

where M^S and M^D are the nominal supply and demand for money, P_t is the price of commodities in terms of money, K is a constant, and $\{g_t\}^\infty_{t=1}$ is a sequence of i.i.d. random variables drawn from a probability distribution with mean $\bar{g}$.

a. Let m_t be the real value of money at date t. Find a functional difference equation that characterizes sequences of probability distributions for m_t that constitute a rational expectations equilibrium of this model.

b. Consider the case in which g_t is nonrandom and equal to its mean in every period. Also suppose that $c = 1$. For this special case find explicit formulas for the two steady state nonstochastic equilibria of the model.

c. Let m_1 and m_2 be the two steady state values of real balances in the model for which m_t is equal to its mean in every period. Further let m_2 be greater than m_1. Define the inflation factor as

$$\Pi_t = \frac{P_t}{P_{t-1}}.$$

Find the two steady values of Π associated with m_1 and m_2.

d. Draw a graph of the revenue from the inflation tax (in the steady state) against the inflation factor. (This graph is sometimes called an "inflationary Laffer curve"). Show that the two stationary equilibria are on different sides of the Laffer curve.

e. Using the definition

$$y_t = \begin{bmatrix} \log(m_t) - \log(m_2) \\ \log(\Pi_{t+1}) - \log(\Pi_2) \end{bmatrix},$$

find a first-order linear stochastic difference equation in the vector y_t that represents an approximation to the stochastic version of the model in the neighborhood of m_2. That is, find an equation of the form

$$y_t = A y_{t+1} + B e_{t+1}.$$

What are the elements of e_{t+1}? (You may assume that $C = 1$).

f. Find the elements of the matrices A and B in terms of the parameters of the model.

g. Find a rational expectations equilibrium of the linearized model (linearized around m_2). Is this equilibrium (locally) unique? Explain your answer.

h. Using your answer to 3g explain what is meant by "the Lucas critique."

3. This question involves computer simulation of an economy. It is suggested that you use a matrix based language such as GAUSS or MATLAB. There is a representative family that solves the following problem:

$$\max E_t \left\{ \sum_{t=0}^{\infty} \left(\frac{1}{1+\rho} \right)^t \left[\log(C_t) - \frac{L_t^{1+\gamma}}{1+\gamma} \right] \right\}.$$

The family produces output Y_t using the technology

$$Y_t = A_t K_t^\alpha L_t^{1-\alpha},$$

$$A_t = A_{t-1}^\lambda u_t,$$

$$\log(u_t) \sim N(0, \sigma_u^2).$$

The aggregate resource constraint is given by the equation

$$Y_t = C_t + I_t + G_t.$$

Government expenditures are financed by lump-sum taxes, and the government budget is always in equilibrium:

$$G_t = T_t.$$

Government purchases are generated by the following rule:

$$G_{t+1} = B G_t^\theta \varepsilon_{t+1},$$

$$\log(\varepsilon_t) \sim N(0, \sigma_\varepsilon^2).$$

The law of motion of the capital stock is

$$K_{t+1} = K_t(1-\delta) + I_t.$$

a. Write down the first-order conditions to this problem.

b. Compute the steady state for the nonstochastic version of the economy.

c. Compute a log linearized version of the model around the values obtained in 4b. (*Hint*: You should arrive at a linear stochastic difference equation in the variables k, c, l, g, y, and a driven by innovations u and e where lowercase letters denote logs.)

4. Assume the following parameter values:

$$\rho = 0.0163 \quad \gamma = 0 \quad \alpha = 0.4 \quad \lambda = 0.98 \quad \sigma_u^2 = 0.07$$

$$\theta = 0.9 \quad B = 0.9957 \quad \sigma_\varepsilon^2 = 0.01 \quad \delta = 0.0272$$

Compute graphs of the logarithms of the variables G, C, K, L, I, and Y for 40 periods given the following alternative assumptions about the processes for the shock processes.

a. Suppose that the innovation to government spending, ε_t, equals zero for all t. Suppose that the log innovation to the productivity shock, u_t, takes a value equal to one positive standard deviation from its mean in period 1 and is equal to zero for all subsequent periods. Suppose that K_1 and G_1 are equal to their steady state values in the absence of any shocks.

b. Refer to 4a, but instead of a technology shock use a one standard deviation government expenditure shock.

c. Starting from the steady state values, simulate a single time path for the economy drawing the shocks from their respective distributions; that is, simulate two sequences of shocks for each of the innovation variables e_t and u_t drawn from normal distributions with the appropriate variances.

4 General Equilibrium Theory Under Certainty

4.1 Introduction

In the next three chapters of the book I am going change tack and examine more closely a theory that underlies the linear econometric models we studied in chapters 2 and 3. Since these models are derived by linearizing nonlinear economies, our study will take us into the realm of nonlinear simultaneous equations, and since macroeconomics is intimately connected with problems that involve the passage of time these equations will typically be systems of difference or differential equations.

Before looking closely at intertemporal general equilibrium theory, it is a good idea to have some understanding of the static model on which intertemporal general equilibrium theory is based. With this end in mind, this chapter will provide an introduction to a modern treatment of general equilibrium—the Arrow-Debreu model of exchange.[1]

The central ideas that I will focus on in the chapter are grouped around the concepts of equilibrium, of determinacy, and of Pareto optimality. The building block of the chapter is the idea of an equilibrium, which forms the foundation for thinking about modern macroeconomic theory. Related ideas, which develop from this concept, are concerned with the properties of an equilibrium. Two ideas will receive particular mention, since they play a key role in helping to understand the behavior of the linear econometric models that are the bread and butter of applied econometrics. The first is that the equilibria that arise in Arrow-Debreu economies are generically[2] *determinate*. The second is that they are *Pareto optimal*.

All social sciences must grapple with the problem that societies consist of individuals who make decisions based on their perceptions of social constraints. But the social constraints themselves are the result of the interactions of millions of individuals. In economics we have been able to make some headway into the problem of social interaction by choosing to isolate only that part of human behavior that takes place in markets. In general equilibrium theory the social constraints on behavior are summarized by market prices. The decisions of agents are summarized by plans that specify how much of each commodity to buy or sell as functions of market prices. The solution to the problem of understanding the economic dimension of the relationship between the individual and society is the theory of general equilibrium.

To describe the behavior of individuals, economists assume that no one person is large enough to influence a commodity's price. In the pure trade version of the theory, one assumes that the supply of each good is fixed and then summarizes the choices of a typical household by its *demand function*. The demand function describes how the household's plan, to buy or sell a good, depends on the prices of all of the commodities at all points in time. By adding up the demand functions of all of the households and subtracting the fixed supply, one arrives at the *aggregate excess demand function*.

The aggregate excess demand function has as many components as commodities. It is a list with elements that indicate how much of a shortage exists for each commodity, in society as a whole, given a particular structure of relative prices. If we can find prices at which every element of this list is equal to zero, then we will have found an equilibrium. Since the elements in the list vary in a complicated nonlinear way as we change the prices, an equilibrium can be thought of as a solution to a system of nonlinear simultaneous equations.

One of the key ideas that has evolved from the study of economic equilibrium is connected with the relationship between the prices at which commodities are traded and the properties of the economy that *determine* those prices. For example, the number of people in the economy, the preferences of these people, and the amount of each commodity with which they are endowed are all features of the environment that are likely to influence equilibrium prices. In order for our theory of equilibrium to be a useful one, we would like the connection between the things that determine prices, and the prices themselves, to be a continuous function. This property is essential if we are to use the theory to predict, since it enables us to make coherent statements about the way in which equilibrium prices are likely to change if, for example, the supply of a commodity increases.

In general equilibrium theory there is an obvious set of candidates for the determinants of equilibrium prices. This is the set of preferences and endowments of the agents, sometimes referred to as *fundamentals*. It would be useful if general equilibrium theory were to provide a unique answer to the question; what are the equilibrium prices for any given set of fundamentals? Unfortunately this is not typically the case, and it is fairly easy to find simple examples of economies in which there is more than one equilibrium. But the fact that equilibrium may not be unique does not necessarily imply that general equilibrium theory has no predictive content. If equilibrium prices are continuous functions of fundamentals, then the economist can trace out the way in which any particular equilibrium will move as fundamentals change. As long as the movement is small, the economist can retain some confidence that equilibrium prices will move to track the change in fundamentals rather than jumping off to some other equilibrium that might also be consistent with the change.

In Arrow-Debreu economies, although there may be multiple equilibria, there is a sense in which there are never very many of them. Furthermore each equilibrium is isolated from its neighbors, and so it makes some sense to think of the local properties of an equilibrium. If we are at one equilibrium, then we are likely to stay there and if something changes a "little bit," so we won't move "very far." This property of an equilibrium being isolated from its neighbors is referred to in the literature as *determinacy* of the equilibrium because it is a property that is necessary if we are to make sense of the idea that equilibrium prices are *determined* by fundamentals. In the chapter I will provide a geometrical introduction to the idea of determinacy, and I will illustrate an important theorem of Arrow-Debreu economies which asserts that the set of equilibria is finite and that every equilibrium must therefore be determinate. This geometrical intuition will also give some insight into what is meant by *indeterminacy*.

Although Arrow-Debreu economies have determinate equilibria, it is not very difficult to find relaxations of the Arrow-Debreu assumptions under which determinacy breaks down. The economies that we will study in chapters 6 and 7 are of exactly this kind. Most economists have looked at this breakdown as a serious shortcoming of the theory, since it means that there is no longer a unique connection between equilibrium prices and the fundamentals of the economy. In this book I am going to take a different point of view. I will argue that the concept of indeterminacy is important because the existence of indeterminate equilibria is associated with the possibility that beliefs can influence outcomes. To understand how agents behave in a world of indeterminate equilibria, we must pin down their beliefs. If we are prepared to grant, to beliefs, the same methodological status that one usually reserves for preferences and endowments, there is a simple solution to the problem of indeterminacy. Beliefs pick the equilibrium, and each possible belief is associated with a different possible realization of the observable variables of the model. This theme

will be taken up again in chapter 6 in which I will give a concrete example
of an economy where beliefs matter and I will relate the idea of indeterminacy of equilibrium to the irregular linear models that I introduced in
chapter 3.

General equilibrium theory attempts to provide an idealized description
of a market economy. But one could conceive of other ways in which
societies might allocate resources. In the branch of general equilibrium
theory that studies economic welfare, an attempt is made to compare
alternative allocation mechanisms according to an objective criterion. A
number of alternative criteria have been proposed in the literature, some
of which place weight on the distributional properties of different mechanisms. The weakest efficiency notion, proposed by Pareto [88] in 1906,
makes no such demand. It requires of an allocation mechanism only that
it should be "nonwasteful" in the sense that there is no way of reallocat-
ing social resources in a way that *everyone* would agree to. An allocation
that satisfies this criterion is referred to as *Pareto optimal*.

In the second part of the chapter I am going to introduce the reader
to the relationship of the concept of competitive equilibrium to that of
Pareto optimality. This relationship is formalized in two *welfare theorems*
which assert that every competitive equilibrium is a Pareto optimum and
that every Pareto optimum can be achieved as the outcome of market
exchange through a system of income redistributions. This section is
important for two reasons. The first is that the welfare theorems allow one
to demonstrate that some types of infinite horizon economies have determinate equilibria. A Pareto optimum is a much simpler concept than that
of a competitive equilibrium, since it can be formalized as the solution to
a *single* optimization problem, the problem faced by a benevolent social
planner. A competitive equilibrium, on the other hand, is the fixed point
of a complicated nonlinear map. If a competitive equilibrium can be
represented as a Pareto optimum, then it may also inherit the properties
that are known to characterize solutions to maximization problems, for
example; as long as the maximization problem is concave the solution will
be locally unique. In chapter 5, I will use this idea to show that the difference equations that describe competitive equilibria in certain kinds of
infinite horizon economies are always regular in the sense that we defined
in chapter 3. More important, I will show that there are other classes of
economies in which the welfare theorems do not hold, and I will argue
that an understanding of the concept of Pareto optimality, and a knowl-

edge of when the welfare theorems fail, can help us to understand the dynamics of simple linear econometric models.

4.2   Idea of Equilibrium

The Arrow-Debreu model generalizes the idea that the price of a commodity is determined by the intersection of a demand curve and a supply curve. To fix ideas about the model, it may help to think of a number of agents each of whom arrives at a rural agricultural market for the purpose of trade. Each agent brings to market an *endowment* that consists of a finite collection of commodities. These commodities are traded at a vector of prices that is the same for all agents. The agents leave with an *allocation* consisting of a bundle of commodities acquired through trade at prices determined by the market. An *equilibrium* for the market process consists of an *allocation* and a *price vector* such that no agent wishes to make additional trades at the equilibrium prices.

The importance of general equilibrium theory for macroeconomics lies in an interpretation of the idea of a commodity first discussed by Debreu in chapter 7 of *The Theory of Value* [37]. Debreu suggested that we should attach a date, a location, and a state of nature to each item that is traded. Under this interpretation of the theory agents do not trade oranges, they buy or sell *contingent commodities*. An example of the sale of a contingent commodity might be represented by an offer to deliver oranges on the fourth of July 1995 in Chicago, contingent on the event that the rainfall in Florida is above average. This transaction does not exclude a simultaneous offer to deliver oranges if the rainfall in Florida is below average, although such an offer would be modeled by Debreu as the sale of a distinct commodity that might transact at a different price. This way of conceptualizing trade has the advantage of providing a single unified framework for understanding contemporaneous transactions, intertemporal trades, and the purchase and sale of insurance.

Before discussing the extensions of general equilibrium theory that provide a foundation for macroeconomics, I will introduce the basic concepts of the theory in the context of finite economies. The model that we will examine is of a nonstochastic, pure exchange, economy in which there is a finite number of commodities indexed by $j = 1, \ldots, l$, and a finite number of consumers indexed by $i = 1, \ldots, m$. The fact that both m and l are finite is important. I will return to this point in chapter 5 in which I show that the assumption of an infinite number of commodities does not do great violence to one's intuition. But, if one wishes to model economies in which there may be an infinite number of commodities *and* an infinite number of agents, then there may exist competitive equilibria that are associated with socially inefficient growth paths. This phenomenon is my first example of a potential failure of the welfare theorems in a competitive equilibrium economy, and I will return to the idea in chapter 6.

4.3 Theory of Consumer Choice

Much of the literature of general equilibrium that appears in economic theory journals is concerned with finding the weakest possible assumptions about preferences under which one may establish the existence of equilibrium. In macroeconomics, on the other hand, the focus is different. Macroeconomists *use* general equilibrium theory to test hypotheses about the relationships between economic time series. A typical economic theory article might assume that preferences are discontinuous and intransitive and ask whether an equilibrium might still exist for some abstract economy. A typical macroeconomics article might assume that all choices are made by a single representative agent with logarithmic preferences and ask whether this simple environment can explain why consumption is less volatile than income in U.S. time series. In this book I am going to lean more heavily toward the macroeconomists vision, although I will be rather more careful about the assumptions that we make than most macroeconomics textbooks. My goal is to provide a tool kit for understanding how to *do* macroeconomics.

4.3.1 Assumptions about Preferences

In the spirit of the macroeconomic approach to general equilibrium theory, many of the assumptions that I introduce will be designed to make proofs easy and to rule out difficult cases. I will impose very strong assumptions on the economy and ask if the highly restrictive models that result are consistent with the observed behavior of economic time series. The following four assumptions are in this vein.

ASSUMPTION 4.1 *Preferences are* representable *by a utility function* $u_i : X \equiv R_+^l \mapsto R$. X *is the consumption set that we take to be the nonnegative orthant.*

ASSUMPTION 4.2   Differentiability: *Utility functions u_i are at least C^2.*

ASSUMPTION 4.3   Monotonicity: $Du_i(x) > 0$ *for all $x \in X$.*

ASSUMPTION 4.4   Strict quasi-concavity: $u_i(\lambda x + (1 - \lambda)y) > u_i(y)$ *for all $x, y \in X, u_i(x) \geq u_i(y), \lambda \in (0,1)$.*

Assumption 4.1 is much stronger than is required to establish existence. Much of general equilibrium theory begins with more basic assumptions on choice and characterizes the conditions under which utility functions exist. For our purposes it is acceptable to begin with the utility function as a primitive and to assume that this function is monotonic and differentiable. The notation C^2 in assumption 4.2 means that the function is continuous, and its first and second derivatives exist and are also continuous. The monotonicity assumption says that more is better, and the notation Du means the vector of first derivatives of the function u. When I apply the inequality symbol $x > y$ to two vectors x and y, as in assumption 4.3, I will mean that every element of the vector x is greater than, or equal to, the corresponding element of y, and at least one element is strictly greater. Monotonicity means therefore that more of at least one good is always strictly preferred. The strict quasi-concavity assumption, 4.4, implies that indifference surfaces are strictly convex (we do not allow flat segments).

My own view is that the above assumptions are not particularly strong, although there is a large branch of the literature in mathematical economics and general equilibrium theory that investigates whether one can prove existence of an equilibrium under more general assumptions. For example, preference orderings may be well defined but not representable. Indifference curves may have linear segments and so on. These are interesting questions, but I will leave them to others.

ASSUMPTION 4.5   Positive endowments: $\omega_i \in R^l_{++}$, $i = 1, \ldots, m$.

Assumption 4.5 says that every agent is endowed with a positive amount of every commodity. This assumption *is* strong, particularly in the context of infinite-horizon economies, since it is inconsistent with finite lives. Luckily, however, the assumption can be replaced by a weaker condition known as *resource relatedness*. Resource relatedness says that everyone has something that someone else wants and it is necessary to have something like this in order to generate a motive for individuals to want to trade.

ASSUMPTION 4.6 Interiority: $\|Du_i(x_k)\| \to \infty$ *as* $x_k \to x$ *where some component of* x, $x^j = 0$. *However,* $Du_i(x) \cdot x$ *is bounded for all* x *in any bounded subset of* X.

This is also a strong assumption. It asks you to conceptualize a sequence of commodity bundles that converges to a bundle that is on the boundary of the consumption set and not out at infinity. For all such boundary bundles, every element of the sequence that converges to the bundle must have a finite marginal utility. But the boundary bundle itself must have at least one element with an infinite marginal utility. In the case of just two commodities, this assumption means that indifference curves are tangent to the axes, but they never become vertical, or horizontal, except at infinity. It is a very convenient assumption that allows one to ignore the possibility of corner solutions to the individual's maximization problem.

Armed with this set of assumptions about the way that the agents in our model make choices, we proceed to investigate just what these choices will be.

4.3.2 Consumer's Problem

Each individual chooses a demand vector that maximizes his utility subject to the constraint that the value of his demand must be no greater than the value of his endowment. Formally this problem may be stated as follows:

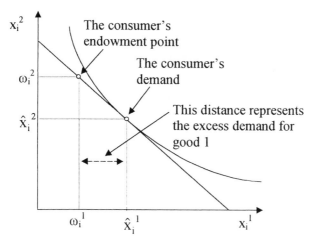

Figure 4.1
Consumer's problem

$$\max_{x_i} u_i(x_i) \tag{4.1}$$

such that

$$p \cdot (x_i - \omega_i) \leq 0, \quad x_i \in X. \tag{4.2}$$

Assumptions 4.1 through 4.6 imply the existence of a unique interior solution to this problem which takes the form

$$x_i^1 = \omega_i^1 + f_i^1(p^1, \ldots, p^l; \omega_i \cdot p),$$

$$\vdots$$

$$x_i^l = \omega_i^l + f_i^l(p^1, \ldots, p^l; \omega_i \cdot p),$$

or, more compactly,

$$x_i = \omega_i + f_i(p). \tag{4.3}$$

Since the programming problem is concave, the following set of first-order conditions is both necessary and sufficient for the existence of a unique solution:

$$Du_i(x_i) = \mu_i p, \tag{4.4}$$

$$p \cdot (x_i - \omega_i) = 0, \tag{4.5}$$

and assumption 4.6 implies that the solution will be strictly interior to the consumption set.

4.4 Excess Demand Functions

4.4.1 Individual Excess Demand Functions

So far we have provided the tools that are necessary to understand how an individual consumer will behave in the face of an exogenously given set of prices. The function that describes his behavior, $f_i(p)$, possesses the following five properties all of which are preserved under the process of aggregating excess demands across consumers:

1. Continuity.

2. Bounded below.

3. $p \cdot f_i(p) = 0$.

4. $f_i(\lambda p) = f_i(p)$, for all $\lambda > 0$.

5. $p_n \to p$ (where some $p^j = 0$) $\Rightarrow \|f_i(p_n)\| \to \infty$.

Properties 1 and 2 are straightforward and follow directly from the assumptions that were placed on utility functions. Continuity relies on the convexity of indifference curves which implies that the tangency of an indifference curve with the budget set varies continuously as the budget constraint is rotated around the endowment point. Property 2 follows from the assumption that endowments are bounded, and property 3 relies on nonsatiation; it says that the consumer will always choose a point on the boundary of his budget set. Property 4, zero-degree homogeneity of excess demand functions in prices, expresses the idea that only relative prices matter. Another way of saying this is that excess demand functions are invariant to the choice of units in which prices are quoted. Finally, property 5 is an implication of monotonicity. It says that if the price of a commodity goes to zero then the norm of the excess demand vector becomes infinite.

The above five properties are not the only restrictions that are placed on excess demand functions by the assumption that they arise from the process of rational agents solving a maximization problem. But they are the only relevant restrictions from the standpoint of macroeconomics because they are the only properties that survive the process of aggregation.

4.4.2 Aggregate Excess Demand Functions

An equilibrium is a vector of prices with the property that the sum of excess demands across consumers, evaluated at equilibrium prices, is equal to zero. A price vector with this property captures the idea that demand equals supply for every commodity simultaneously. Community or *aggregate excess demand functions* are derived by summing the individual functions across all agents:

$$f(p) = \sum_{i=1}^{m} f_i(p).$$
(4.6)

It is important, if one wishes to understand the properties of equilibria, to know something about the properties of the function f. The basic idea that we will pursue is that the five properties of individual excess demands 1 to 5 are all inherited by aggregate excess demands.[3] That is,

1. Continuity.
2. Bounded below.
3. $p \cdot f(p) = 0$.
4. $f(\lambda p) = f(p)$, for all $\lambda > 0$.
5. $p_n \to p$ (where some $p^j = 0$) $\Rightarrow \|f(p_n)\| \to \infty$.

In the context of the *aggregate* excess demand function property 3 is called *Walras's law*. It follows from the idea that every individual will choose to be on his or her budget constraint. Walras's law implies that if $l - 1$ markets are in equilibrium at prices $\hat{p}$, then the lth market must also be in equilibrium. Another way of saying this, in the two good world, is that if all you have is oranges and apples and everyone is happy with the quantity of apples that they are trading, then they must also be happy with the quantity of oranges—since every offer to buy apples is an offer to sell oranges, and vice versa. Walras's law is important because it reduces the dimension of the equilibrium problem by one. If there are l commodities, then we need only establish the existence of an equilibrium for $l - 1$ commodities.

Property 4 says that the units that you measure prices in don't matter. Only relative prices count. In fact the units in which prices are quoted doesn't even have to be a commodity that is actually traded by anyone. It could equally well be astral star dust providing every good that *is* traded has a well-defined price in terms of the numéraire good. In view of this restriction it is normal to quote prices in terms of the bundle of commodities that places equal weight on every good. This normalization is achieved by restricting prices to lie on the open simplex $\Delta(p)$:

$$\Delta(p) = \left\{ p \in R^l_{++} \,\middle|\, \sum_{j=1}^{l} p^j = 1 \right\}. \tag{4.7}$$

In the case of two commodities the Simplex is equivalent to the unit interval. In a three-commodity world it is the triangle that is formed by joining the points $\{0, 0, 1\}$, $\{0, 1, 0\}$, and $\{1, 0, 0\}$. Figure 4.2 illustrates the simplex when there are three commodities.

One way of thinking about the restrictions implied by homogeneity and by Walras's law is that the former reduces, by one, the dimension of the domain of the excess demand function and the latter reduces, by one, the dimension of the co-domain. Rather than describing a function that

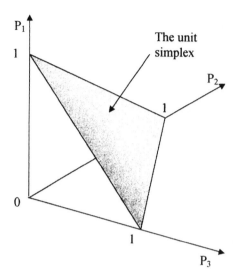

Figure 4.2
Unit simplex in a three-commodity world

maps from R_+^l to R^l, we can think of excess demand functions that map from the $l - 1$ dimension simplex to R^{l-1}. Excess demand functions are continuous functions, bounded below, that satisfy a certain boundary condition.

4.5 Equilibria and Their Properties

The first task of general equilibrium theory is to make sure that the equilibrium formalization of the market mechanism is internally consistent. To establish internal consistency, one must show that there exists a vector of relative prices at which demand equals supply for every commodity simultaneously. In other words, one can express "the existence question" as follows: *Does there exist a vector $\hat{p}$ such that*

$$f(\hat{p}) = 0?$$

The answer is yes. In fact, generically, there is a finite odd number of equilibria. There are many ways of proving the existence of an equilibrium, and in this book I take an informal approach by looking at the geometry of the excess demand function. But before providing a discussion of the existence issue and looking at some of the properties of an equilibrium, I am going to introduce some concepts a little more formally. Some of these concepts have already been described in words, and some of them go beyond our previous discussion.

4.5.1 Some Definitions and Development of Notation

1. A consumer's *characteristic* is a pair $c_i \equiv (u_i, \omega_i)$, where u_i is a utility function and ω_i is an endowment.

2. An *exchange economy*, $\mathscr{E}$, is an m-tuple of characteristics $(c_1, c_2, \ldots, c_m)$.

3. A *allocation* is a vector of consumption bundles $x = (x_1, x_2, \ldots, x_m)$.

4. An allocation is *attainable* if $\sum_{i=1}^m x_i \le \sum_{i=1}^m \omega_i$.

5. An *equilibrium* for $\mathscr{E}$ is an attainable allocation x and a price vector p such that x_i maximizes u_i and $p \cdot (x_i - \omega_i) \le 0$ for all i.

6. An equilibrium $e \equiv (p, x)$ is *indeterminate* if there exists an $\varepsilon > 0$ such that for all $\delta < \varepsilon$ there is another equilibrium $e' \equiv (p'(\delta), x'(\delta))$ such that $\|e' - e\| < \delta$. An equilibrium is *determinate* if it is not indeterminate.

7. An allocation, x, is *Pareto optimal* if it is attainable and there is no other attainable allocation x' such that $u_j(x_j') \ge u_j(x_j)$ for all j and $u_j(x_j') > u_j(x_j)$ for at least one j.

Many of these definitions will not be required until I take up the issue of the welfare theorems in section 4.6. Others, the concept of determinacy, for example, will be useful to bear in mind when I talk about the geometry of the set of equilibria. I have collected them together in this section to provide an easy reference point.

Although I have made use of a formidable array of notation, the definitions themselves introduce some concepts that make the organization of the material of general equilibrium theory relatively simple to understand, and they are not as mystical as they may at first seem. For example, the idea of a characteristic formalizes the important parts of a consumer from the point of view of the theory of demand. A consumer *is* his endowment and his utility function. Similarly an exchange economy *is* a finite collection of consumers.

An allocation is a description of how much of each commodity is given to each consumer, and an attainable allocation is one that is feasible given the resources of society.[4] The definitions of an allocation and of attainability are introduced to facilitate the comparison of alternative economic systems as ways of distributing resources. The competitive mechanism that is formalized in general equilibrium theory is just one member of the set of all possible resource allocation mechanisms, and one could conceptualize many other possible mechanisms that might be designed to achieve the same end. Central planning, for example, is an alternative method that has been widely used in the economies of Eastern Europe. The language of welfare economics is designed in a way that allows one to make comparisons of these alternatives.

Definition 6 formalizes the idea of determinacy of an equilibrium. It says that an indeterminate equilibrium is one that is arbitrarily close to another equilibrium where the concept of closeness is defined by the norm, $\| \ \|$. In finite economies this could be the euclidean distance between one equilibrium and another, where the equilibrium is defined by a vector of prices and a matrix of commodity allocations, that is, a point in an $(m + 1) \times l$ space.

Definition 7 introduces the idea of a Pareto optimal allocation. Pareto optimality is a very weak efficiency notion that says nothing about the ethics of the distribution of resources. The idea is to formalize what it means for a way of allocating resources to be nonwasteful. If there were only one good, the idea of not wasting resources would be obvious; don't throw anything away. The Pareto concept generalizes this idea to a multiple commodity environment. In words, an allocation is Pareto optimal if there is no way of redistributing commodities that would make at least one person better off, without making anyone worse off.

4.5.2   Geometry of Equilibrium

A look at the geometry of the situation is instructive in understanding how an existence proof might work, and it also tells us something about the topological properties of the equilibrium set. Figure 4.3 illustrates some of the properties of equilibria in the three-dimensional case. The triangle represents the price simplex. There are only two components of the excess demand functions to worry about, f^1 and f^2 because of Walras's law. Each of these components describes a two-dimensional surface. We are interested in the points where both of these surfaces intersect the price simplex simultaneously. Points above the simplex are points of positive excess demand; points below the simplex are points of negative excess demand.[5]

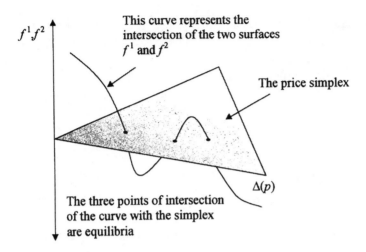

Figure 4.3
Existence of an equilibrium

The intersection of two manifolds (smooth surfaces that are locally like euclidean space) of dimension two is, generically, a manifold of dimension one (a piece of string).[6] This piece of string may have disconnected loops, but it will also have one connected piece that starts above the simplex and ends below the simplex. This can be shown using properties 1 to 5. It follows immediately that there is at least one equilibrium and that the number of equilibria is odd; a rather curious property that does not seem to have much practical importance.[7] Of rather more importance is the fact that equilibria are generically *isolated*. This means that the piece of string almost always crosses the simplex cleanly, and situations in which it runs exactly along the surface for a little ways don't often happen. "Don't often" is made precise by considering a big set of possible economies and showing that the complement of the set in which pathological things occur is open and dense. An equilibrium that is locally isolated is called *determinate*. This property is important because we need it in order to be able to make comparative static predictions. If something changes that shifts the excess demand functions, then the piece of string will move. Suppose that the equilibrium of the economy is one of a large set of possible equilibria characterized by the property that the bit of string lies along the price simplex. In this situation we will be unable to predict what will happen if an exogenous change shifts the set of equilibria. Perhaps the economy will move to track the old equilibrium; or perhaps it will move to an adjacent equilibrium as the string slides along the surface: Comparative statics in this situation does not make much sense.

Although an indeterminate equilibrium is very unlikely in a finite economy, something very much like this is exactly what *can* happen *generically* in overlapping generations economies. We will return to this concept in chapter 7 where we will show how the idea of indeterminacy can be related to the macroeconomic idea of self-fulfilling expectations.

4.5.3 Debreu-Sonnenschein-Mantel Theorem

The ideas that I am going to discuss in this section are most clearly understood in the historical context in which they were developed. In the 1960s there was a considerable interest in testing econometrically the restrictions of demand theory by estimating complete systems of demand equations. This literature took the approach that market data could be treated "as if" they were chosen by a single representative consumer. The results of these studies suggested that the stronger restrictions of consumer theory could be rejected. The work was instrumental in leading economists to inquire into the issue of aggregation. In particular, Hugo Sonnenschein posed a question that subsequently led to the development of work that is known as the Debreu-Sonnenschein-Mantel theorem.[8] Sonnenschein was interested in the question: Can an arbitrary function be an excess demand function for some economy, or does the theory of rational choice impose any additional restrictions?

We have already pointed out that two of the properties of aggregate excess demand functions are taken care of by judiciously choosing the domain and range of the functions one considers. Pick functions that map from the price simplex (an $l - 1$ manifold) to R^l that also satisfy Walras's law. The restriction to functions that satisfy Walras's law effectively reduces the dimension of the range of the functions. Restated, we are looking at functions that map $\Delta \mapsto R^{l-1}$.

Now define the set Δ_ε which is the price simplex excluding a piece around the boundary of width ε:

$$\Delta_\varepsilon = \{p \in \Delta \mid p^j > \varepsilon \text{ for all } j\}.$$

Given this definition:

THEOREM 1 (Debreu-Sonnenschein-Mantel)   *Let $f(p)$ be a continuous function $\Delta \mapsto R^l$ such that*

$p \cdot f(p) = 0.$

Then for any $\varepsilon > 0$ there exists an l consumer exchange economy such that this economy generates f on Δ_ε.

The implication is that *any* continuous function that satisfies Walras's law could be an excess demand function for some economy provided that the economy has at least as many consumers as there are commodities. The boundary condition 5 is taken care of by restricting the domain on which an economy can be found that duplicates the arbitrary aggregate function to a strictly interior portion of the price simplex. The Debreu-Sonnenschein-Mantel theorem has proved to be extremely useful in the study of overlapping generations economies in which it has been used to show that there is a sense in which indeterminate equilibria are very common.

4.6 General Equilibrium Theory and Efficient Allocations of Resources

General equilibrium theory has both positive and normative aspects. The positive part of the theory is a description of how the market mechanism determines prices and how it allocates commodities. The normative part of the theory is an evaluation of how well it performs this task when markets are evaluated as one member of the set of all possible resource allocation mechanisms. In this section I am going to introduce the idea of a social planning problem, and I will state and prove the first and second theorems of welfare economics. These theorems assert that there is, under certain circumstances, an equivalence between the set of a competitive equilibria of an exchange economy and the set of Pareto optimal allocations.

4.6.1 First Welfare Theorem

THEOREM 2 (First welfare theorem) *Every competitive equilibrium is Pareto optimal.*

The proof is simple. It works as follows:

Proof of the first welfare theorem

1. Suppose that a particular allocation x is an equilibrium allocation at prices p.

2. Suppose, in contradiction of the theorem, that there exists an attainable allocation x' that is at least as good as x for all consumers and that is preferred to x by at least one consumer.

3. But if x' is at least as good as x, then it must be either on or outside every consumer's budget set. Since at least one consumer, the jth consumer, strictly prefers x'_j; for this one consumer the allocation x'_j must be strictly outside his or her budget set. If this weren't true, then the allocation x'_j would have been chosen over x_j at prices p, and (x, p) could not have been an equilibrium.

4. It follows that the value of the social allocation $\sum_{j=1}^{m} x_j$ must be greater than or equal to the value of the social endowment $\sum_{j=1}^{m} \omega_j$; that is, $p \cdot \sum_{j=1}^{m} (\omega_j - x'_j) > 0$.

5. Hence x' must be unattainable, which is a contradiction. $\square$

The first welfare theorem holds under very weak conditions. It is already assumed, in the premise of the theorem, that a competitive equilibrium exists. Given this assumption, the theorem requires the assumption of local nonsatiation (more is better) which guarantees that each individual is on his budget constraint.

4.6.2 Second Welfare Theorem

THEOREM 3 (Second welfare theorem) *Every Pareto optimum can be decentralized as a competitive equilibrium.*

The second welfare requires more assumptions since one must have enough structure to guarantee that an equilibrium exists. To represent the set of Pareto optima of our economy, we will consider the problem of a social planner whose goal is to maximize a social welfare function. This problem has the following structure:

$$\max_{x} \sum_{i=1}^{m} \lambda_i u_i(x_i) \quad \text{where} \quad \sum_{i=1}^{m} \lambda_i = 1, \tag{4.8}$$

such that

$$\sum_{i=1}^{m} (\omega_i - x_i) \geq 0, \tag{4.9}$$

$$x_i \geq 0. \tag{4.10}$$

The social planner chooses an $l \times m$ vector x that represents the complete allocation of the l commodities among the m consumers. The m vector λ of social welfare weights represents the importance of each of the i agents to the social welfare.

Now choose an l-dimensional vector p of Lagrange multipliers, one for each of the vector of constraints (4.9). At this point p represents a vector of multipliers. The choice of notation is not arbitrary, however, since we will show that p also represents the vector of competitive prices that will decentralize the solution to the planner's problem. Necessary and sufficient conditions for a unique interior solution to equation 4.8 are given by

$$\lambda_i Du_i(x_i) = p, \qquad i = 1, \ldots, m, \tag{4.11}$$

$$\sum_{i=1}^{m}(\omega_i - x_i) = 0. \tag{4.12}$$

Equation 4.11 consists of m sets of l equations. Equation 4.12 consists of l equations. There are $m + 1 \times l$ unknowns: the l vector p of Lagrange multipliers and the $m \times l$ vector of allocations.

Recall that a competitive equilibrium solves

$$Du_i(x_i) = \mu_i p, \qquad i = 1, \ldots, m, \tag{4.13}$$

$$p \cdot (\omega_i - x_i) = 0, \tag{4.14}$$

$$\sum_{i=1}^{m}(\omega_i - x_i) = 0. \tag{4.15}$$

Equation 4.13 consists of m sets of l equations. Equation 4.14 consists of m equations. Equation 4.15 consists of l market-clearing equations.

Notice that if $\mu_i = (1/\lambda_i)$, and the vector of prices p in the competitive equilibrium is the same as the vector of Lagrange multipliers p in the planners problem, then the sets of first-order conditions 4.11 and 4.13 are identical. The first of the above qualifications equates the Lagrange multiplier in each of the consumer's problems μ_i with the inverse of the social welfare weight $(1/\lambda_i)$.

Notice also that the l first-order conditions 4.12 which tell the social planner to use up all of the l commodities are identical to the market-clearing conditions for a competitive equilibrium, 4.15. The issue of whether a Pareto optimum can be decentralized comes down to whether the social planner can redistribute income in a way that forces the additional m budget identities 4.14 to be satisfied in an equilibrium. Let x^* and p^* be the solution to the social planners problem 4.8. The required redistribution of income will be possible if there exists a set of transfers τ_i, $i = 1, \ldots, m$ such that

$$p^* \cdot (\omega_i - x_i^*) + \tau_i \geq 0$$

for all $i = 1, \ldots, m$. But now the solution is obvious. We know that the consumer will choose to consume x_i^* if he or she is able, since the first-order conditions to the consumer's problem duplicate the first-order conditions to the planners problem that define x^*. Let

$$\tau_i = p^* \cdot (x_i^* - \omega_i).$$

Notice that $\sum_{i=1}^{m} \tau_i = 0$, since x_i^* is attainable. Therefore the set of income transfers $\{\tau_i\}$ is feasible at zero cost. But now 4.14 becomes

$$p^* \cdot (x_i^* - x_i) \geq 0,$$

and x_i^* becomes attainable for the consumer. Since it is attainable, and since 4.13 duplicates 4.11, it follows that x_i^* will be chosen by the ith consumer.

In chapter 5 I will use the same proof of the second welfare theorem in the context of an infinite-horizon economy, and I will present a proof of the first welfare theorem which exploits the idea that the equations which describe a Pareto optimum are a subset of the equations that describe a competitive equilibrium.

4.7 Concluding Remarks

The main ideas in this chapter can be summarized as follows: First, we made a set of six assumptions about the properties of preferences which allowed us to derive the excess demand function of an individual and to discuss its properties. This function describes how the individual responds to opportunities to trade commodities at alternative prices. We proceeded to define the concept of an aggregate excess demand function which describes how the sum of the individuals in society responds to alternative trading opportunities, and we asserted that the process of aggregation destroys many of the properties that rational choice imposes on individual excess demands. We used the properties that do survive aggregation to explain how one can establish that an equilibrium exists and that generically there is an odd finite number of equilibria. This idea is important, since it implies that equilibria are determinate, a topic that we will return to later. Finally we defined the concept of a Pareto optimum and proved the first and second welfare theorems.

4.8 Problems

1. Define the meaning of each of the following terms as it is used in general equilibrium theory:

a. Allocation

b. Feasible allocation

c. Pareto optimal allocation

d. Competitive equilibrium

e. Determinate equilibrium

2. Consider a finite general equilibrium model with three commodities and m agents. Let the excess demand functions for goods 1 and 2 be given by

$$x_1 - \omega_1 = \left(\frac{p_1}{p_2} - 3\right)\left(\frac{p_1}{p_1 + p_2 + p_3}\right)$$

and

$$x_2 - \omega_2 = \left(\frac{p_3}{p_2}\right)^2 + \frac{p_1}{p_1 + p_2}.$$

a. Find the excess demand function for good 3.

b. What is meant by the price simplex?

c. Could the excess demand functions given above represent excess demand functions for an economy in which all of the agents have preferences that satisfy the assumptions discussed in this chapter? If not why not?

d. What is meant by the Debreu-Sonnenschein-Mental theorem? Be careful to state carefully all of the conditions of the theorem. How big must m be (in this example) for the theorem to apply?

3. Consider the constant function $\{x(p) = 1 \mid e < p < 1 - e\}$. Using this example illustrate what is meant by the Debreu-Sonnenschein-Mantel theorem for the case of an economy with two commodities. How is the theorem consistent with the existence of an equilibrium in this example?

4. Let the following two functions represent the first and second components of the aggregate excess demand function for some three-good economy:

$$f^1 = \frac{p_1 - p_2}{p_3}, \quad f^2 = \frac{p_1 p_3}{(p_2)^2}.$$

Find the third component of the excess demand vector.

5. Consider the following three-person pure exchange economy with three commodities. The economy is populated by three people, Mr. A, Mr. B, and Mr. C. There are three goods, denoted by subscripts 1, 2, and 3. The preferences of Mr. A, Mr. B, and Mr. C are given by:

$$U^A = \log(x_1^A) + \log(x_2^A) + \log(x_3^A),$$

$$U^B = x_1^B x_2^B x_3^B,$$

$$U^C = -\left(\frac{1}{x_1^C}\right) - \left(\frac{1}{x_2^C}\right) - \left(\frac{1}{x_3^C}\right).$$

The endowments of A, B, and C are given by

$$\omega^A = \{1, 0, 0\}, \quad \omega^B = \{0, 1, 0\}, \quad \omega^C = \{0, 0, 1\}.$$

Let the price vector be $p = \{p_1, p_2, p_3\}$.

a. Find the set of excess demand functions $f^i(p)$ for $i = 1, 2, 3$.

b. Find an expression for the aggregate excess demand function $f(p)$.

c. Show that your solution is homogenous of degree zero in p and that it satisfies Walras's law.

5 Infinite Horizon Economies and Representative Agents

5.1 Introduction

Frank Ramsey [92] was one of the first economists to study how an infinitely lived agent should allocate his resources over time. His work was at the forefront of mathematical economics at the time that it was written, but his approach has now become a standard part of graduate macroeconomics courses. Many applications of Ramsey's work assume that there is only one agent in the economy and that this "representative agent" can be thought of as a stand-in for the workings of the market mechanism. For this reason I will often refer to infinite horizon–agent models as the representative agent, or RA approach. However, proponents of the RA approach point out that it is much more general than it at first appears. Their claim is based on the fact that economies in which there exists a finite number of infinitely lived families can, under some circumstances, lead to equilibria that replicate the allocation that would be made by a social planner. Under this interpretation the representative agent is a stand-in for this benevolent dictator.

The representative agent model has become the most widely used tool of equilibrium macroeconomic theory, but it is not the only possible approach. A second important class of models assumes that economies consist of a sequence of *overlapping generations*. The first English language paper to introduce the overlapping generations, or OG model, was written by Paul Samuelson [97] in 1958, although Maurice Allais wrote a paper in French in 1947 that predates Samuelson's article. The choice of an RA or OG model is not simply a choice of modeling convenience since the two types of economies behave in very different ways. In chapters 5 and 6 I will be concerned with understanding these differences, and I will pay particular attention to the issues that were raised in the first three chapters of this book. I will show that the representative agent model is a lot like the finite general equilibrium model; in particular, the welfare theorems hold and equilibria are determinate. An important implication of these facts is that RA economies always give rise to economic models with *regular* equilibria. In contrast, overlapping generations models may display equilibria that are not Pareto optimal, and there may be indeterminate steady states. The fact that the OG general equilibrium environment may display indeterminacy implies that linear economic models derived from this environment may lead to linear econometric models with solutions that are *irregular*.

To understand the relationship between determinacy and regular equilibria, it helps to conceptualize an equilibrium, in an infinite horizon economy, as a sequence of vectors $\{y_t\}_{t=1}^{\infty}$. The elements of this sequence are related to each other by a difference equation, $y_t = f(y_{t-1})$, that may be locally approximated by a nonstochastic version of the linear difference equation that we studied in chapter 3. To pin down a particular solution to a difference equation, one requires a set of boundary conditions. If the equilibria of an economy are *locally unique* (determinate), then economic theory will specify exactly the right number of boundary conditions to determine a solution to this equation in the neighborhood of a stationary state. Local uniqueness holds generically in representative agent models that satisfy the same kinds of assumptions that one imposes in finite general equilibrium theory. But in overlapping generations economies, or in representative agent economies in which there are externalities of one kind or another, it is possible for there to be fewer boundary conditions than one requires to pick a single equilibrium based solely on the technology, preferences, and endowments of the economy.

Figure 5.1 compares the kinds of linearized dynamics that occur in RA models with the dynamics that *may* arise in OG models or in economies in which the technology is nonconvex.[1] There are two state variables in each model: the stock of capital which is predetermined and the aggregate level of consumption which is a free choice, made by the agents in the model, that depends on their beliefs about the future value of prices. In a representative agent economy one knows that there is a finite odd number of sequences $\{k_t, c_t\}_{t=1}^{\infty}$ that characterizes a competitive equilibrium. If a stationary equilibrium exists, this argument implies that it must be a saddle point; that is, for any k_0 in the neighborhood of a stationary equilibrium, there is a locally unique c_0 associated with sequences that converge to it.[2] The RA case is represented in the first panel of figure 5.1.

In an overlapping generations economy it is possible in a similar example (with two state variables one of which is predetermined) for there to exist a steady state that is a sink. In this case there are not enough boundary conditions to uniquely pin down the difference equation that describes equilibria. For any given initial capital stock there may exist a continuum of initial levels of consumption, each of which is consistent with a sequence of pairs, $\{c_t, k_t\}_{t=1}^{\infty}$, that characterizes a competitive equilibrium. This situation is described in the second panel of figure 5.1. For any equilibrium sequence that converges to the steady state, there is

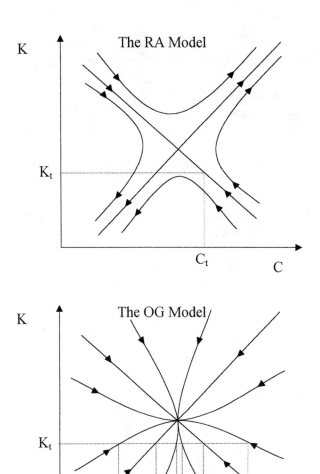

Figure 5.1
Comparative dynamics of RA and OG Models

another sequence that is arbitrarily close. The steady state and each of the nonstationary equilibria that converge to this steady state are examples of indeterminate equilibria.

In the first part of this chapter I will introduce the assumptions that one requires to talk about general equilibrium theory when choices are made by families that plan for the future, and I will prove that the welfare theorems hold in this environment. The fact that the welfare theorems hold under some circumstances implies that we can describe a competitive equilibrium as the solution to a single maximization problem. This is the starting point for the theory of *real business cycles* in which it is assumed that the observed time series of consumption, investment, labor supply, and output can be modeled *as if* they were chosen by a single infinite horizon maximizer. The maximization problem is thought of as the solution to the social planner's problem, and the first-order conditions to the planner's problem describe both the allocations and the prices that can be supported as a competitive equilibrium. In the second part of the chapter I will introduce some of the methods that are used in the real business cycle research program and explain how these methods are linked to the representative agent model of Frank Ramsey.

5.2 Representative Agent Economy

5.2.1 Assumptions about Structure

A general formulation of an RA economy assumes that the world consists of a finite number, m, of infinitely lived families each of which consumes a bundle of l commodities in every period, t, where $t = 1, \ldots, \infty$. There are two alternative interpretations of the market structure in which trades occur. In the first interpretation, markets open once at the beginning of time and agents trade commodities that are indexed by date of delivery. The market closes, and trades are executed. This way of thinking about the economy is important because it allows the infinite horizon economy to be treated in the same way as the finite general equilibrium model. The problem with the contingent commodity interpretation is that it is unrealistic. In the real world markets are open at many different dates, and there is no real world analog of the single market at the dawn of history.

In a second interpretation of general equilibrium theory one thinks of a sequence of markets, one that opens in every period. This sequential structure is known as *temporary equilibrium* theory, and it was first discussed by Sir John Hicks [60] in an important book that appeared in 1939.[3] Temporary equilibrium theory, in its most general form, allows for the possibility that agents may act on the basis of expectations about the future which later turn out to have been incorrect. But recently there has been a movement in economics that insists on beginning with the premise that expectations are correct. This approach, *the rational expectations approach*, leads to the conclusion that the equilibria that arise in temporary equilibrium theory are the same as the equilibria that arise in a world of one timeless market.

To understand this equivalence, it helps to try to conceptualize an economy in which there are no uncertain events and in which the future unfolds in a manner that is known at every date. In a world of this nature, sequential markets can be connected together by the trade of a single asset. In *Value and Capital* Hicks asks us to think of "weeks" during which agents produce and consume. At the end of each week all of the agents in the economy come together at a central market to trade their produce. These markets take place on a sequence of Saturdays. If there was no way of transferring wealth from one Saturday to the next, then the decisions made at each date would be unconnected. But if agents can trade an asset, for example, which they might borrow and lend with each other, then the sequence of budget constraints faced by each of the agents can be collapsed to a single lifetime constraint. The single constraint implies that the decisions made by each of the agents, based on their (correct) predictions of future prices, will be the same as the decisions that they would make if all future trades were made by contract in a single market at the dawn of time. It follows that the equilibria that occur in the single market model are identical to the equilibria that occur in the sequential market world.

The assumption that there is no uncertainty is important in developing the above argument, although a similar equivalence can be shown to hold in a world that is uncertain but subject to known laws of probability. In this more complicated world the assumption that agents know that future prices is replaced by the assumption that agents know the *probability distribution of future prices*. To establish an equivalence of the two types of equilibria in this more complicated environment, one requires a much richer set of assets for transferring resources into each of the possible futures that might unfold. I will introduce economies with uncertainty in chapter 9 where I will explain the idea of *complete markets* under which a single trading date is sufficient to summarize the allocations that occur in equilibrium.

5.2.2 Assumptions about Preferences

I will begin by extending the preference assumptions of finite general equilibrium theory to cover the case where the commodity space may have an infinite number of dimensions. Conceptually this introduces some additional difficulties if we wish to restrict the ways in which the quantity of commodities at very different dates can interact with each other. For example, I would not wish to place a high value on the possibility that an increase in the quantity of apples that I consume today might have a big impact on the marginal utility of apples that might be consumed by my descendants in the next century. Formally this idea is represented by assuming that preferences are *additively separable*. Nevertheless, the separability assumption is much stronger than one requires, and it does have some unpleasant implications which I describe below.

ASSUMPTION 5.1 (Representability) *Preferences are* representable *by a utility function:* $\bar{u}_i = \sum_{t=0}^{\infty} \beta^t u_i(x_{it}), \beta \in [0, 1)$. *The period utility function* u_i *maps from X to R, where* $X \equiv R_{++}^l$.

ASSUMPTION 5.2 (Differentiability) $u_i : X = R_{++}^l : \mapsto R$ *is* c^2.

ASSUMPTION 5.3 (Monotonicity) $Du_i(x_{it}) > 0$ *for all* $x_{it} \in X$.

These three assumptions mirror those made in chapter 4 for the finite case. Notice, however, that the function u_i is a period utility function, that the function $\bar{u}_i$ is separable across periods, and that all agents have the same rate of discount. These are the strong separability assumptions that I alluded to above. Many of the results that we talk about can be extended to the case where agents have different discount rates, but I have avoided this generalization because a model of heterogeneous discount rates leads to strongly counterfactual implications for the evolution of the distribution of wealth over time. It implies that the agent with the lowest discount rate will, asymptotically, own all of society's wealth.[4]

It *is* possible to extend the infinite family model to allow for heterogeneity of rates of time preference among agents, but the mathematics that one requires to describe an equilibrium becomes correspondingly more complicated. The basic idea is to allow the discount rate to depend on the wealth of the family. If this dependence occurs in the right way, then a model of heterogeneous agents may lead to a nondegenerate wealth distribution. The "right way" means that as families become wealthier, they must also become less patient.

Formally the dependence of discount rates on wealth can be captured with a class of *recursive* preferences in which utility is defined by an *aggregator function*

$$\tilde{u}_{it} = w(x_{it}, \tilde{u}_{it+1}).$$

Separability is a special case of recursive preferences in which the aggregator function $w : X \times R \mapsto R$ takes the form[5]

$$w(x, \tilde{u}) = u(x) + \beta\tilde{u}.$$

For much of this book I will restrict my attention to the class of separable preferences for which the discount rate is common across agents and is strictly less than one. This restriction implies that agents place more weight on present than on future consumption. Although one can construct models in which agents do not discount the future, these models generate considerable mathematical difficulties because the value of utility will not usually be finite. There will typically be many different plans that lead to infinite utility, and the criterion of utility maximization, as a way of describing rational behavior, will no longer work.[6]

Although the assumption of positive discounting goes some way toward solving the problem of ensuring that utility has a well-defined maximum, it does not go all of the way and there are many examples of infinite horizon growth models in which this becomes a practical problem. Recall that utility is a weighted sum of period utilities with weights that are declining geometrically through time (the fact that the weights are declining follows from the fact that β is less than one). As long as the period utility function, $u_i(x_{it})$, is bounded, one can ensure that utility is bounded, and this fact, together with geometrically declining weights, can be used to show that the utility maximization problem has a well-defined solution. But many of the most important examples of period utility functions are *unbounded*, for example, logarithmic utility. This issue can generate considerable technical difficulties if one allows the value of $u_i(x_{it})$ to grow bigger through time without limit. In this book I avoid problems of this nature by studying pure trade economies in which the resources of society are finite. Even if the utility function is unbounded, no agent can consume more resources in any period than the finite limit imposed by the social endowment.[7]

ASSUMPTION   5.4   (Strict   concavity) $u_i(\lambda x + (1 - \lambda)y) > \lambda u_i(x) + (1 - \lambda)u_i(y)$ *for all* $x, y \in X, \lambda \in (0, 1)$.

Assumption 5.4 appears to be stronger than the quasi-concavity assumption that we introduced in chapter 4, but notice that 5.4 deals with the *period* utility function u_i. The assumption that u_i is strictly concave is equivalent to assuming that $\tilde{u}_i$ is strictly *quasi-concave*, since the sum of strictly concave functions is strictly quasi-concave.[8] This is another example of the fact that the additive separability assumption, made for tractability, is not as innocuous as it may at first appear. The final two assumptions are analogues of the assumptions that we introduced in chapter 4, and they are introduced for the same reasons.

ASSUMPTION 5.5 (Strictly positive endowments) $\omega_{it} \in X = R_{++}^l$ *for all* $i = 1, \ldots, m, \ t = 0, \ldots, \infty$.

ASSUMPTION 5.6 (Interiority) $\|Du_i(x_k)\| \to \infty$ *as* $x_k \to x$ *where some* $x^j = 0, j = 1, \ldots, l$. $Du_i(x) \cdot x$ *is bounded for* x *in any bounded subset of* X.

5.2.3   Budget Sets and Market Structure

In this section I am going to develop the relationship between the budget constraints that are faced by an agent in a sequence of markets and the single budget constraint that arises in a market for dated commodities. In the economies that we are studying in this chapter and in chapters 6 and 7 in which there is no uncertainty, this relationship is not very difficult to describe. It is worth paying attention to the details, however, since something very similar will apply in the economies that we study in chapters 9 and 10 in which we will introduce uncertainty.

In a world of sequential markets there is a separate budget constraint in each period. Each of these constraints takes the form

$$p_t \cdot (x_{it} - \omega_{it}) + (b_{it} - R_{t-1}b_{it-1}) \leq 0, \quad t = 1, \ldots, \infty, \tag{5.1}$$

where the term p_t is a vector of l prices denominated in units of account and b_{it} denotes assets transferred between periods. If the unit of account is the dollar; then p_t is a vector of money prices and b_{it} is denominated in dollars. It is important to realize that nobody in this economy will ever hold dollars between periods. Nevertheless, one is free to quote prices in dollars, since only relative prices influence demands.

By convention, I will assume that there is a single financial asset in each period called a one-period bond. A bond costs one period t dollar and represents a claim to $R_t = (1 + r_t)$ period $t + 1$ dollars. The term R_t is called the nominal interest factor, and r_t is the nominal interest rate. Individuals may either buy or sell bonds. The dating convention that we are using refers to the bonds that are used to transfer wealth between periods t and $t + 1$ as b_t. Similarly R_t is the interest factor that applies to bonds that are issued in period t, redeemable in period $t + 1$.

To understand the relationship between the budget constraint that occurs in a single market and the constraints that apply in a sequence of markets, it is useful to introduce the idea of *present value prices*. The present value (or period t value) of a period s commodity is its relative price in terms of period t dollars. I will use the notation Q_t^s to refer to the vector of prices of period s commodities valued in period t dollars:

$$Q_t^t \equiv p_t,$$

$$Q_t^s \equiv \frac{p_s}{\prod_{v=t}^{s-1} R_v} \qquad \text{for all } s > t.$$

Using this definition, we are in a position to impose two additional constraints on the consumer's choices that arise in the context of infinite commodity spaces. The first assumption limits the set of prices for which the consumer's problem is well defined:

ASSUMPTION 5.7

$$\lim_{\tau \to \infty} \sum_{t=1}^{\tau} Q_1^t \omega_{it} < \infty.$$

In other words, the wealth of every agent exists and is bounded.[9] If wealth were not bounded, then the agent's demand for every commodity would be infinite. In economies without growth, assumption 5.7 implies that the real interest rate is positive. In economies in which endowments are growing through time, it requires that the real rate of interest should be greater than the growth rate.

In the economy in which agents face a sequence of constraints, it is also necessary to place a bound on the amount that they may borrow at any point in time. The assumption that we will impose is as follows:

ASSUMPTION 5.8

$$\lim_{\tau \to \infty} \frac{b_{i\tau}}{\prod_{v=t}^{\tau-1} R_v} \geq 0.$$

Assumption 5.8 is an infinite horizon analogue of the finite horizon assumption that no agent may die in debt. Notice that the assumption allows agents to borrow, and it even allows the value of their debts to grow through time. What is *not possible*, if assumption 5.8 holds, is for the value of a family's debt to grow faster than the rate of interest.

Using the definition of present value prices, one can construct a compound budget constraint at any date τ in terms of period 1 prices:

$$\sum_{t=1}^{\tau} Q_1^t \cdot (x_{it} - \omega_{it}) + \frac{b_{i\tau}}{\prod_{v=t}^{\tau-1} R_v} \leq 0. \tag{5.2}$$

It follows from assumptions 5.7 and 5.8 that the limit of this compound constraint is well defined as $\tau \to \infty$. The equivalence of a sequential market structure with an Arrow-Debreu economy in which there is a single market for dated commodities follows directly by showing that the set of allocations that can be attained in the two economies is identical. The budget constraint in a single market economy takes the form

$$\sum_{t=1}^{\infty} Q_1^t \cdot (x_{it} - \omega_{it}) \leq 0, \tag{5.3}$$

which can be derived from the sequence model by taking the limit of 5.2 as $\tau \to \infty$.

5.2.4 Consumer's Problem

We now have enough notation to define the problem that is faced by an agent in a representative agent economy. Rather than write out the sequence of constraints, I will assume directly that agents trade dated commodities and that they maximize utility subject to a single budget constraint. By this convention, the ith family solves the problem

$$\max_{\{x_{it}\}_{t=1}^{\infty}} \sum_{t=1}^{\infty} \beta^t u_i(x_{it}) \tag{5.4}$$

subject to the constraint

$$\sum_{t=1}^{\infty} (x_{it} - \omega_{it}) \cdot Q_1^t \le 0. \tag{5.5}$$

This leads to a set of first-order conditions that characterize an equilibrium. The first-order conditions are necessary and sufficient to define a maximum, given that the problem is concave:

$$D\beta^t u_i(x_{it}) = \mu_i Q_1^t, \qquad i = 1, \ldots m, \, t = 1, \ldots, \infty, \tag{5.6}$$

$$\sum_{t=1}^{\infty} Q_1^t \cdot (x_{it} - \omega_{it}) = 0, \qquad i = 1, \ldots, m. \tag{5.7}$$

5.3   Competitive Equilibrium and the Planner's Problem

5.3.1   Competitive Equilibrium

In this section I will develop the infinite horizon version of the planner's problem and prove versions of the first and second welfare theorems that hold in infinite horizon economies. I begin by generalizing the definition of a competitive equilibrium to the infinite horizon case.

A competitive equilibrium is characterized by three sets of equations. The first two sets are the solutions to the m agents' optimization problems. These are described by 5.6 and 5.7. In addition one must establish that at present value prices $\{Q_1^t\}_{t=1}^{\infty}$, all markets clear at all dates:

$$\sum_{i=1}^{m} (x_{it} - \omega_{it}) = 0, \qquad t = 1, \ldots, \infty. \tag{5.8}$$

Equations 5.6 and 5.7 generate a set of individual excess demand functions of the form:

$$x_{i1} - \omega_{i1} = f_i^t(Q_1^1, Q_1^2, \ldots, Q_1^t, \ldots)$$

$$\vdots$$

$$x_{it} - \omega_{it} = f_i^t(Q_1^1, Q_1^2, \ldots, Q_1^t, \ldots)$$

$$\vdots$$

Aggregating these equations across individuals using the definition

$$f^t = \sum_{i=1}^{m} f_i^t,$$

one may write down a set of nonlinear equations in present value prices that must be satisfied by a competitive equilibrium sequence of present value prices $\{Q_1^t\}_{t=1}^{\infty}$:

$$f^1(Q_1^1, Q_1^2, \ldots) = 0$$
$$f^2(Q_1^1, Q_1^2, \ldots) = 0$$
$$\vdots \qquad\qquad\qquad\qquad (5.9)$$
$$f^t(Q_1^1, Q_1^2, \ldots) = 0$$
$$\vdots$$

This system describes an infinite number of market-clearing equations in an infinite number of unknowns. But now we face a problem. In the finite commodity case we used geometrical techniques to argue that an equilibrium exists, that there is a finite odd number of equilibria, and that equilibria are generically determinate. The techniques that are used to formalize these arguments use differential topology, and they do not extend in a straightforward way to infinite commodity spaces.

In the case of representative agent models, however, there is a way of reducing the description of equilibrium to a finite dimension problem by appealing to the idea that equilibria can be represented as the solution to a planner's problem It is this issue to which we now turn.

5.3.2 Planner's Problem

To establish that an equilibrium exists and that the number of equilibria is finite I am going to apply a technique originally used by Negishi [86]. The idea is to show that the proof of the first welfare theorem can be reduced to a statement about the existence of a solution to a particular system of equations that has all of the properties of excess demand equations but is in a different dimensional space. In the case of a representative agent model the technique allows us to reduce the infinite dimensional system of equations 5.9 to a finite system.

The notation is the same as that which was developed in chapter 4. The planner is assumed to solve

$$\max_{\{x_{it}\}} \sum_{i=1}^{m} \lambda_i \sum_{t=1}^{\infty} \beta^t u_i(x_{it}) \qquad\qquad (5.10)$$

such that

$$\sum_{i=1}^{m} x_{it} \leq \sum_{i=1}^{m} \omega_{it}, \quad t = 1, \ldots. \tag{5.11}$$

The first-order conditions to this problem are given by

$$\lambda_i \beta^t Du_i(x_{it}) = Q_1^t, \qquad t = 1, \ldots, \tag{5.12a}$$

$$\sum_{i=1}^{m} x_{it} = \sum_{i=1}^{m} \omega_{it}, \qquad t = 1, \ldots \tag{5.12b}$$

The terms Q_1^t represent the vectors of Lagrange multipliers that are associated with each of the constraints 5.11. Notice that if these multipliers are equal to the prices that are faced by agents in the competitive economy, and if each of the multipliers μ_i in equations 5.6 are equal to the inverse of the welfare weights λ_i in the planner's problem, then the set of first-order conditions, 5.6, that define how consumers behave in a competitive equilibrium is identical to the set of equations 5.12a that defines the solution to the planner's problem.

It is also true that the set of feasibility constraints that the planner will choose to hold with equality (equations 5.12b) are identical with the market-clearing equations that define a competitive equilibrium, 5.8. The equivalence between a competitive equilibrium and the solution to a planner's problem comes down to two questions:

1. Is it possible to find a set of welfare weights λ_i, $i = 1, \ldots, m$, such that the vectors x_{it}^* and Q_1^{*t} that solve the planner's problem constitute a competitive equilibrium for a given distribution of resources?

2. Is it possible to find a redistributive system of taxes and transfers such that the solution to the planner's problem for a given set of welfare weights λ_i, $i = 1, \ldots, m$, is supportable as a competitive equilibrium?

That is, do the first and second welfare theorems hold.

Second Welfare Theorem To establish the second welfare theorem, let $(Q_1^{*t}(\lambda), x_{it}^*(\lambda))$ be the solution to (5.12a) and (5.12b) for some vector of welfare weights λ. We have fixed the welfare weights, and we are looking for a set of transfers that makes the budget constraints hold when the prices and allocations solve the planner's problem for given welfare weights. To establish that such a set of transfers exists, we define

$$\tau_i(\lambda) = \sum_{t=1}^{\infty} Q_1^{*t}(\lambda) \cdot [\omega_{it} - x_{it}^*] \tag{5.13}$$

to be the dollar value of the transfer to the ith family that would just enable it to purchase the solution to the planner's problem $\{x_{it}^*(\lambda)\}_{t=1}^{\infty}$ for welfare weights λ when prices are equal to $Q_1^{*t}(\lambda)$. The second welfare theorem follows immediately by the same argument that was used for the finite case. For any vector of weights there exists a feasible set of lump-sum taxes and transfers that enables the solution to the planner's problem to be decentralized as a competitive equilibrium.

First Welfare Theorem   To establish the first welfare theorem, we need to be able to go in the other direction. Let $(Q_1^{*t}(\lambda), x_{it}^*(\lambda))$ be the prices and allocations that solve 5.12a and 5.12b *as functions of* λ. Now consider the following system of equations:

$$\tau_1(\lambda_1, \ldots, \lambda_m) = 0$$
$$\vdots \tag{5.14}$$
$$\tau_m(\lambda_1, \ldots, \lambda_m) = 0.$$

As we vary the vector λ the left-hand side of this equation traces out how far each individual will be from balancing his budget at prices $Q_1^{*t}(\lambda)$ if he wishes to purchase the allocation $x_{it}^*(\lambda)$ *given the existing distribution of endowments*. If the system of equations has a solution, then the vector of welfare weights λ^* that solves the system must constitute a parametric specification of the planner's problem that is consistent with a competitive equilibrium. Negishi pointed out, however, that the equation system 5.14 in which the m welfare weights λ are the independent variables has the same properties exactly as the system of market excess demand equations:

$$f(p) = 0,$$

where the vector p represents the prices that arise in a finite Arrow-Debreu exchange economy. It follows that generically there is an odd finite number of possible vectors of weights that could represent the competitive equilibria associated with a representative agent economy for any given distribution of endowments. Negishi's proof takes an infinite-dimensional system of excess demand equations and shows that the existence of a solution to these equations is equivalent to the existence of a solution to a finite set of budget equations.

5.4   Using the Representative Agent Model to Explain Time Series Data

In this part of the chapter I am going to shift track a little and describe to you how the representative agent model has been used to provide a description of U.S. time series. The method begins by writing down an objective function that is supposed to represent the problem faced by the social planner, and in order to implement the theory, one must make some relatively strong assumptions about the form that this function takes. For example, all agents are identical, preferences are logarithmic, and technology is Cobb-Douglas. The basic idea of the real business cycle (RBC) agenda is to begin with simple assumptions and to relax them gradually if they conflict with evidence.

5.4.1   Removing the Trend from Data

I am going to begin with a part of theory that would require its own book if I were to do justice to everything that has been written in the area. This has to do with the theory of how to remove the trend from economic time series, and it is closely related to the theory of economic growth. Since I am trying to keep this book relatively short, I will restrict myself to telling you about two different ways that economists have used to describe growth, and then I am going to do something that is very common in the literature on economic fluctuations: I am going to ignore it.

Until relatively recently, economic time series were modeled as processes of the form

$$y_t = a + bt + e_t, \tag{5.15}$$

where y_t represents an economic time series, t is a time trend, and e_t is a stationary disturbance. The word stationary, means that the probability distribution of e_t does not depend *explicitly* on time. It was well known that a statistical model of this kind could be used to remove the *trend* from an economic time series by running a regression of y_t on a constant and a time dummy. But in order to make this statistical model fit the facts of most economic data, it is necessary to assume that the disturbance to the equation, e_t, is highly autocorrelated. Another way of saying this is that the *conditional distribution* of e_t may depend on e_{t-1}.[10] The result of a regression of GNP on a trend is depicted in the figure 5.2. Notice that the residual from this regression may depart from the trend line for relatively long periods of time.

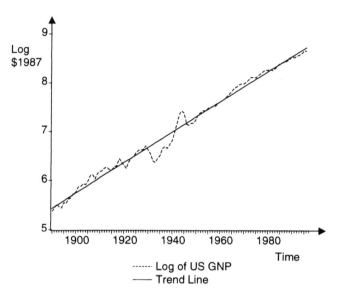

Figure 5.2
Removing the trend from GNP

In 1982 Nelson and Plosser [87] wrote a very influential article in which they argued that most economic time series are not *level stationary* but *difference stationary*. If Nelson and Plosser are right, then economic time series should not be regressed on a time trend to remove drift. Instead, one should build models that are based around data that have been detrended by taking first differences, and one should allow for the fact the time series arise from a common model by making sure that the time series do not drift apart from each other over time. Technically first difference stationary time series that are coupled in this way are called *co-integrated*.

The trend stationary and difference stationary models can be captured in the same framework if one assumes that the disturbance term, e_t, is autocorrelated and that it is described by the model

$$e_t = \rho e_{t-1} + u_t.$$

The trend stationary model implies that ρ is less than one. The difference stationary model implies that ρ is equal to one. In either case the state vector, $\{y_t, e_t\}$, will be described by a linear model

$$\begin{pmatrix} y_t \\ e_t \end{pmatrix} = A \begin{pmatrix} y_{t-1} \\ e_{t-1} \end{pmatrix} + \begin{pmatrix} b \\ 0 \end{pmatrix} t.$$

But a value of unity for the coefficient ρ leads to a very different implication for the econometric procedures that are appropriate if one is interested in inference, since for $\rho = 1$, the matrix

$$A = \begin{pmatrix} 0 & 1 \\ 0 & \rho \end{pmatrix}$$

has a unit root. In this situation it is not possible to use repeated observations of the stochastic process $\{y, e\}$ to draw inferences on the value of parameters of the data-generation process because this process is changing through time.

Now that we have two clear-cut statistical models of the data, one might think that it is a relatively easy task to find which model provides a better fit. Unfortunately, this is not the case. Theoretically it is possible to tell the difference between the model in which $\rho = 1$ and the model in which $\rho < 1$, since the asymptotic behavior of time series that arise from each model is very different. But, when ρ is close to one (e.g., 0.97), a very large amount of data is needed to get precise information. And this is exactly the situation that occurs in practice. We know, with a very high degree of confidence, that ρ is not equal to zero but that there is not enough data to tell the difference between 0.97 and 1 in the relatively short time in which we have been collecting information.

So how should we proceed in practice if we want to build models of the U.S. economy. My own view is that it really doesn't make much difference for most of the questions in which we are interested, so the approach that I have taken in this book is to assume that data are trend stationary. There is an important qualification to this statement, however, which is related to the relationship between data and theory. Although it does not matter much whether one assumes that data are trend or difference stationary, it *is* important that one's model of the data should start from a logically coherent model of individual behavior. This is good econometric practice because it forces one to take a stand about exactly what is generating the source of uncertainty. It is not likely to make much sense if one uses one detrending procedure on GNP and a different detrending procedure on consumption!

5.4.2 Simple RBC Model and Its Implications

The work on real business cycles began with two papers, one by Kydland and Prescott [72] and the other by Long and Plosser [74], in which they demonstrated that simple maximizing models that incorporate market clearing and rational expectations can capture many of the observed features of economic time series. Both of the original papers presented models with multisector technologies, although much of the recent research in the field has worked with less elaborate economies. A stripped down version of a real business cycle model can be represented by a social planner who solves the problem

$$\max_{\{c_t, l_t\}} \left\{ \sum_{s=1}^{\infty} E_t \beta^{s-t} \left[\log(c_t) - \frac{l_t^{1+\chi}}{1+\chi} \right] \right\}$$

such that

$$c_t + k_{t+1} \leq s_t k_t^{\alpha} (\gamma^t l_t)^{1-\alpha} + (1-\delta)k_t,$$

$$k_0 = \bar{k}_0, \quad s_0 = \bar{s}_0.$$

This is essentially the economy that we studied in chapter 3 with the additional complication that I am now allowing the supply of labor, l_t, to be a choice variable. The term k_t is capital, c_t is consumption, δ $(0 \leq \delta < 1)$ represents depreciation, β $(0 \leq \beta < 1)$ is the discount factor, γ $(\gamma > 1)$ is the growth factor, χ $(\chi \geq 0)$ is the inverse of the labor supply elasticity, and s_t is a productivity disturbance which is typically assumed to be autocorrelated and to follow the process

$$s_t = s_{t-1}^{\rho} v_t,$$

where ρ $(0 < \rho < 1)$ captures the persistence of technology shocks and v_t is an i.i.d. innovation to these shocks. An economy that solves this problem can be described by the equations

$$k_{t+1} = y_t + (1-\delta)k_t - c_t, \tag{5.16}$$

$$y_t = s_t k_t^{\alpha} (\gamma^t l_t)^{1-\alpha}, \tag{5.17}$$

$$(1-\alpha)\frac{y_t}{l_t} = c_t l_t^{\chi}, \tag{5.18}$$

$$\frac{1}{c_t} = \beta E_t \left[\frac{1}{c_{t+1}} \left(1 - \delta + \alpha \frac{y_{t+1}}{k_{t+1}} \right) \right] \tag{5.19}$$

$$s_t = s_{t-1}^p v_t. \tag{5.20}$$

In these equations we have exploited the assumption that the technology, described in equation 5.17, is Cobb-Douglas in order to write the marginal products of labor and capital as

$$(1 - \alpha) \frac{y_t}{l_t} \quad \text{and} \quad \alpha \frac{y_t}{k_t}$$

in equations 5.18 and 5.19.[11] Equations 5.16 to 5.20 are very similar to the model that we introduced in chapter 3. The only difference is that we have added a static first-order condition, 5.18, that tells the social planner to equate the marginal product of labor, $(1 - \alpha) y_t / l_t$, to the slope of the agent's indifference curve between consumption and leisure. This latter object is the ratio of the marginal disutility of labor supply, l_t^χ, to the marginal utility of consumption, $1/c_t$.

5.4.3 Regression on a Common Trend: What the Model Tells Us to Do

Before we can begin to think about econometric inference, we are going to have to find a way of writing down a model that implies that we are observing repeated draws from an invariant distribution; that is, we are looking for a transformation of the data that makes it stationary. By choosing to assume that utility is logarithmic and separable in consumption and leisure, and by choosing to assume that technology is Cobb-Douglas, we have already slipped in some strong assumptions that will help us in this endeavor. Although both of these assumptions can be generalized a little bit, they cannot be generalized a whole lot. Notice also that we have modeled the growth process by assuming that the marginal product of labor depends on the date at which it is applied. This assumption is called *labor-augmenting technical progress*, and it is necessary to assume that growth occurs in this way if the model is going to have a solution in which capital, output, and consumption all grow at the same rate.

To arrive at a stationary model, we are going to divide equations 5.16 to 5.20 by γ^t:

$$\gamma \left(\frac{k_{t+1}}{\gamma^{t+1}} \right) = \left(\frac{y_t}{\gamma^t} \right) + (1 - \delta) \left(\frac{k_t}{\gamma^t} \right) - \left(\frac{c_t}{\gamma^t} \right), \tag{5.21}$$

$$\left(\frac{y_t}{\gamma^t}\right) = s_t \left(\frac{k_t}{\gamma^t}\right)^\alpha l_t^{1-\alpha}, \tag{5.22}$$

$$(1 - \alpha)\left(\frac{y_t}{\gamma^t}\right) = \left(\frac{c_t}{\gamma^t}\right)l_t^{\chi+1}, \tag{5.23}$$

$$\left(\frac{\gamma^t}{c_t}\right) = \left(\frac{\beta}{\gamma}\right)E_t\left[\left(\frac{\gamma^{t+1}}{c_{t+1}}\right)\left\{1 - \delta + \alpha\left(\frac{y_{t+1}}{\gamma^{t+1}}\right)\left(\frac{\gamma^{t+1}}{k_{t+1}}\right)\right\}\right], \tag{5.24}$$

$$s_t = s_{t-1}^\rho v_t. \tag{5.25}$$

We are now ready to find a steady state for our economy by defining transformed variables

$$\tilde{k}_t \equiv \left(\frac{k_t}{\gamma^t}\right), \quad \tilde{c}_t \equiv \left(\frac{c_t}{\gamma^t}\right), \quad \tilde{y}_t \equiv \left(\frac{y_t}{\gamma^t}\right),$$

just as we did when we introduced the Solow growth model in chapter 2. The steady state is the solution, $\{\bar{k}, \bar{c}, \bar{y}, \bar{l}\}$, to the equations

$$\gamma\bar{k} = \bar{y} + (1 - \delta)\bar{k} - \bar{c}, \tag{5.26}$$

$$\bar{y} = \bar{k}^\alpha \bar{l}^{1-\alpha}, \tag{5.27}$$

$$(1 - \alpha)\bar{y} = \bar{c}\bar{l}^{\chi+1}, \tag{5.28}$$

$$1 = \left(\frac{\beta}{\gamma}\right)\left(1 - \delta + \alpha\frac{\bar{y}}{\bar{k}}\right), \tag{5.29}$$

and it is relatively easy to show, given our functional forms and the restrictions on the parameters, that this solution exists and is unique.

The model that I have described is the one that underlies most of the work on real business cycles. Although it would be unfair to the approach to place too much weight on the implications of the model for the long-run behavior of output, consumption, and capital, it *is* worth pointing out what these implications are and where they come from. The most important econometric implication of a model with a *balanced growth path* is that one should detrend the data by removing a common trend from all of the variables in the model. This implication follows from the fact that each variable can be described as a stationary stochastic process around the same long-run growth factor. In figure 5.3 I have drawn pictures of deviations from trend that are estimated for GNP and consumption in

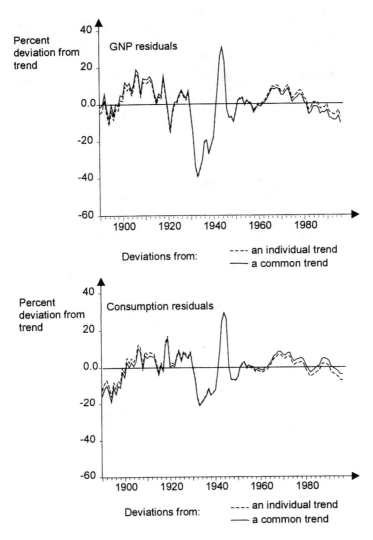

Figure 5.3
Removing the trend from consumption and GNP

two different ways. The upper panel depicts the deviations of GNP from a linear trend and the lower panel depicts the deviation of consumption from a linear trend. In each case the solid line represents residuals from a common trend and the dashed lines represent residuals when GNP and consumption are allowed to have two different linear trends. The coefficient on the common trend is equal to 0.0317 when estimated by least squares, and the coefficients on the trends in income and consumption, when estimated separately, are equal to 0.0323 and 0.0311, respectively.[12] These numbers may seem to be similar, but the *probability value* of the restriction that they are equal, is less than 1%! Another way of saying this is that the data tell us to reject the hypothesis of a common trend.

5.4.4 Hodrick-Prescott Filter: What RBC Economists Actually Do

The equations that we have written constitute a fully specified general equilibrium model of an economy. This model has implications for the behavior of the time series data, and these implications can be tested econometrically by estimating the model and checking its goodness of fit. The model is nonlinear, and it is not quite of the same form as the econometric models that come from Keynesian economics. But there has been a lot of recent work in econometrics that has evolved to handle models of this kind, and a number of researchers have checked how well they fit U.S. time series data. One approach, called *generalized method of moments*, tries to check the restrictions that the model places on certain selected moments of the data and jiggles around the parameters of the model until it finds the *best fit*. You will have to take a course in econometrics if you want to find out what "best fit" means, what "moments" are, and how to jiggle parameters in the most efficient way. One way that econometricians use to tell whether a model is a good one is by looking at a summary statistic from the data and seeing if the statistic could have reasonably been generated by the theoretical model in question. The general conclusion, when these methods are applied to the simple model that I have outlined above, is that it fails rather dramatically. One dimension in which it fails is in the prediction that economic time series can be described as fluctuations around a common trend growth path.

The fact that the RBC model is rejected by the data is pointed to by critics as a significant failure of the research agenda. While I am not, a big advocate of the RBC approach, I do not think that the fact that the model is rejected by formal statistical tests should lead us to reject prematurely the approach. My reasons for this position have to do with the difference between *economic significance* and *statistical significance*. The RBC model is rejected by some kinds of statistical tests, but the reasons why the model fails could quite easily be due to factors that are not of much economic significance. Incorrect theories can be very useful theories as long as we are aware of the dimensions in which they fail and the limitations of their predictions. We are quite confident in the answer when we use Newtonian theories of dynamics to predict how long it will take to get from New York to London on the Concord, even though Newtonian physics is known to be false and has been superseded by Einstein's theory of relativity.

In the context of economic theories, the common trend hypothesis is an example of a feature of the model that is viewed as a useful first approximation. Although an estimated growth rate of 0.0323 is statistically different from an estimated growth rate of 0.0311, these two numbers are not very different from an economic point of view, at least over relatively short time horizons. It is not very difficult to modify the model to account for different growth rates, for example, by including two different sources of growth, by allowing growth to enter the production technology in a way that does more than augment the productive capacity of labor, or by allowing the utility function to be more complicated than the separable logarithmic example that we used in the chapter. Since real business cycle theorists wish to emphasize the predictions of their models for the theory of economic fluctuations, they have adopted a procedure that removes a different trend from each of the time series in the data. And since they are not willing to commit themselves to the assumption of a time invariant linear trend, the detrending procedure that is favored in the literature is more flexible.

In figure 5.4 I have depicted the detrending procedure that is commonly used. The idea behind this procedure is that the business cycle deals with fluctuations of a certain frequency that is typically defined as somewhere between four and eight years. Smoother movements than this are subsumed into the trend. The *Hodrick-Prescott filter* [61] allows the data to determine the trend by splitting the series $\{x_t\}_{t=1}^T$ into two parts, $\{s_t\}_{t=1}^T$ and $\{x_t - s_t\}_{t=1}^T$, in a way that solves the problem:

$$\min\left\{\frac{I}{T}\sum_{t=1}^{T}(x_t - s_t)^2 + \frac{\lambda}{T}\sum_{t=2}^{T-1}[(s_{t+1} - s_t) - (s_t - s_{t-1})]^2\right\},$$

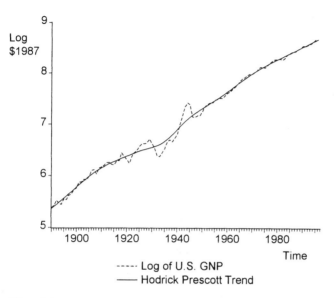

Figure 5.4
Applying the Hodrick-Prescott filter to U.S. GNP

where $\lambda > 0$ penalizes fluctuations of the trend series $\{s_t\}$. The parameter λ is usually picked to equal 100 in annual data, and this is the value that I have used in figure 5.4. A larger value of λ will result in a smoother trend.

5.4.5 Calibration and Summary Statistics: How RBC Theorists Measure Success

Real business cycle theorists are unwilling to concede that a model has failed simply because it does not pass a formal hypothesis test. As an alternative to formal econometric testing, advocates of the approach suggest that a theoretical model should be *calibrated* and *simulated* and that selected moments of the time series from the simulated model should be checked against the moments of U.S. data. Since RBC theories are exclusively concerned with fluctuations at business cycle frequencies, their proponents suggest that all of the series involved, both simulated series and real world series, should be passed through the Hodrick-Prescott filter to remove low-frequency components. This research agenda is known as calibration.

To pick the parameters of a model that is to be calibrated, an RBC theorist will try to draw on information that is outside of the immediate data set. For example, the model predicts that the interest factor should be equal, on average, to $1/\beta$. By observing that the real rate of interest in the U.S. economy has fluctuated around 4% per annum one is able to guess that β, (the discount factor) should be set at around 0.99 in a quarterly model. Similar arguments can be made for the other parameters of the model. For example, a competitive economy will set $(1 - \alpha)$ equal to labor's share of national income which is roughly two-thirds in the postwar United States. Gary Hansen's [58] paper is a good example of the calibration technique, and his work is widely cited in the literature because it solved a significant puzzle in the research agenda. Earlier work in RBC theory had trouble in accounting for the volatility of employment fluctuations in U.S. data, since cross-sectional studies suggest that the labor supply elasticity is rather low. Gary drew on an argument by Richard Rogerson [93] who pointed out that there is a significant non-convexity in the labor market that arises from the fact that there is a fixed cost of traveling to work. This fixed cost implies that the social planner would rather lay off workers than smoothly vary hours, and it implies that the social planner's utility function is linear in l even when individuals face quite low labor supply elasticities.

The bottom line of all of this is that in some dimensions the RBC model does quite well. In particular, it can generate time series that have roughly the right second moments as the time series data, using parameter values that are in accord with a variety of other evidence. In chapter 7, I will present some evidence of the dimensions on which the model succeeds, and I will also point out a dimension on which it does not do so well. Since this book is about self-fulfilling prophecies, and since I have tied this idea to irregular equilibria, you might have guessed that the way in which the RBC model fails has something to do with these concepts. You would be guessing correctly, but you will have to wait until chapter 7 before I can explain these ideas further.

5.5 Concluding Remarks

I opened this chapter with a discussion of the difference between RA and OG economies, and I pointed out that the fact that a representative agent economy solves a planner's problem has implications for macroeconomics. Roughly speaking, these implications come down to the idea that equilibria of RA models are locally determinate. Let us take, for instance, a model with a finite number of representative agents. Typically the equilibria will be described by a difference equation:

$$y_t = f(y_{t-1}), \qquad y_t \in R^n, \tag{5.30}$$

plus some initial or end point conditions. The economic assumptions will *always* give exactly enough initial and end point conditions to ensure that there is a unique equilibrium, or at least an odd finite number of equilibria.[13] I also introduced some of the ideas that have become important in the theory of real business cycles, the branch of macro-economics that uses the RA model to understand the behavior of economic time series. In chapter 7, I will return to these ideas and contrast the RBC model, based on a determinate equilibrium, with a related model in which there may be an indeterminate steady state.

5.6   Appendix: Transversality Condition

There is an additional necessary condition to a maximization problem, the transversality condition. This appendix explains transversality. Suppose that we study the finite problem

$$\max_{X_T} J(X_T)$$

over all admissible sequences

$$X_T \equiv \{x_t\}_{t=1}^T,$$

with $J(\ )$ defined as

$$J(X_T) = \sum_{t=0}^{T} \left(\frac{1}{1+\rho}\right)^t V(x_t, x_{t+1}).$$

The optimal growth model is a special example of this problem in which $\{x\}$ is a sequence of capital stocks and $V(\ )$ represents the indirect utility in period t of choosing the capital stock k_{t+1}. In the optimal growth example the function $V(\ )$ is given by

$$V(k_t, k_{t+1}) = U(k_t(1-\delta) + F(k_t, l_t) - k_{t+1}, l_t).$$

We will consider the simpler case in which labor is inelastically supplied ($l_t = 1$), although the addition of variable labor simply adds an additional contemporaneous first-order condition to the problem. Returning to the more compact notation, suppose that $\tilde{X}_t$ represents the *optimal* sequence. Then

$$J(\tilde{X}_T) \geq J(X_T),$$

and expanding the value of an arbitrary sequence X_T around the value of the optimal sequence leads to the Taylor series

$$J(X_T) - J(\tilde{X}_T) = \frac{\partial J(X_T)}{\partial X_T}\bigg|_{X_T=\tilde{X}_T} (X_T - \tilde{X}_T) + O(x^2).$$

Writing out the first-order terms explicitly leads to the expression:

$$\begin{aligned}
\frac{\partial J(X_T)}{\partial X_T}\bigg|_{X_T=\tilde{X}_T} &(X_T - \tilde{X}_T) \\
&= \sum_{t=1}^{T-1} \left(\frac{1}{1+\rho}\right)^{t-1} \left(V_2(\tilde{x}_{t-1}, \tilde{x}_t) + \frac{1}{1+\rho} V_1(\tilde{x}_t, \tilde{x}_{t+1}) \right) (x_t - \tilde{x}_t) \\
&+ \left(\frac{1}{1+\rho}\right)^T V_2(\tilde{x}_{T-1}, \tilde{x}_T)(x_T - \tilde{x}_T),
\end{aligned} \tag{5.31}$$

where the terms $V_1(\tilde{x}_t, \tilde{x}_{t+1})$ and $V_2(\tilde{x}_{t-1}, \tilde{x}_t)$ refer to partial derivatives of $V(\ )$ evaluated at the optimal values. In a finite problem these terms are set to zero as first-order conditions for a maximum. In other words, in the finite problem

$$V_2(\tilde{x}_{t-1}, \tilde{x}_t) + \frac{1}{1+\rho} V_1(\tilde{x}_t, \tilde{x}_{t+1}) = 0, \qquad t = 1, 2, \ldots, T-1,$$

$$V_2(\tilde{x}_{T-1}, \tilde{x}_T) = 0. \tag{5.32}$$

Equation 5.32 says that the marginal benefit of ending up with positive capital at date T should equal zero. In the infinite horizon problem the analogue of this condition is that

$$\lim_{T \to \infty} -\left[\left(\frac{1}{1+\rho}\right)^T V_2(\tilde{x}_{T-1}, \tilde{x}_T)\tilde{x}_T \right] = 0. \tag{5.33}$$

It is this expression that is known as the transversality condition.

Equation 5.31 defines the slope of the objective function with respect to small changes of the sequence $\{x\}$ in the neighborhood of the optimum.

The last term of equation 5.31 has two parts. The first part multiplies $V_2(\ )$ evaluated at the optimal sequence by the Tth element of an arbitrary sequence X_T, and the second part subtracts $V_2(\ )$ evaluated at the optimum multiplied by the Tth element of the optimal sequence $\tilde{X}_T$.

Since V_2 is negative, the term

$$\lim_{T \to \infty} \left[\left(\frac{1}{1+\rho} \right)^T V_2(\tilde{x}_{T-1}, \tilde{x}_T) x_T \right],$$

where x_T is an element of some arbitrary (positive) sequence, cannot possibly increase the value of the optimal program. There is still the term

$$\lim_{T \to \infty} - \left[\left(\frac{1}{1+\rho} \right)^T V_2(\tilde{x}_{T-1}, \tilde{x}_T) \tilde{x}_T \right]$$

to consider. In the finite problem one simply sets $V_2(\ )$ to zero. In the infinite horizon problem, however, it is not enough that the limit of the marginal utility should go to zero; that is, it is not enough that

$$\lim_{T \to \infty} - V_2(\tilde{x}_{T-1}, \tilde{x}_T) = 0,$$

since the discounted value of capital [the term $(1/(1+\rho))^T \tilde{x}_T$] could be going to infinity faster than V_2 goes to zero. The required condition is given by equation 5.33.

5.7 Problems

1. What is meant by "present value prices"? If R_t is the nominal interest factor on a one-period bond, how would you express the present value price of a period 5 commodity in terms of the period 1 commodity?

2. This problem concerns a representative agent economy. Technology is given by

$$Y_t = K_t^{\alpha} L_t^{1-\alpha},$$

where K_t is capital, C_t is consumption, and L_t is labor supply. The representative agent maximizes discounted utility

$$U = \sum_{t=1}^{\infty} \beta^{t-1} [C_t - L_t^{\gamma}] \qquad 0 \le \beta \le 1, \gamma > 1,$$

where C_t is consumption subject to the capital accumulation equation

$$K_{t+1} = K_t(1 - \delta) + Y_t - C_t, K_1 = \bar{K}_1,$$

where δ is the rate of depreciation and $\bar{K}_1$ is the initial capital stock.

a. Find a set of four equations in the variables $C_t, K_t, L_t,$ and Y_t that characterizes a competitive equilibrium for this economy.

b. What is meant by the transversality condition? What is the transversality condition for this problem?

c. Find the steady state value of K as a function of the parameters of the model.

d. Assuming that $\bar{K}_1$ is positive but less than the steady state stock of capital, describe the path that the economy would follow to the steady state. Your answer should explain how the four variables $C, L, Y,$ and K will adjust over time from their initial values to their steady state values.

e. Now suppose that the equilibrium in this economy were to be decentralized by competitive markets. Describe the path of (1) the rental rate, (2) the real rate of interest, and (3) the real wage that you would observe in a competitive equilibrium. (Hint: In a competitive market the real wage will equal the marginal product of labor, the rental rate will equal the marginal product of capital, and the real interest rate will equal the rental rate plus the depreciation rate.)

f. Consider the special case in which the preference parameter $\gamma = 1$. Are there parameter configurations for which this economy can grow even when productivity is constant? If so, what are they?

3. Briefly contrast the differences between the assumptions that we made on preferences in the case of infinite horizon economy with those for the finite economy in chapter 5.

a. What would be the consequence for the implications of the model of dropping the assumption that all agents have the same rate of time preference?

b. You are asked to consider a two-country model in which each country is represented by a representative agent with the same infinite horizon utility function but with different rates of time preference. Describe the limiting behavior of trade between the two countries.

6 Infinite Horizon Economies and Overlapping Generations

6.1 Introduction

Although representative agent economies behave a lot like the finite commodity general equilibrium model of Arrow and Debreu, it is *not true* that this statement applies to all temporary equilibrium models even if one assumes market clearing and rational expectations. A second important class of models, overlapping generations economies, can behave in very different ways. Overlapping generations models have been used widely as a research tool in monetary theory, and their theoretical properties have been explored in the theory journals. As vehicles for developing quantitative empirical predictions, OG models have been less successful, mainly for reasons of tractability. There have been some attempts to address quantitative issues in the public finance area, using overlapping generations economies in which agents live for many periods,[1] but the main use of the model has been to provide theoretical examples of what might be possible in an equilibrium model, based on simple examples in which one assumes that agents live for only two periods.

In chapter 5 we demonstrated that the equilibria of representative agent economies are Pareto optimal and determinate. In this chapter I will introduce the idea that in an overlapping generations economy, both of these properties may fail to hold. The way in which Pareto optimality may fail, referred to in the literature as *dynamic inefficiency*, has been widely discussed in theoretical research on economic growth. Since I am going to deal exclusively with pure trade economies, dynamic inefficiency will manifest itself as the possibility that the rate of interest may be "too low." In these pure trade economies society's resources are fixed, and an inefficient equilibrium is one in which a reallocation of these resources may make everyone better off.

In economies in which agents may accumulate physical capital, not only can the distribution of resources be improved but society can have more of everything. In these economies, an interest rate that is too low implies that agents will choose to accumulate "too much capital." "Too low" and "too much" are made precise by asking if there is a way of re-allocating social resources that produces *more physical output* in *every* period. If interest rates are low, then firms will be induced to produce using a larger quantity of physical capital than would otherwise be the case. In this event it may be possible for society to consume part of the capital stock in the current period and still have more output in subsequent periods. This increase in the future is achieved by the fact that at a lower stock of capital, fewer resources will be required for replacement investment and the resulting increase in consumption may more than offset the loss of output that occurs from the fact that production occurs using a lower input of capital.

Some authors have tried to develop econometric tests of over accumulation based on the criterion that an inefficient economy will be one in which the rate of interest is less than the rate of growth.[2] The main purpose of this chapter is not, however, to suggest that an inefficient growth path, due to overaccumulation of capital, is a likely state of affairs in the U.S. economy. Indeed in chapter 7 we will investigate a second kind of inefficiency, due to externalities in production, that suggests that the economy may be underinvesting rather than overinvesting. The point is to develop a theory in which these issues can be addressed and to get the reader to learn how to construct models from a general equilibrium perspective that allow for the possibility that any particular equilibrium is not necessarily the best possible outcome that society can achieve.

A major theme of this book, and a second important theme of the chapter, is the idea that beliefs may independently influence events. The overlapping generations model will provide our first introduction to this idea in the context of a general equilibrium model in which all agents are optimizing and expectations are rational. In subsequent chapters I will show that the phenomenon of indeterminacy may also occur in economies with externalities, and I will argue that indeterminate equilibria may be exploited to help us to explain important features of the real world.

6.2 Structure of the Overlapping Generations Economy

I will begin the chapter by studying a special case of the overlapping generations model in which there is a single commodity in each period, and a single agent in each generation with a life span of only two periods. In models with more than one agent and more than one good, the assumption that agents live for two periods is unrestrictive; it is possible to write a model where agents live for T periods as a two-period model by redefining agents and goods. In section 6.8, I will introduce an example that demonstrates how to carry out this transformation.

In the two-period, two-agent, two-commodity model, some of the results that I will derive are special. However, the main features that I am going to concentrate on are the properties of indeterminacy and possible nonoptimality of equilibria, and both of these properties may be shown to hold in more general models. I will use the two period example to build up some intuition about the model, and in the latter part of chapter I will sketch out some results due to Kehoe and Levine that illustrate which of the properties of the two-period model can be generalized.

6.3 Consumer's Problem

The overlapping generations model differs from a representative agent economy in a number of ways, one of which is the heterogeneity that is captured by the fact that at any point in time there are agents of different ages transacting with each other. It is assumed that trade takes place in a sequence of periods, indexed by the subscript, $t = 1 \ldots \infty$ and that there is an infinite set of agents, partitioned into sets of generations. Generation t is born in period t and lives for two periods. Figure 6.1 depicts the generational structure; G_t refers to generation t.

6.3.1 Problem of a Young Agent

To keep things simple, I will assume that all agents born in generation t have identical preferences, and I will describe the representative agent's life cycle choices by solving the problem:

$$\max u(x_t^t, x_{t+1}^t) \tag{6.1}$$

such that

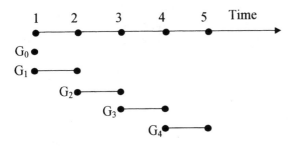

Figure 6.1
Generational structure in the OG model

$$p_t \cdot (x_t^t - \omega^0) + b_t \leq 0, \tag{6.2}$$

$$p_{t+1} \cdot (x_{t+1}^t - \omega^1) - R_t b_t \leq 0. \tag{6.3}$$

The function $u : X \times X \mapsto R$ satisfies all of the properties that were imposed on preferences in chapter 4. The notation X represents the consumption set, which I take to be all of R_+, x_s^t is the demand of generation t at date s, and (ω^0, ω^1) is the agent's endowment of the single commodity in youth (superscript 0) and old age (superscript 1). Notice that endowments and utilities are not indexed by time, since I am assuming that these aspects of the environment do not change from one period to the next.

The physical characteristics of the endowment are important in overlapping generations economies, since durable goods represent an alternative technology for transferring resources through time. I am going to study an economy with a nonstorable commodity, and I will force all intertemporal transfers to occur by borrowing or lending with other agents at a *gross* money rate of interest R_t. This assumption implies that there is a single financial asset, a one-period nominal bond, that represents a promise to pay R_t dollars in period $t + 1$. We will use the symbol b_t to represent the quantity of such bonds purchased by an agent of generation t, and p_t, to denote prices in dollars where the dollar is the unit of account.

The budget sets 6.2 and 6.3 reflect the opportunities for trade that are perceived by an agent of generation t. In youth he is able to borrow or lend his endowment in return for nominally denominated bonds. These promises may be issued by other (identical) young agents, or they may be issued by the government. There are two special and important cases of the model. The first case is when the government does not enter the loan market, and in this case the net supply of nominal bonds will be equal to zero in equilibrium. The second case is when the government issues nominal liabilities that pay a zero nominal rate of interest, and these liabilities are willingly held in equilibrium. This is the case of positively valued fiat money.

6.3.2 Problem of an Old Agent

For all periods other than period 1, the problem solved by a young agent (in conjunction with the assumption of perfect foresight) serves to define the actions that will be taken by the old. But in the first period of the model, one must explain the actions of the initial old generation. These people are assumed to be born old and to live for only one period. They solve the problem

$$\max u(x_1^0) \tag{6.4}$$

such that

$$p_1 \cdot (x_1^0 - \omega^1) - R_0 b_0 \leq 0, \tag{6.5}$$

where the term $R_0 b_0$ represents the initial money value of nominal liabilities. If b is interpreted as money, then $R_0 = 1$, and the term $R_0 b_0$ is simply the value of the stock of money that is owned by the initial old. Since utility is assumed to be increasing in x, these agents face a trivial problem which is solved by trading the money value of their nominal assets in exchange for commodities.

6.4   Example of a Pareto Inferior Equilibrium

6.4.1   Case of Early Endowments

I am going to begin with a very simple example of a model that demonstrates the problems that can arise when the commodity space *and* the number of agents are infinite. The example is characterized by a particular assumption about the aggregate endowment pattern that has been generalized by David Gale [52] who refers to economies of this type as *Samuelson economies*. I describe Gale's generalization in section 6.6.2.

The economy that I am going to look at is one where all generations, greater than or equal to 1, have an endowment pattern of $(1, 0)$ so that these agents have one unit when young and no units of the commodity when old. I will assume that generation 0 is born old with no endowment of commodities and that there is no such thing as money. In this economy there is a competitive equilibrium in which the relative price of a period t commodity in terms of a period $t + 1$ commodity is zero.

The competitive equilibrium of this economy is one of no trade. The old have nothing to give, and they will thus be forced to consume nothing. The young would like to trade some of their endowment in youth in exchange for some consumption in old age at any positive price. But since the price is zero and the market value of their endowment is zero, they may as well consume their endowment. In this extreme example the price of commodities in terms of the numéraire, money, is infinite and every individual consumes one unit when young and nothing in old age.

But it does not take much thought to come up with an allocation that Pareto dominates autarky. Suppose, for example, that a Social Planner were to take half of the allocation of the initial young generation and that he were to give these resources to the initial old. The initial old would be made better off by this transfer, since they have gone from zero to a half. But suppose that the transfer is repeated in every period into the infinite future, that is, each generation is offered the allocation $(1/2, 1/2)$ instead of the allocation $(0, 1)$. This proposal is feasible because it can be supported by taking half a unit from the young generation in every period and giving it to the old. If individuals have convex preferences, then the allocation is welfare improving for *every* generation. I have given an example of an economy in which there exists a competitive equilibrium that is not Pareto optimal.

6.4.2   Case of Late Endowments

Suppose now that the economy is one in which the endowment of each agent is tilted toward old age rather than toward youth. Gale calls an economy like this *classical*. For example, let the endowment vector be $(0, 1)$ for each generation greater than or equal to 1, and let the initial old generation be endowed with one unit rather than with nothing. Once again, there is a competitive equilibrium in which each generation consumes its endowment. But consider the reallocation that gives each generation $(1/2, 1/2)$ instead of $(0, 1)$. This reallocation is welfare improving for every generation other than the initial old, but in order to support the reallocation, it is necessary to take resources away from generation zero. Here we have an example of an economy in which the autarkic equilibrium is Pareto optimal.

What distinguishes the above two examples from each other? When are the equilibria of overlapping generations economies Pareto optimal, and why does the first welfare theorem sometimes break down? These are the topics that I take up below in section 6.6.2.

6.5   Institutions That May Improve Allocations

The idea that a competitive equilibrium may be Pareto inferior to some other allocation mechanism is an important one, since it suggests that the design of social institutions is an important issue. The market failure that occurs in the overlapping generations model under perfect foresight is only one of the potential market failures that may occur when we depart in mild ways from any one of the assumptions of the finite Arrow-Debreu model. In economies with physical capital, the same kinds of failure can occur, and in this case the failure implies that the long-run growth path of the economy will be inefficient. A number of alternative institutions have been suggested, as ways of solving the problem.

For example, a simple reallocation by redistributive taxes and transfers looks a lot like the real world institution of social security. Perhaps the overlapping generations model should be taken as an explanation of why government should be in the pension business. Alternatively, it has been suggested that the model should be taken as an explanation for valued fiat money, since in his 1958 [97] article Samuelson pointed out that one way that a private market might achieve an efficient allocation would be to introduce an asset that was valued simply because agents believe that it will have value in the future.

Samuelson's social institution of money works as follows: Suppose that we are in the first environment described above in which agents are endowed with one unit of the commodity in youth and no units in old age. Suppose now that the initial old generation invents an object that they call money which is a piece of paper that bears an inscription. The piece of paper is not valued for its own sake, but it will have value if other individuals believe that it has value.[3] This piece of paper can support the Pareto-improving allocation that we attributed to the social planner simply by the process of passing money from one generation to the next in exchange for commodities.

There is a considerable branch of literature that uses this idea to address questions in monetary theory, and there is an equally large body of economists who eschew such practices. Distrust of the overlapping generations model as a model of money arises from the observation that the model cannot explain why one paper asset is held over another. For example, the object called money in the overlapping generations model could equally well represent a title to land or to a Rembrandt painting. Skeptics point out that money has many characteristics and the overlapping generations model captures only one of these: It explains why an intrinsically useless object may come to have value. It explains the store-of-wealth function of money but not the medium of exchange. In an economy in which there coexist two paper assets, one of which pays interest and the other of which does not, the overlapping generations model cannot explain the value of the asset that is dominated in rate of return.

The response to these criticisms, by those who defend the model, is that the explanation of the value of an unbacked paper asset is primary and the question of rate of return dominance is a separate question that must be faced by *any* model of money. We will sidestep these issues in this chapter by modeling a single paper asset that we think of interchangeably as money or debt. The appropriate empirical counterpart of the object in our model is an aggregate of all of the paper liabilities of the federal government, and to keep things simple, we will take the money rate of interest on these liabilities to be zero.

6.6   Set of Equilibria in the Overlapping Generations Model

In chapter 5 I showed that equilibria of representative agent economies could typically be described by difference equations together with a transversality condition. I am going to look at the equilibria in the overlapping generations model in a similar light and once again obtain a simple difference equation that characterizes equilibrium paths of prices. The difference, in the overlapping generations case, is that the difference equation is no longer associated with a unique boundary condition.

6.6.1   Equilibria as Solutions to Difference Equations

To generalize the examples presented in the above sections, I will define the excess demand function $f(p_t/p_{t+1})$ as the solution to the agent's optimization problem:

$$z_t^t \equiv \hat{x}_t^t - \omega^0 = f\left(\frac{p_t}{p_{t+1}}\right). \tag{6.6}$$

This definition may be combined with the following characterization of an equilibrium to arrive at an excess demand function for each commodity that must be set equal to zero.

An *equilibrium* is an allocation $\hat{x} \equiv (\{\hat{x}_t^t\}_{t=1}^{\infty}, \{\hat{x}_{t+1}^t\}_{t=0}^{\infty})$ and a price system $\hat{p} \equiv \{\hat{p}_t\}_{t=1}^{\infty}$ such that:

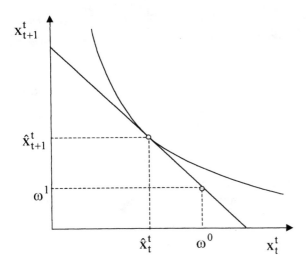

Figure 6.2
Consumer's problem

1. $\hat{x}$ solves the consumer's problems when $p = \hat{p}$ (rational choice); see figure 6.2.

2. $\hat{x}_t^t + \hat{x}_t^{t-1} = \omega^0 + \omega^1$ (market clearing).

It is now relatively simple to show that the set of competitive equilibria can be represented by the solutions to a difference equation. Let us take the simple case in which the government issues fiat money to the initial old generation and assume that this money passes down the generations from one period to the next. Let the quantity of money be M. Then the initial old generation has the following trivial excess demand function:

$$z_1^0 = \frac{M}{p_1}.\tag{6.7}$$

Equilibrium in the first period of the model requires that the sum of the excess demand of the old and the excess demand of the young should be equal to zero. That is,

$$\frac{M}{p_1} + f\left(\frac{p_1}{p_2}\right) = 0.\tag{6.8}$$

For every subsequent period one can compute the excess demand of the old in terms of the function f by observing that each agent will choose a point that is on his life cycle budget constraint:

$$(\omega^1 - \hat{x}_t^{t-1}) + \left(\frac{p_{t-1}}{p_t}\right)(\omega^0 - \hat{x}_{t-1}^{t-1}) = 0. \tag{6.9}$$

But the market-clearing assumption implies that

$$(\omega^1 - \hat{x}_t^{t-1}) + (\omega^0 - \hat{x}_t^t) = 0. \tag{6.10}$$

Combining these two pieces of information, one arrives at the following equation in price ratios that describes the equilibrium conditions in periods t for $t \geq 2$:

$$\frac{p_{t-1}}{p_t} f\left(\frac{p_{t-1}}{p_t}\right) - f\left(\frac{p_t}{p_{t+1}}\right) = 0. \tag{6.11}$$

6.6.2 Stationary Equilibria

An equilibrium sequence of prices can be generated by beginning with an initial price p_1 and exploiting the market-clearing conditions in period 1 given by equation (6.8) to find a price in period 2 that is consistent with the assumptions of perfect foresight and market clearing. Given the period 2 price, one can then iterate the difference equation (6.11) to generate a sequence of prices that is consistent with market clearing and with perfect foresight for all time.

Some realizations of this process will be special in the sense that they will lead to an allocation across generations that is independent of time. This observation suggests that one should define a *stationary equilibrium* to be an equilibrium with the additional property that it may be characterized by a pair of numbers (x^0, x^1) such that $(x_t^t = x^0, x_{t+1}^t = x^1)$ for all t. This definition implies that the price ratio p_{t+1}/p_t will also be independent of time, since all generations are identical, endowments do not vary through time, and the excess demand of each young generation depends only on the price ratio.

I will refer to the price ratio p_{t+1}/p_t as π_{t+1} and the price ratio associated with a stationary equilibrium as π. This definition of a stationary equilibrium leads directly to the following proposition:

PROPOSITION 6.1 *There are two possible inflation factors that may be associated with a stationary equilibrium. These are given by the roots of the equation*:

$$\frac{1}{\pi}f'\left(\frac{1}{\pi}\right) - f\left(\frac{1}{\pi}\right) = 0. \tag{6.12}$$

There are two possible types of solution to this equation. The first solution occurs when $f(1/\pi) = 0$, and a solution of this type is referred to as *generationally autarkic*, since it involves no intergenerational trade. A solution of this type always exists.

It is also possible for there to be another type of solution when $\pi = 1$. This solution is often referred to as the *golden rule equilibrium*, since it may be shown to maximize steady state per-capita consumption. In more general economies the golden rule equilibrium equates the real rate of return to the rate of population growth. In our example, however, the rate of population growth is zero and the monetary interest factor is one. Since the real interest factor is equal to the ratio of the nominal interest factor to the inflation factor, the golden rule prescription reduces to the proposition that prices should be constant through time.[4]

I have been careful to assert that there *may* exist two types of solution to the above equation. The reason for this choice of language is that the golden rule equilibrium cannot always be supported by positively valued fiat money. This observation holds the key to the question that we posed in the first part of this chapter of how to generalize the observation that some equilibria may be Pareto optimal and some may not.

6.6.3   Classifying Economies by Types of Stationary Equilibria

Whether or not the golden rule equilibrium can be supported as a competitive equilibrium with fiat money has to do with whether the initial young generation can be induced, in aggregate, to give up some of their endowment to the initial old when they correctly believe that the terms of trade between periods are equal to one. Figure 6.3 depicts two possible situations. The first frame depicts an economy in which the young agent would like to save if he were faced with a price ratio of one. The second frame depicts the reverse situation in which he would like to be a borrower. The first economy type is one that Gale [52] defines as *Samuelson* and the second type is one that he defines as *classical*. It is only Samuelson economies that will support positively valued fiat money.

Other things equal, an economy is more likely to be Samuelson the more heavily tilted toward youth is the endowment profile and the lower

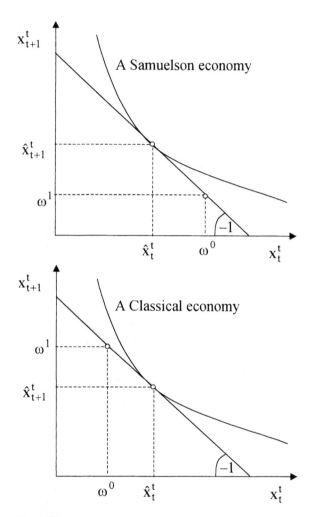

Figure 6.3
Types of OG economies

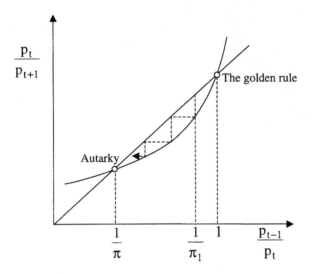

Figure 6.4
Nonstationary equilibria in a Samuelson economy

is the rate of time preference. This observation explains why our simple examples in which an agent had all of his endowment, either in youth or in old age, provided cases in which there was or was not a possibility of a Pareto-improving reallocation over the autarkic equilibrium.

6.6.4 Dynamic Equilibria

Figure 6.4 depicts the set of solutions to the difference equation 6.11 for the case of a Samuelson economy. A typical solution to 6.11 is represented by the sequence that begins at $1/\pi_1$ and converges to the autarkic steady state, $1/\bar{\pi}$. This sequence is an example of an indeterminate equilibrium, since it is arbitrarily close to another equilibrium sequence that is constructed by beginning with an initial value of inflation within a distance ε of π_1. The steady state $1/\bar{\pi}$ is also indeterminate since it is arbitrarily close to a large set of nonstationary equilibria.

What determines which of the many equilibria the economy will follow? The answer is that it depends on the beliefs of the initial generation and that there are many possible sets of beliefs that are consistent with the existence of a rational expectations equilibrium. Suppose, for example, that generation 1 believes that the rate of inflation between periods 1 and 2 will be given by π_1. They will demand real balances equal to $-f(1/\pi_1)$,

and equilibrium in the asset markets will cause the price level to equate
demand and supply at an initial price of $-f(1/\pi_1)/M$.

Now suppose that future generations observe past prices and that they
use the forecast rule

$$\frac{p_t}{p_{t+1}} = f^{-1}\left[\left(\frac{p_{t-1}}{p_t}\right)f\left(\frac{p_{t-1}}{p_t}\right)\right], \tag{6.13}$$

to forecast future prices. It follows that the demand for money in period t
will be given by

$$-\left(\frac{p_{t-1}}{p_t}\right)f\left(\frac{p_{t-1}}{p_t}\right), \tag{6.14}$$

which must equal M/p_t in equilibrium. By equating 6.14 with M/p_t, one
obtains an expression that determines the sequence of equilibrium prices
as functions of past prices and the money stock. What we have shown is
that there exists a simple rule for predicting the future that is consistent
with a large number of possible equilibria.

The above analysis is considered by many people to be a problem
for macroeconomics, and a vast amount of effort has been devoted to
the exercise of trying to show that most of the equilibria that we have
constructed do not make sense. One could, for example, take the per-
fectly defensible position that nonstationary equilibria are unlikely to be
observed in practice because the passage of time would cause the economy to move to the steady state. But this line of argument comes unstuck
once one moves to stochastic models because, as we will see in chapter 10,
indeterminate steady states are associated with many *stationary* stochastic
equilibria. An alternative approach, which I will be arguing for in this
book, is that the possibility of multiple equilibria is a symptom of the fact
that we have failed to properly specify beliefs. In practical models, each of
the possible equilibria that we will look at has a different implication for
the time series movement of the data. Looked at in this light, the issue of
which of the many possible rules agents select for forecasting the future is
a question that can be settled empirically.

6.7   Some Questions about the Model

One is entitled to ask whether the problem of indeterminate equilibria is a
peculiarity of simple two period models. Perhaps the problem only occurs

in monetary economies. Maybe one can forget about indeterminate equilibria, since, in the example we have looked at, all of the nonstationary equilibria eventually lead to a situation in which money has no value. One might also wonder why the proof of the first welfare theorem fails. We address some of these questions below, beginning with the issue of Pareto optimality.

6.7.1   Why Does the First Welfare Theorem Break Down?

When Samuelson's paper first appeared, a number of authors attributed the breakdown of the first welfare theorem to the fact that the overlapping generations model does not permit generations to meet in a single market. This issue was finally laid to rest by Karl Shell [104] who showed how to reinterpret the overlapping generations model as a single market model. Shell pointed out that agents who face a single lifetime budget constraint can be thought of as trading in a market that takes place at the beginning of time. Looked at in this way the overlapping generations model *is* an Arrow-Debreu economy with the simple difference that the commodity space *and* the number of agents is infinite. This double infinity turns out to be the key to the failure of the first welfare theorem.

The proof of the welfare theorem relies on the impossibility of constructing a feasible allocation that dominates the equilibrium allocation. One shows that the value of a candidate allocation, valued at equilibrium prices, must be greater than the value of the endowment of at least one agent and that it must be at least as expensive as the endowment for all other agents. One then sums these inequalities over all agents and concludes that the value of the proposed allocation is greater than the value of the endowment for society as a whole and that the proposed Pareto-improving allocation is, therefore, infeasible.

This proof breaks down in the case of a double infinity of commodities and agents, since the infinite sum of endowments weighted by Arrow-Debreu prices across all agents may not be finite. There is a sense in which society has infinite resources, and as a consequence one may no longer conclude that a proposed Pareto dominating allocation is unattainable.

6.7.2   When Does Indeterminacy Occur?

Another fallacy that arose in early work on the overlapping generations model was the idea that there might be some connection between inde-

terminacy and Pareto optimality of steady state equilibria. This is also
false. One example that has been pursued by a number of authors is the
case where there are strong income effects. For example, there may be a
single representative agent in each generation with preferences given by

$$U = \frac{(x_t^t)^{1-\rho}}{1 - \rho} + \frac{(x_t^{t+1})^{1-\rho}}{1 - \rho}. \tag{6.15}$$

For the case of $\rho = 1$ the function $x^{1-\rho}/(1 - \rho)$ is equal to the natural
logarithm of x. In this case the excess demand function for period 1 consumption depends only on wealth as the income effect on demand of a
relative price increase is exactly canceled by the substitution effect. As ρ
gets larger, the income effect increases, and for high values of ρ the excess
demand function $f(\cdot)$ is no longer monotonic. This can lead to a situation
in which there are two possible values of π_{t+1} that are consistent with the
same value of π_t.

The implication of strong income effects for the dynamics of equilibria
is that the difference equation that describes competitive equilibrium
sequences may be oscillatory at the golden rule steady state. One such
possibility is depicted in figure 6.5. In this picture the golden rule steady
state is indeterminate, and there exist perfect foresight paths that begin
close to the golden rule steady state and oscillate in toward it. Jean-
Michel Grandmont [55] has studied this economy in great depth in an
article in which he suggests that deterministic equations of this class may
be used to explain business cycles. Unlike the previous example, all of the
equilibrium paths in this economy may be shown to be Pareto optimal by
a method that we will discuss briefly in the following section.

6.7.3 When Are Equilibria Efficient?

The idea that some capital accumulation paths may be inefficient was
studied by Phelps [91] and Koopmans [70] in the context of growth
models in which preferences are not made explicit. They looked at concept of productive efficiency that says nothing about the distribution
of resources across different agents. It asks a more basic question: Is the
economy allocating resources correctly between the activities of consumption and investment.

To talk about a productively efficient allocation, we first need to define
the golden rule. In the context of a simple one-sector growth model the

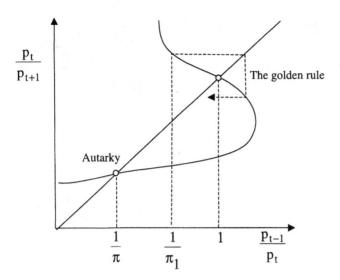

Figure 6.5
Oscillating equilibria in a Samuelson economy

golden rule is that allocation of resources between consumption and investment that maximizes the steady state resources available for consumption. One of the basic results in growth theory is that this allocation can be achieved as a competitive allocation in an economy in which the rate of interest is equal to the rate of growth. An economy is said to be *productively dynamically inefficient* if the stock of capital is greater than the golden rule stock of capital and if it remains bounded away from the golden rule, from above, for all time. The reason for dynamic inefficiency is easy to see. If the economy has more capital than the amount that would maximize steady state consumption then it can run down this capital stock and consume the resources without adversely affecting the resources available for consumption in any future period.

The contributions of Malinvaud [79] and David Cass [31] to this area involved a statement of the conditions under which an economic equilibrium would or would not be *Pareto efficient* in terms of the infinite sequence of Arrow-Debreu prices that prevails in equilibrium. Using the notation that I introduced in chapter 5, and restricting it to the case of a single commodity, Malinvaud showed that if an economy is dynamically inefficient in an economy with zero population growth, then

$$\lim_{s \to \infty} \frac{1}{Q_t^s} \equiv \lim_{s \to \infty} \prod_{v=t}^{s-1} R_v = 0.$$

This means that the current period Arrow-Debreu price of resources for delivery in the infinite future is infinite. Alternatively stated, it says that the rate of interest will eventually become negative and stay negative for most of the time.[5] If there is an agent in the model who owns a positive amount of resources in the infinite future and if this individual has preferences that include period t consumption, then an infinite Arrow-Debreu price cannot be an equilibrium price. The agent would try to consume an infinite amount in period t, since he has infinite wealth.

Although an inefficient allocation implies that the Arrow-Debreu price for delivery of a commodity dated in the infinite future is infinite, the reverse statement does not hold. A precise statement of the converse of Malinvaud's theorem is due to Cass [31] who showed that if

$$\sum_{v=t}^{\infty} R_v < \infty,$$

then the corresponding allocation is Pareto inefficient. The *Malinvaud-Cass criterion* for identifying inefficient equilibria is directly applicable to the overlapping generations economy. Notice that equilibria in which the interest rate is equal to zero in the limit are efficient, since the sequence of interest *factors* (one plus the interest rate) converges to 1 and the sum of an infinite sequence of ones is infinite.

The Malinvaud-Cass criterion can also be applied to sequences of oscillating interest factors that converge to zero. This is the situation in all of the indeterminate equilibria that occur in the economy studied by Grandmont [55] which we looked at briefly above. Applying the criterion to these equilibria, one can show that since all of the nonstationary equilibria converge to the golden rule, the sum of the associated interest factors in every such equilibrium is infinite. This is an example of an economy with a set of indeterminate equilibria each of which is Pareto optimal.

6.8   More General Examples of Overlapping Generations Economies

A treatment of more general versions of the overlapping generations model is found in a paper by Balasko, Cass, and Shell [10] and an inves-

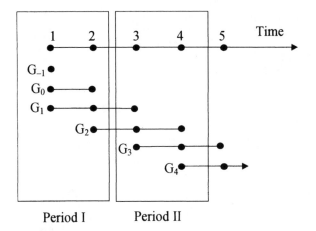

Figure 6.6
Redefining periods in the general model

tigation of indeterminacy in the model is found in a paper by Kehoe and Levine [64]. The general model has l goods in each period and m agents. This structure is broad enough to subsume any finite lived model with pure trade, since one may reduce higher-order models to two periods by a simple redefinition of commodities and periods. In this section I am going to provide a brief outline of the conditions under which indeterminacy can occur.

To begin with, I am going to show how to reduce a general model, with agents who live for T periods, to a simpler model in which agents live for only two periods. This result is explained in the paper by Balasko, Cass, and Shell [10]. I will work with an example in which each person lives for three periods and there are m people. The basic idea is outlined in figure 6.6. The original periods of the model are represented by the arabic numerals, $1, 2, \ldots$, and the new periods by the roman numerals I, II, $\ldots$, so that period I is equal to the union of periods 1 and 2, period II to the union of 3 and 4, and so on. If there are l commodities in each of the original periods then there will be $2 \times l$ commodities in each of the new combined periods. By suitably relabeling commodities, one can reduce any T period model to two periods.

One thing that is important to note is that this process will also multiply the number of types of consumer. For example, suppose that the original model has a representative consumer in each generation with preferences

$$u = u(x_t, x_{t+1}, x_{t+2}) : R_+^{3 \times l} \mapsto R.$$

The new model will have two types of consumer. The first of these individuals is born in the first half of period I with preferences defined over the commodities in both halves of period I and over commodities that occur in the first half of period II. Generations $1, 3, 5, \ldots$, are of this type. The second type of consumer is born in the second part of period I, and his preferences are for commodities in the second half of period I and both halves of period II. Even-numbered generations are of this type. This observation is important because, although the two-period model with many agents and many goods is not restrictive, the two-period model with one agent and one good *is very* restrictive.

6.8.1 Kehoe-Levine Approach

Kehoe-Levine do not specify preferences directly. Instead they appeal to the theorem of Debreu-Sonnenschein-Mantel which we described in chapter 4. In the present context this means that we do not have to worry about the preferences that generated the excess demand functions, since we know that there is some finite set of consumers (with at least as many consumers as commodities) that generated these excess demand functions as the outcome of maximizing behavior. Taking this approach, we can completely summarize the behavior of generation t by a vector of excess demand equations:

$$y(p_t, p_{t+1}) \in R^l, \tag{6.16}$$

$$z(p_t, p_{t+1}) \in R^l, \tag{6.17}$$

where $y(\cdot)$ is the aggregate excess demand function of the young generation at date t and $z(\cdot)$ is the aggregate excess demand function of these same agents one period later at date $t + 1$. Each of these functions maps from $R_{++}^{2 \times l}$ to R^l.

By applying the appropriate market-clearing equations, we can define an equilibrium in the general OG model as the solution to a difference equation of the form:

$$z(p_{t-1}, p_t) + y(p_t, p_{t+1}) = 0,$$

subject to a set of initial conditions that are determined, in part, by the behavior of the initial old generation.

An equilibrium is said to be stationary if it satisfies the following additional restriction:

$$p_t = \pi p_{t-1}$$

for all t. In the one-commodity world we showed that stationary allocations were associated with a stationary inflation factor that was equal to the ratio of the price at date t (in terms of the numéraire) to the price at date $t + 1$. In a multiple commodity world something similar is true, but there are l prices in each period. The above definition of stationarity amounts to the assumption that prices are being scaled up in each period by a common rate of inflation.

6.8.2   Indeterminacy in the OG Model

Kehoe and Levine distinguish between steady states in which money has value and steady states in which it does not. They show that the overlapping generations model generically has a finite odd number of each type of equilibria. Further there are open dense sets of economies in which one or more of these equilibria may be indeterminate. In the general case indeterminacy can be of differing degrees, since the initial conditions are associated with a vector of nonpredetermined variables that represent relative prices in the initial period. These results suggest that the indeterminacy problem is unlikely to be disposed of easily.

One position that many macroeconomists have taken is that models with indeterminate steady states are simply bad models. It has also been asserted that none of the models that we use in practice suffer from indeterminacy, and so we may, for all practical purposes, ignore the problem. In this book I will argue that indeterminacy, rather than being a nuisance, is actually a useful property of a large class of practical models and that by exploiting indeterminacy one is able to explain a number of otherwise anomalous features of the data.

6.9   Concluding Remarks

So far I have demonstrated that simple dynamic general equilibrium models may behave very differently from the finite Arrow-Debreu paradigm. In particular, the welfare theorems may break down and the set of equilibria may be very large. I have illustrated these features in the context of the overlapping generations model, mainly for historical reasons. Until very recently most of the interesting examples of indeterminacy and of nonoptimality of equilibria had been constructed using elaborations of this structure. A number of authors have discovered that similar features occur in models with infinitely lived agents if the aggregate economy is characterized by the existence of important externalities. Since models with externalities are much closer to the real business cycle paradigm that has become the industry standard, these examples are potentially much more interesting. Many of the examples that I will introduce in the later part of the book will be of this latter type.

6.10 Problems

1. Consider an overlapping generations model in which there exists a single type of agent who lives for two periods. There is no population growth. Each agent has an endowment of the unique perishable commodity of a units when young and b units when old. Preferences are given by

$$U = \log(c_t^t) + \beta \log(c_{t+1}^t),$$

where superscripts refer to date of birth and subscripts refer to date of consumption. In period 1 there is an existing old generation with preferences

$$U = \log(c_1^0),$$

an endowment of b units of the commodity, and M units of money. Let $\{p_t\}_{t=1}^{\infty}$ be the sequence of prices at which money trades for goods. Define $R_t = p_t/p_{t+1}$ to be the relative price of consumption at dates t and $t + 1$. Let $S(R_t)$ be the demand for money by a young person at date t.

a. Write down the life cycle budget constraint of a young person at date t.

b. Find an expression for the function $S(R_t)$.

c. Find a difference equation in R_t that characterizes equilibrium sequences. What is the initial condition for this difference equation?

d. For what values of a, b, and β does there exist a stationary equilibrium in which money has value?

e. For what values of a, b and β is there a unique equilibrium? Is it determinate? Explain your answer.

2. Consider an overlapping generations economy in which there are two types of agents indexed by superscripts, 1 and 2. The utility functions and endowments of types 1 and 2 are given by

$$U^1 = \log(x_t^{1t}) + \beta \log(x_{t+1}^{1t}), \qquad \omega_1 = \{1, 0\},$$

$$U^2 = \log(x_t^{2t}) + \beta \log(x_{t+1}^{2t}), \qquad \omega_2 = \{0, 1\},$$

where β is a positive parameter. In period 1 there exists an initial generation with the preferences and period 1 endowments

$$U^1 = -\frac{1}{x_1^{10}}, \qquad \omega = 0,$$

$$U^2 = \log(x_1^{20}), \qquad \omega = 1,$$

where the superscripts 10 and 20 mean type 1 generation 0 and type 2 generation 0. Assume that individuals can trade consumption loans with each other. Suppose that a loan of one unit of consumption in period t must be repaid with R_t units of the consumption commodity in period $t + 1$.

a. Find an expression for the intertemporal budget constraint of each type of agent.

b. Find an expression for the aggregate excess demand function of the young generation:

$$\hat{x}_t^i - \omega_t = f(R_t).$$

(*Hint*: This is the sum of the excess demands of each type of agent.)

c. Define a competitive equilibrium for this economy and find an equilibrium.

d. How many equilibria are there?

e. Are they (is it) efficient? How does you answer depend on the parameter β?

f. Is there any trade in your equilibrium (equilibria)?

g. Now suppose that each member of generation 0 is endowed with M units of money. Define a monetary equilibrium for this economy, and characterize the set of monetary equilibria as the solution to a difference equation.

h. What is meant by a stationary equilibrium?

i. How many stationary equilibria are there? How does your answer depend on β?

3. Consider the two-period overlapping generations model (with no population growth) in which agents live for two periods. Agents have preferences given by

$$U = -n_t^2 + c_{t+1},$$

where n_t is labor supplied to the market when young and c_{t+1} is consumption when old. (In this model the young work and the old consume.) Output is produced from labor with the technology

$$y_t = n_t.$$

a. Define Pareto efficiency in the context of an infinite horizon model of this kind.

b. Prove that in the absence of money the unique competitive equilibrium of the model is Pareto inefficient.

c. Explain how the introduction of money can potentially restore Pareto efficiency.

4. Consider the overlapping generations model in which there is a single perishable commodity, two-period lives, and in which there is a single type of agent in each generation with the preferences

$$U = c_t^t c_{t+1}^t.$$

(Superscripts index generation and subscripts index calendar time.) Time runs from 1 to infinity. There is an initial generation that owns a fixed stock of fiat money, M, and none of the commodity. All other generations have an endowment of the commodity in youth and old age:

$$\{\omega_t^t, \omega_t^{t+1}\} = \{\omega_0, \omega_1\}, \qquad \omega_0 > \omega_1.$$

a. Define what is meant by a competitive equilibrium for this economy, and find the set of all competitive equilibria.

b. If there was no money in the economy, describe the properties of the equilibrium. Is this equilibrium Pareto efficient? If not, suggest a Pareto improving allocation.

c. What is the importance of the assumption $\omega_0 > \omega_1$ to your answers to parts a and b.

d. Repeat your answers to parts a and b using the alternative assumption that $\omega_0 < \omega_1$.

7 Infinite Horizon Economies with Nonconvexities

7.1 Introduction

We have looked at the two models that are frequently used in the macroeconomics literature and compared their properties. Although it is well known that the overlapping generations model can behave in very different ways from representative agent economies, there has not been a great deal of work that has successfully exploited these differences to explain empirical phenomena. The biggest obstacle to the empirical implementation of overlapping generations economies is the fact that realistic versions of the model require a very high dimensional state vector. One might summarize an equilibrium by a difference equation, but the dimension of this difference equation will typically be as large as the number of periods of life of an agent in the model. As a practical matter, most empirical work in applied general equilibrium theory has taken the representative agent approach.

Although the representative agent model has dominated the real business cycle literature, there have been a number of attempts to modify the model to account for features of the data that are hard to understand in the standard framework. Later in this chapter I will introduce some empirical puzzles that the RBC agenda has encountered, and I will describe one way in which researchers in the field have modified the model to account for these empirical features. This modification involves the assumption that the aggregate technology set may be nonconvex, and it leads to a class of economies that behave a lot like overlapping generations economies but are relatively easy to study empirically.

The idea that the aggregate technology might be subject to increasing returns-to-scale has been around for a long time in the literature. But there are difficulties in understanding how to reconcile increasing returns with a competitive theory of income distribution and these difficulties placed a barrier that, until relatively recently, prevented much progress on the topic of incorporating nonconvexities into general equilibrium models. The stimulus to a renewed study of the increasing returns hypothesis came from work on the theory of growth by Paul Romer [94] and Robert Lucas [77], and its implications for a theory of fluctuations were pointed out by Robert Hall [57].

In this chapter I am going to study two alternative ways in which one can reconcile increasing returns with a competitive theory of distribution. The first approach assumes that there are significant externalities in the production process, and the second introduces important noncompetitive elements to explain how a profit-maximizing firm may attain an interior optimum in the presence of a nonconvex technology.[1] Both avenues lead to a set of equations to describe the evolution of the variables in the economy that are similar to the equations studied in chapter 5. Although these equations have the same form as the equations that describe a representative agent economy, they contain different restrictions on the parameters of these equations. These restrictions are the key to understanding a range of behavior that may be displayed by the increasing returns economies that cannot occur in the standard model.

7.2 Growth Model with Increasing Returns

7.2.1 Equations That Characterize an Equilibrium

I am going to begin by describing the implications of increasing returns for the equations that describe the aggregate economy. These equations are laid out below:

$$k_{t+1} = y_t + (1 - \delta)k_t - c_t, \tag{7.1}$$

$$y_t = s_t k_t^\mu (\gamma^t l_t)^\nu, \tag{7.2}$$

$$n\frac{y_t}{l_t} = c_t l_t^\chi, \tag{7.3}$$

$$\frac{1}{c_t} = \beta E_t \left[\frac{1}{c_{t+1}} \left(1 - \delta + m\frac{y_{t+1}}{k_{t+1}} \right) \right], \tag{7.4}$$

$$s_t = s_{t-1}^\rho v_t, \tag{7.5}$$

where the parameters δ and γ are subject to the restrictions

$$0 < \delta < 1 \quad \text{and} \quad \gamma \geq 1.$$

Equation 7.1 is an aggregate capital accumulation equation, k_t is capital, y_t is output, c_t is consumption, and δ is the rate of depreciation. Equation 7.2 is an aggregate production function where s_t is an aggregate shock to the technology, γ is an exogenous growth factor, and l_t represents labor hours. This technology differs from the production function that we studied in chapter 5, since I will not restrict the marginal product of labor, represented by v, to be equal to one minus the marginal product of capital, represented by μ. The increasing returns hypothesis is represented, instead, by the assumption that

$$\mu + v > 1.$$

The two behavioral equations of the model are given by 7.4 and 7.3. These equations are similar, with one significant difference, to the representative agent economy that we described in chapter 5. In the increasing returns economy, the share of capital in national income is represented by a parameter, m, and the share of labor is represented by the parameter, n. These parameters are no longer equal to the marginal products of capital and labor, μ and v. In section 7.5.3 I will show how the fact that the share parameters can depart from marginal products can alter the dynamics of equilibrium paths in a way that makes the representative agent economy behave a lot like the overlapping generations economies that we studied in chapter 6.

7.2.2   Behavior of the Representative Family

I am going to work with a simple example that assumes that the representative agent has preferences that are separable in leisure and consumption, separable across periods, and logarithmic in consumption. These are not the most general preferences that have been studied in the literature, but they are not uncommon assumptions to make. The economy is characterized by a large number of identical producer-consumers, indexed by $i \in [0, 1]$, each of whom maximizes the utility function[2]

$$U_i = \sum_{t=1}^{\infty} E_1 \beta^{t-1} \left[\log(c_{it}) - \frac{l_{it}^{1+\chi}}{1+\chi} \right] \tag{7.6}$$

subject to the sequence of constraints

$$c_{it} + k_{it+1} \le k_{it}(1-\delta) + p_{it} y_{it}, \qquad t = 1, \ldots, \infty. \tag{7.7}$$

The variable p_{it} represents the price of the ith family unit's own produced commodity relative to the price of the commodity that it consumes—we will give two different interpretations to these commodities in the following two parts of the chapter.

We are going to examine two possible assumptions about the aggregate technology, each of which generates the equations that I have outlined in the previous section, but the two assumptions have different implications for the share parameters m and n. Later in the chapter I will build an artificial economy that is based on the monopolistically competitive model, and I will compare some simulated time series from this artificial economy with the U.S. data and with simulations from a more standard RBC approach. Both the externalities approach and the noncompetitive approach to increasing returns have been studied in the literature, and I have included both interpretations because there is no consensus among researchers in the field as to which is a better avenue for understanding the macroeconomy.

7.2.3 Interpretation 1: Externalities in Production

In this section, and in the following section of this chapter, I will describe a theory of the organization of production that explains how equations 7.1 to 7.5 can be derived from a model in which individual agents maximize expected utility, taking prices as given. The first model that I will look at has been investigated extensively in the literature on endogenous growth, and there has been a fair amount of recent work that has tested the implications of the model for the behavior of production functions at a disaggregated level.[3] The idea is that each of the individual families produces an identical final commodity using a technology

$$y_{it} = A_t s_t k_{it}^m (\gamma^t l_{it})^{1-m}. \tag{7.8}$$

The technology described in 7.8 is a standard neoclassical production function that is subject to constant returns to scale. The fact that each family produces the same commodity under competitive conditions implies that, in equilibrium, the law of one price will hold and that

$$p_{it} = p_{jt} = 1,$$

where we have chosen final output as the numéraire.

Although each family in our economy is competitive, we will assume that the economy as a whole is affected by organizational synergies that cause the output of the ith family firm to be higher if all other firms in the economy are producing more. These external effects are outside of the scope of the market, and they cannot be priced or traded. The effects of externalities are captured by the assumption that

$$A_t = \left[\int_i k_{it}^m (\gamma^t l_{it})^{1-m} di \right]^\theta, \tag{7.9}$$

where the terms in the square bracket represent the average output of all other agents in the economy, net of the productivity shock, and the interaction effects. Putting together equation 7.9 with the technology, 7.8, and recognizing that all agents are identical, leads to a description of the aggregate technology that takes the form

$$y_t = s_t k_t^\mu (\gamma^t l_t)^\nu, \tag{7.10}$$

where

$$\mu \equiv m(1 + \theta), \quad \nu \equiv (1 - m)(1 + \theta).$$

The first big difference of 7.10 from the RA model is that the parameters μ and ν may sum to more than one. In a standard model with no externalities, this assumption would preclude the existence of a competitive equilibrium, since the marginal productivity theory of distribution rests on the assumption of a concave production function. By introducing nonconvexities through an externality, we have preserved the neoclassical conclusion that the returns to labor and capital exhaust the national income when the private technology is subject to constant returns to scale. That is, the share parameters, m and n, sum to one. But we have allowed for the possibility that the aggregate technology may display marginal products, μ and ν, that sum to more than one. The externalities model leads to standard first-order conditions to each agent's optimization problem which are represented in equations 7.3 and 7.4. Although the factor shares sum to one, the fact that the aggregate technology displays increasing returns accounts for the possibility that the externalities economy may display very different dynamic behavior from a standard real business cycle model.

7.2.4 Interpretation 2: Monopolistic Competition

A second approach to increasing returns makes the assumption that each of the families in the economy produces a distinct intermediate commodity that is combined, in a competitive final sector, and uses the technology

$$y_t = \left[\int y_{it}^\lambda \, di \right]^{1/\lambda}.$$

This model is a little different from the externalities approach, since we are going to internalize the nonconvexities by allowing each family to take account of the impact of its decisions on the price of its own output. Since each producer faces a nonconvex technology, it will also face a downward-sloping marginal cost curve. But we have also assumed that producers have market power, and this assumption leads to a downward-sloping marginal revenue schedule. As long as the ith producer's market power is large enough, relative to the nonconvexity in its technology, the monopolistically competitive family firm will arrive at an interior optimum in the face of increasing returns.

Although we require the assumption of monopoly power and the existence of multiple differentiated commodities to tolerate increasing returns, it is an inconvenient assumption when we are dealing with final commodities, since one would like a model that produces an analogue of familiar concepts like GNP, consumption, and investment. For this reason we are assuming that the families have monopoly power only over intermediate commodities, and we introduce a device for aggregating these commodities which we refer to as a final goods technology. By aggregating the intermediate goods with a single aggregator, we are assuming that investment and consumption goods use the same mix of intermediate commodities—an assumption that is almost certainly false but is a good initial simplification since it leads to a tractable model that can be compared with the standard RA economy.

Notice that the final goods technology is subject to constant returns to scale and that it uses only intermediate commodities; that is, one does not require labor or capital to produce a unit of the final good. Any firm that sets up in business in the production of final goods will potentially make profits defined by

$$\Pi = p_t y_t - \int p_{it} y_{it} \, di,$$

although the assumption of free entry implies that these profits will equal zero in an equilibrium. By manipulating the first-order conditions for the firm's problem, one can demonstrate that a competitive final goods producer will adjust the ratio of inputs in such a way that

$$p_{it} = \left(\frac{y_{it}}{y_t}\right)^{\lambda - 1}. \tag{7.11}$$

Notice that when $\lambda = 1$, the technology collapses to a competitive model, since none of the intermediate goods producers will be able to exploit monopoly power. The interesting case, of imperfect substitutability in intermediate inputs, occurs when $0 < \lambda < 1$.

Although the final goods sector is competitive, we are assuming that each of the families is a monopoly producer of its own intermediate input. Since each family is small relative to the economy, it is possible to take the social output, which we represent as y_t, parametrically. Equation 7.11 can then be interpreted as an inverse demand curve for the family's product. We will let the ith family produce using a technology:

$$y_{it} = s_t k_{it}^{\mu} (\gamma^t l_{it})^{\nu},\tag{7.12}$$

where

$$\mu + \nu > 1,$$

which implies that the *intermediate technology* is subject to *increasing returns to scale*. The profit-maximizing problem of the ith family firm is given by

$$\max \left\{ \Pi_{it} = \left(\frac{y_{it}}{y}\right)^{\lambda-1} y_{it} - \omega_t l_{it} - r_t k_{it} \right\},$$

where ω_t is the competitive wage rate and r_t is the competitive rental rate on capital.

Acting in its capacity *as a consumer* the household will set the real wage rate, ω_t, equal to the slope of its utility trade-off between leisure and consumption, that is,[4]

$$\omega_t = c_{it} l_{it}^{\chi}.\tag{7.13}$$

Similarly the household will take account of r_{t+1} in its intertemporal plans by equating the discounted covariance of r_{t+1}, with the marginal utility of $t + 1$ consumption, to the period t marginal utility:

$$\frac{1}{c_{it}} = \beta E_t \left[\frac{1}{c_{it+1}} (1 - \delta + r_{t+1})\right].\tag{7.14}$$

Acting *as a producer*, the ith family will try to maximize profits taking the technology 7.12 and the demand equation 7.11 as given. Although the technology is not convex, the family may still face a concave programming problem, since the demand for its product is downward sloping. To see this, one may combine the technology 7.12 with a definition of the profit maximizing problem to yield:

$$\max\left\{\Pi_{it} = \frac{s_t^\lambda k_{it}^{\lambda\mu}(\gamma^t l_{it})^{v\lambda}}{y^{\lambda-1}} - \omega_t l_{it} - r_t k_{it}\right\},$$

where the maximand is jointly concave in k_{it} and l_{it} whenever

$$\lambda(\mu + v) \leq 1.$$

The first-order conditions from the firm's profit maximization condition direct it to set

$$\frac{\lambda\mu y_{it} p_{it}}{k_{it}} = r_t$$

and

$$\frac{\lambda v y_{it} p_{it}}{l_{it}} = \omega_t.$$

There might potentially be equilibria in which different firms make different production decisions even though they are otherwise identical. However, in view of the symmetry of the environment, it seems reasonable to look for a symmetric equilibrium. In the discussion that follows we will impose this condition by requiring that, in equilibrium,

$$k_{it} = k_{jt} \equiv k_t, \quad l_{it} = l_{jt} \equiv l_t, \quad \text{and} \quad p_{it} = p_{jt} = 1,$$

where the final equality follows from the zero profit condition for the competitive final goods sector.[5]

By combining the first-order conditions for a firm with the first-order conditions for a household, equations 7.13 and 7.14, one arrives at the following two equations:

$$\frac{1}{c_t} = \beta E_t\left[\frac{1}{c_{t+1}}\left(1 - \delta + \lambda\mu\frac{y_{t+1}}{k_{t+1}}\right)\right]$$

and

$$\lambda v\frac{y_t}{l_t} = c_t l_t^\chi,$$

which are the equations 7.3 and 7.4 that we began with in section 7.2.1, with the additional parameter definitions

$$m \equiv \lambda\mu \quad \text{and} \quad n \equiv \lambda v.$$

In the monopolistic competition version of this model, it is not necessarily true that the share of capital and the share of labor in the economy sum to one, since the intermediate goods producers may make positive profits but otherwise the model makes the same predictions for the behavior of aggregate variables as the externalities version that we introduced above.

7.3 Empirical Evidence for Increasing Returns

One is entitled to ask why we are pursuing a model of the economy in which the aggregate technology is subject to increasing returns. The answer to this question is that the increasing returns model has been put forward as a possible explanation of the observation that output, in the U.S. data, is roughly one and a third times more volatile than hours. In figure 7.1 I have depicted the logarithms of output and hours in annual data—both variables have been passed through the Hodrick-Prescott filter, described in chapter 5, to remove low-frequency components. In the lower panel of figure 7.1, I have drawn the ordinary least squares regression line from a regression of output on hours. This line has a slope equal to 1.27. If all movements of hours and output could be attributed to movements *along* a fixed production function, then this coefficient would be an unbiased estimate of the slope of the production function. Since the slope is greater than one, this interpretation of the data would cause one to doubt the assumption of diminishing returns to labor.

The fact that output is more variable than hours is often referred to as the puzzle of pro-cyclical productivity, since it implies that the ratio of output to hours (productivity) goes up when output goes up.[6] Why is this a puzzle? First, take a look at figure 7.2 which gives two possible ways in which we might explain the relative movements of output and hours. The lower panel of this diagram illustrates the explanation for pro-cyclical productivity that emerges from a standard real business cycle model. In this explanation output and hours both go up, because of a productivity shock that raises the production function at every level of hours. Given this increase in productivity, workers choose to increase their hours from h to h', and output goes up from y to y'. Notice that it is possible, if the increase in hours is small enough, for this productivity shock to raise the *ratio* of output to hours, and this is indeed what happens as the figure has been drawn in figure 7.2.

Why then should one be concerned with any other explanation for procyclical productivity? The answer is that the neoclassical explanation

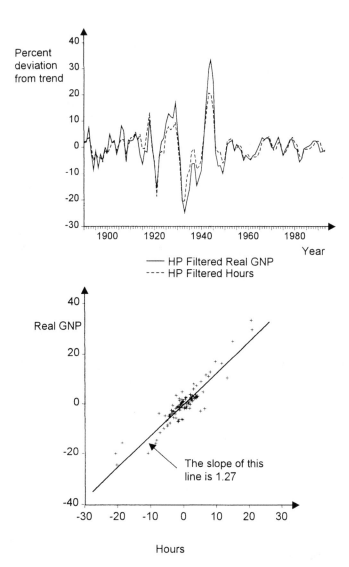

Figure 7.1
GNP and hours in the United States

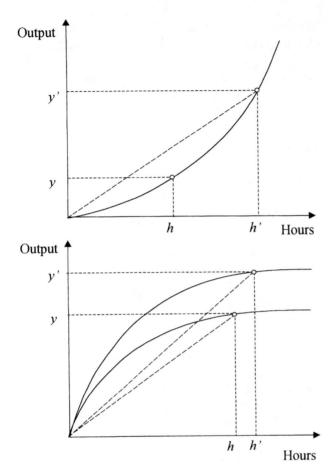

Figure 7.2
Two alternative explanations for pro-cyclical productivity

has a number of other implications that are contradicted by the facts. For example, rather than rely on the observation of correlations between variables one can write down an explicit model and try to estimate the coefficients of the structural equations directly. This direct approach uses more sophisticated estimators than ordinary least squares as a way around simultaneity problems. When one follows an instrumental variables approach to directly estimating the coefficients of the technology, one typically arrives at estimates of the marginal product of labor that are well above one.

A second more direct approach to investigating the increasing returns-to-scale hypothesis is to look at disaggregated data and to try to find effects of *aggregate output* on *individual* industry production technologies. This approach was followed by Caballero and Lyons [29] who found evidence of external effects that should not be present if the neoclassical model is correct. Roughly speaking, they found that a regression of industry output on industry inputs and aggregate output comes up with a positive coefficient on aggregate output in most manufacturing industries. A final indirect piece of evidence against the real business cycle model comes from the properties of the Solow residual which is supposed to be an unbiased estimate of the production disturbance. Recall that this residual, which we discussed in chapter 3, is constructed by subtracting a weighted index of input growth from output growth. Robert Hall [57] has pointed out that the Solow residual is predicted to be uncorrelated with any variable that is uncorrelated with the true productivity disturbance. But a convincing array of evidence shows that there are a number of variables that could reasonably be expected to be uncorrelated with productivity shocks that are nevertheless highly correlated with the Solow residual; for example, an index of military purchases. For all these reasons there has been considerable interest in alternative explanations of pro-cyclical productivity of which one of the more prominent is the increasing returns assumption depicted in the upper panel of figure 7.2.[7]

7.4 Equilibria in the Increasing Returns Economy

7.4.1 Finding a Balanced Growth Path

The techniques that I will use to analyze an equilibrium in the increasing returns (IR) economy are very similar to those that we have already used in the RA economy studied in chapter 5. The first step is to find a balanced growth path around which to linearize. In the increasing returns economy this can be done by dividing the equations 7.1 to 7.4 through by ϕ^t, where

$$\phi \equiv \gamma^{\nu/(1-\mu)}.$$

Notice that the growth rate in this economy is not equal to γ; it is equal to $\gamma^{\nu/(1-\mu)}$, since increasing returns magnifies the effect of labor augmenting technical progress by the factor of $\nu/(1-\mu)$. The transformation, defined by dividing each equation by ϕ^t, leads to the growth equations

$$\phi\tilde{k}_{t+1} = \tilde{y}_t + (1-\delta)\tilde{k}_t - \tilde{c}_t, \tag{7.15}$$

$$\tilde{y}_t = s_t\tilde{k}_t^\mu l_t^\nu, \tag{7.16}$$

$$n\frac{\tilde{y}_t}{l_t} = \tilde{c}_t l_t^\chi, \tag{7.17}$$

$$\frac{1}{\tilde{c}_t} = \frac{\beta}{\phi}E_t\left[\frac{1}{\tilde{c}_{t+1}}\left(1-\delta+m\frac{\tilde{y}_{t+1}}{\tilde{k}_{t+1}}\right)\right], \tag{7.18}$$

$$s_t = s_{t-1}^\rho v_t, \tag{7.19}$$

where

$$\tilde{c}_t \equiv \left(\frac{c_t}{\phi^t}\right), \quad \tilde{k}_t \equiv \left(\frac{k_t}{\phi^t}\right), \quad \text{and} \quad \tilde{y}_t \equiv \left(\frac{y_t}{\phi^t}\right).$$

Now define the *balanced growth path*, $\{\bar{c}, \bar{k}, \bar{y}, \bar{l}\}$, to be the unique solution to the equations

$$\phi\bar{k} = \bar{y} + (1-\delta)\bar{k} - \bar{c}, \tag{7.20}$$

$$\bar{y} = s\bar{k}^\mu\bar{l}^\nu, \tag{7.21}$$

$$n\frac{\bar{y}}{\bar{l}} = \bar{c}\bar{l}^\chi, \tag{7.22}$$

$$1 = \frac{\beta}{\phi}\left(1-\delta+m\frac{\bar{y}}{\bar{k}}\right), \tag{7.23}$$

and define a linearized rational expectations equilibrium by taking a first-order Taylor series approximation to 7.15 to 7.19 in the neighborhood of $\{\bar{c}, \bar{k}, \bar{y}, \bar{l}\}$.[8]

7.4.2 Approximate Linear Model

The linearized model for the increasing returns economy looks a lot like the RA model. In fact the representative agent model is a special case that imposes the parameter restrictions $v + \mu = 1$, $m = \mu$, and $n = v$. To arrive at the linear model, one can use equations 7.16 and 7.17 to eliminate $\tilde{y}$ and l from 7.15 and 7.18. Letting hats over variables denote deviations from the balanced growth path, that is;

$$\hat{k} \equiv \frac{(\tilde{k}_t - \bar{k})}{\bar{k}}, \quad \hat{c} \equiv \frac{(\tilde{c}_t - \bar{c})}{\bar{c}}, \quad \hat{s} \equiv \frac{(\tilde{s}_t - 1)}{1}, \quad \hat{v} \equiv \frac{(\tilde{v}_t - 1)}{1},$$

we can define the vector of expectational errors, just as we did in chapter 3:

$$w_{t+1} \equiv \begin{bmatrix} E_t[\hat{k}_{t+1}] - \hat{k}_{t+1} \\ E_t[\hat{c}_{t+1}] - \hat{c}_{t+1} \\ E_t[\hat{s}_{t+1}] - \hat{s}_{t+1} \end{bmatrix}.$$

Using these definitions, we may write the linearized system in the form:

$$\begin{bmatrix} \hat{k}_t \\ \hat{c}_t \\ \hat{s}_t \end{bmatrix} = J \begin{bmatrix} \hat{k}_{t+1} \\ \hat{c}_{t+1} \\ \hat{s}_{t+1} \end{bmatrix} + R \begin{bmatrix} \hat{v}_{t+1} \\ w_{t+1} \end{bmatrix}. \tag{7.24}$$

The matrices J and R contain coefficients that come from linearizing the equations of the model, and as an exercise, you should make sure that you can derive these coefficients using the techniques that we discussed in chapters 2 and 3. Remember that J has dimension 3×3 and R has dimension 3×2.

Although we have chosen $\hat{k}_t$ and $\hat{c}_t$ as state variables, we could equally well have chosen $\hat{y}_t$ and/or $\hat{l}_t$. Sticking with $\hat{k}_t$ and $\hat{c}_t$ for the moment, we can describe the variables $\hat{y}_t$ and $\hat{l}_t$ as functions of the state:

$$\begin{bmatrix} \hat{y}_t \\ \hat{l}_t \end{bmatrix} = M \begin{bmatrix} \hat{k}_t \\ \hat{c}_t \\ \hat{s}_t \end{bmatrix}, \tag{7.25}$$

where the elements of the 2×3 matrix M are found by taking a Taylor series expansion to 7.16 and 7.17.

7.5 Comparing the Theoretical Properties of RA and IR Models

I am going to begin this section by reviewing the economics of an irregular equilibrium in the model with increasing returns. Although it is difficult to give an intuitive explanation for the complete behavior of a dynamical system, some insight can be gained by looking at the behavior of the labor market when there are increasing returns to scale and comparing it with a more familiar model in which the production function is concave.

Following this discussion, we will look at the matrix algebra of standard rational expectations models. This should be familiar fare by now since we covered these topics in chapter 3, and you may want to skip ahead fairly quickly. Following a discussion of the real business cycle economy, I will cover the dynamics of increasing returns and the bottom line. I'm going to tell you in this section that the IR model does not necessarily deliver a model in which the steady state of the unshocked economy is a saddle point. Instead, it may be a sink. We are going to exploit this idea to show that the IR economy is capable of delivering a model of business cycles that has a lot in common with Keynesian models, in the sense that fluctuations may be generated by the beliefs of the agents in the model, and we will present some evidence from dynamic simulations which suggest that this account may not be too far fetched.

7.5.1 Why Does the IR Model Display Different Dynamics?

After a couple of decades of playing with simple rational expectations economies, most economists have become comfortable with the way that these models behave and the saddle point property, which seemed unfamiliar at first, is now well understood.[9] The puzzle, from a contemporary perspective, is to explain how any other kind of behavior could possibly occur in an equilibrium. A partial answer to this question can be gleaned from a result in the paper by Benhabib and Farmer [17] who show that in the context of a continuous time version of this model, the steady state can only become indeterminate if

$$v - 1 > \chi. \tag{7.26}$$

This condition has a rather simple interpretation which is depicted in figure 7.3. The first-order condition for the problem of a consumer who supplies labor to a competitive labor market for wage ω_t, is given by[10]

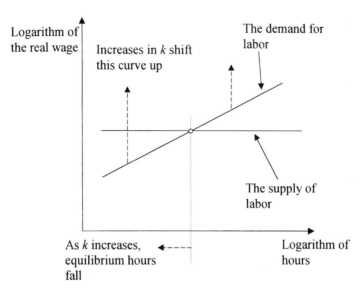

Figure 7.3
Labor market in an IR economy

$$\log(c_t) + \chi \log(l_t) = \log(\omega_t).$$

This first-order condition is graphed in figure 7.3 as the supply of labor The slope of this curve is equal to χ, and for the models that we are looking at, this slope is zero since we assume that utility is linear in leisure. Notice that the position of the labor supply curve depends on the level of consumption, which in turn depends on the beliefs of the agent about future prices.

One can also write down the first-order conditions for the problem of a firm that equates the marginal product of labor to the real wage. When this condition is aggregated across firms it leads to an economywide demand curve for labor:

$$a + (v - 1)\log(l_t) + \mu \log(k_t) = \log(\omega_t),$$

where a is a constant. When there are increasing returns in the economy, the aggregate demand for labor will *slope up* as a function of the real wage if v is greater than one. The necessary condition for indeterminacy that is discussed in Benhabib and Farmer [17] requires that the labor demand curve should slope up more steeply than the labor supply curve.

The relevance of 7.26 for the dynamics of equilibria can be seen in figure 7.3 by thinking about what happens as the stock of capital expands. In a standard model an expansion of this kind would lead to explosive growth as the increased capital drove up hours. But in the IR economy the expansion in capital may be self-damping as hours contract to maintain an equilibrium in the labor market.

7.5.2 RA Model: An Example of a Regular Equilibrium

In the next two sections we are going to develop the RA and IR models and explain how their dynamics may differ. This analysis will involve an understanding of what can happen to the roots of the matrix J, since it is this matrix that determines the linearized dynamics of the model. To begin with I am going to look at the case when the parameter restrictions of the RA model are known to hold; that is, when $m = \mu$, $n = v$, and $m + n = 1$. Because of the fact that there is no feedback in the model, from consumption or capital to the technology shock, the equation that describes the residual, $\hat{s}_t$, is uncoupled from the rest of the system. This property implies that one root of the matrix J will always be determined by the process that governs s_t, and given our assumptions in equation 7.5, this root is equal to $1/\rho$. As long as the productivity disturbance is stationary, the root $1/\rho$ will be bigger than one.

This leaves two more roots to be accounted for, and the arguments that we gave in chapter 5 imply that one of these roots will be bigger than one and the other will be smaller than one, in absolute value. If we premultiply equation 7.24 by Q^{-1}, the inverse of the matrix of eigenvectors of J, we can write the system as three uncoupled equations in the transformed variables, z_t, and η_t, where

$$z_t = Q^{-1} \begin{bmatrix} \hat{k}_t \\ \hat{c}_t \\ \hat{s}_t \end{bmatrix}, \quad \text{and} \quad \eta_t = Q^{-1} R \begin{bmatrix} \hat{v}_t \\ w_t \end{bmatrix}.$$

The system written in this way,

$$\begin{bmatrix} z_t^1 \\ z_t^2 \\ z_t^3 \end{bmatrix} = \begin{bmatrix} \lambda^1 & 0 & 0 \\ 0 & \lambda^2 & 0 \\ 0 & 0 & \lambda^3 \end{bmatrix} \begin{bmatrix} z_{t+1}^1 \\ z_{t+1}^2 \\ z_{t+1}^3 \end{bmatrix} + \begin{bmatrix} \eta_{t+1}^1 \\ \eta_{t+1}^2 \\ \eta_{t+1}^3 \end{bmatrix},$$

has one equation with a root that is less than one that can be iterated into the future to obtain a restriction on the state variables. Suppose that λ^1 is the stable root. Then iterating the first equation into the future, taking expectations, and recognizing that

$$E_t[\eta_{t+j}] = 0, \qquad j \geq 1,$$

leads to the single linear restriction:

$$z_t^1 = 0.$$

But since z_t^1 is a linear combinations of $\hat{k}_t$, $\hat{c}_t$, and $\hat{s}_t$, this restriction implies that $\hat{c}_t$, is a linear function of $\hat{k}_t$ and $\hat{s}_t$.

In the real business cycle model one substitutes the linear restriction that determines $\hat{c}_t$ back into the capital accumulation equation to arrive at a model of business cycles with two state variables, $\hat{k}_t$, and $\hat{s}_t$:

$$\begin{bmatrix} \hat{k}_{t+1} \\ \hat{s}_{t+1} \end{bmatrix} = A \begin{bmatrix} \hat{k}_t \\ \hat{s}_t \end{bmatrix} + B\hat{v}_{t+1},$$

where the coefficient matrix

$$A \equiv \begin{bmatrix} a_{11} & a_{12} \\ 0 & \rho \end{bmatrix}$$

is upper triangular, since the capital stock does not feed back into the technology shock. Although the RBC assumptions deliver a model in which the steady state is a saddle, this is not generally true when one allows for the presence of increasing returns. In the next section I am going to describe a set of parameter values that leads to a matrix J that has all of its roots outside of the unit circle. Before describing these values, we will look a little further at the implications of the model in this situation.

7.5.3 IR Model: An Example of an Irregular Equilibrium

A rational expectations equilibrium is a stochastic process that remains bounded and satisfies 7.24 and 7.25. In chapter 1, I discussed the idea of an irregular economic model in which one might construct a rational expectations equilibrium by taking an arbitrary initial value for the state variable and iterating the equations of the model. I explained conditions under which this process would, and would not, succeed.

We are now in a position to extend the argument of chapter to the case in which the state is described by a multidimensional vector. Let us take the simplest case in which the economy is deterministic, and there are no fundamental disturbances of any kind. This assumption, in the context of the IR model, can be stated as a restriction on the productivity disturbance

$$s_t = 1 \quad \text{for all } t.$$

A rational expectations equilibrium is a sequence of probability distributions

$$\{F_t(\hat{k}_t, \hat{c}_t)\}_{t=1}^{\infty},$$

with the property that sequences of state variables that are drawn from $\{F_t\}$ satisfy the functional equation:

$$\begin{bmatrix} \hat{k}_t \\ \hat{c}_t \\ \hat{s}_t \end{bmatrix} = J \begin{bmatrix} \hat{k}_{t+1} \\ \hat{c}_{t+1} \\ \hat{s}_{t+1} \end{bmatrix} + R \begin{bmatrix} \hat{v}_{t+1} \\ w_{t+1} \end{bmatrix}.$$

or in the case of no fundamental uncertainty,[11]

$$\begin{bmatrix} \hat{k}_t \\ \hat{c}_t \end{bmatrix} = \tilde{J} \begin{bmatrix} \hat{k}_{t+1} \\ \hat{c}_{t+1} \end{bmatrix} + \tilde{R} w_{t+1},$$

where

$$\tilde{w}_{t+1} = \begin{bmatrix} E_t[\hat{k}_{t+1}] - \hat{k}_{t+1} \\ E_t[\hat{c}_{t+1}] - \hat{c}_{t+1} \end{bmatrix}, \tag{7.27}$$

and $\tilde{J}$ and $\tilde{R}$ are conformable partitions of J and R. The rational expectations assumption is contained in the fact that the expectations operator in equation 7.27 is defined with respect to the sequence of true distribution functions $\{F_t\}$.

Now suppose that the matrix $\tilde{J}$ has two eigenvalues *both of which are outside of the unit circle*, and let e_{t+1} be any random variable that is unforecastable at date t. Let us generate the sequence of values $\{\hat{k}_t, \hat{c}_t\}_{t=1}^{\infty}$ for given initial value $\hat{k}_1$ by taking an arbitrary value of $\hat{c}_1$ and iterating the equation

$$\begin{bmatrix} \hat{k}_{t+1} \\ \hat{c}_{t+1} \end{bmatrix} = \tilde{J}^{-1} \begin{bmatrix} \hat{k}_t \\ \hat{c}_t \end{bmatrix} + \begin{bmatrix} 0 \\ e_{t+1} \end{bmatrix}, \qquad t = 2, \ldots. \tag{7.28}$$

Since the roots of $\tilde{J}^{-1}$ are the inverses of the roots of $\tilde{J}$, it follows that equation 7.28 defines a stable Markov process. We have shown that if the roots of $\tilde{J}$ are outside the unit circle, then the IR model is capable of generating a model of business cycles that is driven by a nonfundamental random variable. If one interprets the variable e_{t+1} as the self-fulfilling beliefs of individual agents, then the IR model provides an *equilibrium* interpretation of Keynes's central hypothesis, that business fluctuations are driven by the "animal spirits" of speculators.

7.6 Comparing Some Empirical Predictions of RA and IR Models

We have pointed out that the increasing returns model could have very different implications for the properties of the dynamic equations that describe equilibria. In this section I am going to compare some of the empirical implications of the two types of models using the method of simulation of calibrated economies that has been favored by some of the advocates of the RBC school. I will begin by choosing parameters for two alternative simulations, and I will report the volatility of output, consumption, investment, hours, and productivity that the two sets of parameters will produce. One of these simulations is a fairly standard RBC model which is driven by an autocorrelated productivity shock and the other is an IR model which is driven by i.i.d. self-fulfilling beliefs.

7.6.1 Contemporaneous Statistics

In table 7.1, I have laid out two sets of parameter values for the production economy around which the simulations that I will describe are based. The first set, referred to as the RBC economy, makes a standard assumption about the marginal product of labor that comes from observing that labor's share of national income has been around 0.64 in postwar data. In the RBC economy this observation is sufficient to fix n, m, μ, and v because factor shares equal marginal products and they sum to one.

In the increasing returns economy we have set labor's share at 0.7, which is still within a range that is consistent with observation since there is some ambiguity in interpreting certain categories of income in the

Table 7.1
Parameters of production

	λ	n	v	m	μ	Root 1	Root 2
RBC model	1	0.64	0.64	0.36	0.36	0.93	1.06
IR model	0.58	0.7	1.21	0.23	0.4	$1.07 + 0.11i$	$1.07 - 0.011i$

national income and product accounts and matching them up with data. For example, proprietor's income could reasonably be treated as wages or as profits. The IR economy reported in table 7.1 is based on the monopolistically competitive model, and it arbitrarily sets the share of rents in the economy (monopoly profits) at 7%. This accounts for the fact that the sum of labor's share, 0.7, and capital's share, 0.23, comes to only 0.93. The other 7% is assumed to be a monopoly rent.[12] To find the relationship between marginal products and factor shares, we set λ at 0.58 following estimates of monopoly markups in work by Domowitz, Hubbard, and Peterson [41].[13] In both economies the other parameters are set at values that are standard in the RBC literature, for example, $\beta = 0.99$, $\delta = 0.025$, and $\chi = 0$.[14]

In the last two columns of table 7.1, I have reported the roots of the matrix $\tilde{J}$ that follow from the parametrizations in the first part of the table. Notice that in the RBC model these roots split around unity as we would expect. But in the IR model there is a pair of complex roots that is outside of the unit circle. The fact that the IR model is capable of generating complex roots is the key to understanding why the IR model can capture certain dynamic features of the data better than the standard RBC economy.

One way in which RBC models are often compared with data is by simulating time series from an artificial calibrated economy and comparing the relative volatility of output, investment, hours, and GNP from the simulated economy with the same quantities in the data. The result of this exercise for the RBC and IR economies is set out in table 7.2, which is reproduced from the paper by Farmer and Guo [49]. The two economies that we can simulate to present the results in this table both satisfy the functional equation 7.24, although the parameter values in this equation are different for the two solutions. The RBC model, in which $\tilde{J}$ has two roots that split around unity, has been solved using standard techniques to yield the RBC model:

Table 7.2
Relative volatilities in the RA and IR models

Variables	U.S. data	RA model	IR model
GNP	1.73	1.76	1.74
Consumption	0.86	0.51	0.41
Investment	7.78	5.73	8.91
Hours	1.5	1.34	1.44
Productivity	0.88	0.51	0.41

$$\begin{bmatrix} \hat{k}_{t+1} \\ \hat{s}_{t+1} \end{bmatrix} = A \begin{bmatrix} \hat{k}_t \\ \hat{s}_t \end{bmatrix} + B\hat{v}_{t+1}, \tag{7.29}$$

where A is upper triangular and B is a 2×1 vector. The elements of A and B are found by the techniques described in chapter 3.[15] To simulate the time series, whose volatilities are reported in table 7.2, we can simulate a series of innovations to the technology shock, $\{\hat{v}_t\}$, with a standard deviation of 0.007 and set the persistence parameter, ρ, equal to 0.95. These figures are chosen to cause the output series, which is generated from the side conditions 7.25, to have a volatility that matches postwar quarterly U.S. GNP. The persistence figure of 0.95 is chosen to conform with the properties of the Solow residual in the U.S. case.

To generate the IR time series whose volatilities are also reported in the table, we can simulate the model

$$\begin{bmatrix} \hat{k}_{t+1} \\ \hat{c}_{t+1} \end{bmatrix} = \tilde{J}^{-1} \begin{bmatrix} \hat{k}_t \\ \hat{c}_t \end{bmatrix} + \begin{bmatrix} 0 \\ e_{t+1} \end{bmatrix},$$

where we interpret the random variable e_t as a self-fulfilling prophecy. Notice that in the IR model we have completely shut down the fundamental shock, $\hat{v}_t$, but we are still able to generate persistent time series for the endogenous variables because the model displays endogenously persistent dynamics. The shock that we used to simulate the data reported in table 7.2 has a standard deviation of 0.002. We chose that number the same way that RBC economists choose the volatility of the driving shock—it generates time series that match the volatility of output in the U.S. case.

Are these models good or bad? This is a matter of interpretation, since they are both certainly false on some dimensions. Notice, however, that the two economies are roughly comparable when it comes to matching the second moments of the data. Both models produce consumption fluctuations that are a little too smooth, this follows from the assumption of logarithmic preferences. Both economies understate the volatility of hours by a little and understate the volatility of productivity by quite a lot and the IR economy is a little better at matching the observed investment volatility.

7.6.2 Dynamic Responses—The Impulse Response Function

Contemporaneous moments are not the only dimension on which one might try to compare a model with data. Since all of the models that we are looking at are explicitly dynamic, they will also have implications for the cross moments between variables dated at different points in time. One of the most important tools in the applied macroeconomists tool kit is the *impulse response function* which is designed to capture exactly these intertemporal correlations.

The impulse function is a property of a model in the class

$$y_t = \sum_{s=1}^{M} A_s y_{t-s} + u_t,$$

where y_t is an $n \times 1$ vector of variables and u_t is a vector of innovations that is typically assumed to be independently distributed through time but to have a contemporaneous covariance matrix, Ω. Roughly speaking, the impulse response function addresses the following question: If you were to displace the vector y_t from its rest position at zero in any given direction in n space, how would the variables y_t^i, $i \in n$, return to the steady state as $t \to \infty$? The issue of which n directions to pick is called the normalization problem, and it arises from the fact that the typical disturbances to a system will be correlated; that is, Ω is not generally diagonal. To completely describe the responses in an n space, one must pick n different displacements, and many economists ascribe these displacements to the effects of a shock to each of the n equations. But when shocks are contemporaneously correlated, there is no unique way of sorting out how much of a typical shock is due to one influence and how much is due to another.

A simple resolution to the normalization issue seems to be to ignore the contemporaneous correlations in the data and to ask how the system in the absence of shocks would return to the steady state if it were displaced in each of the n dimensions that correspond to the coordinate axes. Strictly speaking, this object is not an impulse response function; it gives just as much information about the dynamics of the system. In figure 7.4, I have depicted the impulse response functions in the U.S. data and compared it with impulse response functions for artificial data that are generated from each of the RA and IR models. Each panel of figure 7.4 contains four pictures. The pictures represent the effects through time on investment, output, hours, and consumption of displacing the model

$$y_t = \sum_{i=1}^{5} A_i y_{t-i},$$

by increasing the initial value of output by one unit.[16] The vector y_t represents the four vectors whose elements are investment, output, hours, and consumption, and the elements of the matrices $A_1, \ldots, A_5$ are found by estimating a vector autoregression using ordinary least squares on three different data sets. The first data set is postwar quarterly U.S. GNP, and the second two data sets are simulated from the RA and IR model, respectively.

There is a striking feature of these pictures that I want to draw attention to because it represents one dimension on which the standard real business cycle model does not do very well. This concerns the fact that the U.S. data favors a model with complex roots—the evidence for this statement is the fact that the impulse response functions in the data clearly cycle in their return to the steady state. But the RA model depicted in the second panel cannot capture this cyclical response: The model *necessarily* contains a pair of real roots, since the matrix A in equation 7.29 is upper triangular. The IR economy, on the other hand, can pick up this feature of the data, and the qualitative features of the response in this model are quite similar to U.S. time series.

7.7 Concluding Remarks

A lot of the things that I have talked about in this chapter are relatively new, and there is still a lot of disagreement amongst research economists about the role of nonconvexities and self-fulfilling beliefs. I mention these qualifications because this book is directed at graduate students, and

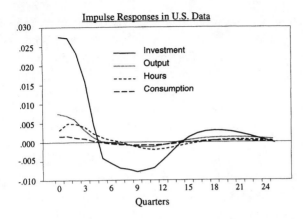

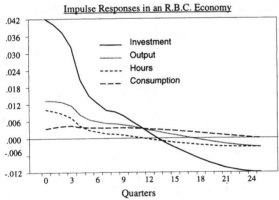

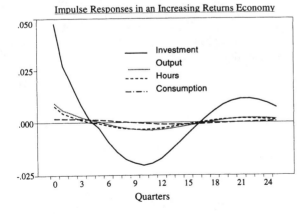

Figure 7.4
Impulse responses in the data compared with two models

graduate students need to be aware of what is generally accepted and what is not. So what should you take away from the material that I have covered? First of all there is the approach of constructing economic environments that are populated by rational actors and using these models to generate artificial data. Although this approach is considered by some to be pretentious pseudoscience, there is growing acceptance of the tools and methods of applied equilibrium economics at a large number of graduate schools.[17]

As for the models that I have described in the chapter, obviously I believe very strongly that they are the way of the future, since a good deal of my own research career has been directed at showing that self-fulfilling prophecies can have important implications in macroeconomics. But the fact that I believe this does not mean that I am right, and you would do equally well in pursuing your own future in macroeconomics if you were to spend some time showing on which dimensions the models that I have introduced might fail. I alluded briefly in the chapter to work on labor hoarding, and the class of models that takes the labor-hoarding approach is currently being vigorously pursued at a number of institutions.

7.8 Problems

1. What are the two principal explanations for procyclical productivity? Explain each of them using a production function diagram.

2. Suppose that a firm produces output using the production function

$$Y = AK^\alpha L^\beta,$$

where $\alpha + \beta = \theta > 1$. Assume that the firm takes prices as given and operates in competitive factor and product markets.

a. Find the least cost way of producing output $\bar{Y}$ by solving the problem

$\min wL + rK$

such that

$$AK^\alpha L^\beta \geq \bar{Y},$$

and w and r refer to the nominal wage and the nominal rental rate.

b. Draw a graph of the cost function $C(\bar{Y})$. Is this function convex or concave?

c. Assume that the firm is a monopolistic competitor in the output market and that price of output is a function

$$p = Y^{-\lambda}.$$

For what values of λ and θ is the firm's problem concave at the optimum?

d. Draw the marginal cost and marginal revenue curves on a graph, and interpret your condition in terms of the slopes of these two curves.

3. Consider the following model in which there exist a large number of identical representative agents each of which maximizes the utility function

$$U = E_t \sum_{t=1}^{\infty} \beta^{t-1}[\log(C_t) - L_t],$$

using the technology

$$Y_t = (K_t)^{1/3}(L_t)^{2/3} A_t \tag{7.30}$$

and the capital accumulation equation

$$K_{t+1} = (1 - \delta)K_t + Y_t - C_t.$$

The variable L_t is labor supply, C_t is consumption, K_t is capital, and Y_t is output. Equation 7.30 represents the production function of a private producer. However, this economy is subject to externalities and the variable A_t (taken as given by an individual producer) is in fact given by

$$A_t = (\bar{K}_t)^{1/3}(\bar{L}_t)^{2/3}$$

where a bar denotes the economywide average.

a. Find an expression for the social production function.

b. Write down the two first-order conditions for the representative agent's problem that come from choosing L_t, and K_{t+1}.

c. Write down the transversality condition for this problem, and explain what it means.

d. Find the values of C^*, K^*, Y^*, and L^* where the stars denote steady state values.

e. Find a set of approximate linear equations in the deviations of C, K, Y, and L from their steady state values.

f. Find a first-order vector difference equation in the variables $\tilde{C}$ and $\tilde{K}$ where tilde's denote deviations from steady state, and calculate the matrix J where

$$\begin{bmatrix} \tilde{C}_t \\ \tilde{K}_t \end{bmatrix} = J \begin{bmatrix} \tilde{C}_{t+1} \\ \tilde{K}_{t+1} \end{bmatrix}.$$

g. What is meant by "determinacy of equilibrium"? Is the steady state equilibrium of this model determinate or indeterminate?

4. This problem concerns an economy with large number of identical representative families that live forever. The ith family produces a single nonstorable commodity using the technology

$$Y_t^i = (K_t^i)^\alpha (L_t^i)^{1-\alpha} A_t,$$

where $A_t = Y_t^\theta$. Variables Y^i, L^i, and K^i with superscript i refer to individual family production functions and variables Y, L, and K without superscript refer to economywide averages. The family takes A as given, although in a symmetric equilibrium A is determined by the actions of other agents in the economy. The family maximizes discounted utility

$$U = \sum_{t=1}^{\infty} \beta^{t-1} [\log(C_t^i) + \log(1 - L_t^i)]$$

subject to the capital accumulation equation

$$K_{t+1}^i = K_t^i(1 - \delta) + Y_t^i - C_t^i.$$

a. Explain what is meant by the social production function? How does the social production differ from the private production function? Write down the social production function for this economy. (*Note*: This economy has an output externality that is a little different from the input externalities discussed in the chapter.)

b. Substitute the resource constraint into the objective function by eliminating C_t^i. Using this substitution, write down the first-order conditions for this problem with respect to choice of labor supply at each point in time and with respect to the choice of capital. (Be careful to use the derivatives of the appropriate production function in your calculations.)

c. Suppose that you observe that labor's share of GDP is equal to 2/3. Explain how this observation can be used to pin down the parameter α.

d. Write a computer program in Gauss to check if the equilibrium of this model is indeterminate. Assume that $\beta = 0.97$, $\delta = 0.1$, and $\alpha = 0.67$. For what value of θ does the equilibrium become indeterminate? (*Note*: Your result will not be identical to the Benhabib-Farmer condition that slopes of labor demand and supply are reversed because their result only holds exactly in a continuous time model.)

8 Some Recent Developments

8.1 Introduction

The increasing returns model which I discussed in chapter 7 was stimulated by the empirical papers of Robert Hall [56, 57] who had found evidence of a high degree of increasing returns to scale in U.S. data. Since the first edition of this book was published in 1993, there has been a tremendous growth of interest in equilibrium models with increasing returns to scale in production, much of it geared to showing that equilibria in these models can be indeterminate and that these indeterminate equilibria might mimic various features of actual business cycles.[1] Some of the papers in this literature assume that there are externalities in production. Others assume internal increasing returns to scale and monopolistically competitive firms either with fixed or variable markups. The literature is discussed by Schmidt-Grohé [101] who compares four different models and finds that those with countercyclical markups need a lower degrees of increasing returns to scale to generate indeterminate equilibria than those that have constant markups or externalities.

The degree of returns to scale required to generate indeterminacy has become the main focus of several recent theoretical papers because a number of recent studies have found that the degree of increasing returns to scale in U.S. manufacturing is not as high as Hall originally claimed. Hall's evidence suggested that the upward-sloping labor demand curve that was necessary to cause equilibrium to be indeterminate in the model of Benhabib and Farmer [17] might be a good approximation to actual data. But subsequent studies suggest that Hall's estimates were too large. The impetus from this new empirical work led to a further burst of theoretical activity that studied alternative routes to indeterminacy. It is this second round that we will take up in this chapter.

8.2 New Evidence against Big Increasing Returns

Early work on one-sector models with increasing returns to scale, for example, the work by Hall [57, 56], Domowitz et al. [41], Caballero and Lyons [29], and Baxter and King [14], suggested that the elasticity of aggregated output with respect to inputs should be higher than that suggested by factor shares by a factor of 40%–60%. More recent work by Basu and Fernald [12, 13] is critical of the earlier methodologies that estimate external effects and increasing returns. Basu and Fernald argue that the earlier work ignores the share of intermediate goods in computing the Solow residual. Using data that correct this problem, they estimate the degree of returns to scale in individual industries to be of the order of 1.03, much lower than the values of 1.5 or more that are required for indeterminacy in single sector models.

Work by John Shea [103] and Burnside et al. [28] throws further doubt on the large estimates of increasing returns by Hall. Using input-output structures to identify demand shocks, Shea finds that in 16 of 26 manufacturing industries, supply curves slope up, contrary to the implications of a model with increasing returns. Burnside et al., using electricity consumption as a proxy for capital services, are unable to reject the hypothesis of constant returns in manufacturing industries. Both papers can be viewed as providing evidence against steeply declining short-run marginal cost curves.

Some recent studies find higher estimates. Bartlesman, Caballero, and Lyons [11], for example, using gross output data that does not suffer from the Basu-Fernald criticism, find external effects associated with aggregate output measures to be around 1.12 in the short-run and 1.30 over the longer horizon. Furthermore, as Basu and Fernald [13] point out, if intermediate goods are produced with increasing returns, then the elasticity of aggregated outputs like consumption or investment with respect to capital and labor inputs will be higher than the estimates that are based on disaggregated outputs. It is possible that external effects and markups implicit in intermediate goods will pile up in aggregation, causing the magnitude of increasing returns for the aggregated sectoral outputs to be closer to the higher estimates obtained by Baxter and King [14]. But although the estimate of 1.03 of Basu and Fernald is at the low end of the spectrum, it is unlikely that the data will support the magnitudes of externalities that are necessary to generate indeterminacy in the one sector model.

The main impact of the new estimates of Basu and Fernald has been to stimulate a series of papers that argue that indeterminacy can be obtained with much lower degrees of increasing returns to scale once one departs slightly from the single-sector closed economy model with separable preferences. For example, Benhabib and Farmer [18] and Benhabib and Nishimura [19] present multi-sector models with indeterminacy, Pelloni and Waldmann [89a] and Bennett and Farmer [15] show that dropping the assumption that preferences are separable in consumption and leisure allows indeterminacy to occur more easily, and Lahiri [73] shows that indeterminacy occurs more easily in an open economy model.

8.3 Nonseparable Preferences

One route to indeterminacy that has been explored in a paper by Bennett and Farmer [15] is the possibility that with nonseparable preferences, the condition for indeterminacy may be more easily satisfied. The model in their paper is identical to the one-sector model that we studied in Chapter 7, with the exception that preferences are modeled as nonseparable in consumption and leisure. The model that I will describe in this section is based on their work.*

8.3.1 Households

I will suppose that the economy contains a large number of identical families, each of which derives utility each period from the function,

$$U(c_{it}, l_{it}) = \frac{[c_{it} V(l_{it})]^{1-\sigma} - 1}{1 - \sigma},$$
(8.1)

where $\sigma > 0$, $\sigma \neq 1$, and $V(\ )$ is a nonnegative, strictly decreasing concave function, bounded above, that maps $[0, \bar{l}] \to R$. I will also assume that $V'(0)$ is bounded and that $V(0) > 0$. $\bar{l}$ has the interpretation of the consumer's endowment of leisure, and I allow for the possibility (since certain simple examples have this feature) that $\bar{l} = \infty$. The function $U(\ )$ displays a constant intertemporal elasticity of substitution and generalizes the utility function used in Chapter 7,

$$U(c_{it}, l_{it}) = \log c_{it} - \frac{l_{it}^{1+\chi}}{1 + \chi}.$$
(8.2)

It is important that the function U is homogeneous in consumption, since this property implies that the consumer will choose to supply the same number of hours to the market when the wage grows. In the U.S. data,

---

* In a related paper, Pelloni and Waldmann study an endogenous growth model and show that indeterminacy can occur whenever the elasticity of substitution between consumption and leisure is less than one. Their model is a limiting case of the model I consider here, which applies when capital externalities are large enough for the social technology to be linear in capital. Pelloni and Waldmann have no labor externalities in their model.

hours per person supplied to the market has been approximately constant in a century of data, even though the real wage has grown at 1.6% per year.

In utility-maximizing models there are two effects on labor supply of an increasing wage. The substitution effect causes the representative household to supply more labor as the wage increases and leisure becomes more expensive. The income effect causes it to supply less labor to the market (consume more leisure) as the value of the household's time increases and the family feels wealthier, thereby inducing it to spend more on all goods, including leisure. The class of preferences given in equation 8.1 has the property that these two effects exactly balance each other and it is the most general class of preferences for which this is the case.[2]

Most work on the representative family model uses additively separable preferences, and as $\sigma \to 1$, the utility function 8.1 can be shown, using L'Hospital's rule, to converge to a separable function that is logarithmic in consumption.[3] If the function $V(\ )$ is given by

$$V(l_{it}) = \exp\left(-\frac{l_{it}^{1+\gamma}}{1+\gamma}\right),$$

the function 8.1 reduces to equation 8.2 which is the utility function used in chapter 7.

To model household decisions, I assume that the ith household maximizes the present discounted value of expected utility

$$U_i = \sum_{\tau=t}^{\infty} E_t \beta^{\tau-t}[U(c_{i\tau}, l_{i\tau})] \tag{8.3}$$

subject to the sequence of budget constraints $c_{i\tau} + k_{i\tau+1} \leq k_{i\tau}(1 - \delta + r_\tau) + \omega_\tau l_{i\tau}$, and the initial condition $k_{it} = \bar{k}_{it}$. Here I assume that the household sells labor and rents capital to a firm for real wage ω_t and rental rate r_t.

8.3.2 Technology

To describe production, I assume that there is a large number of firms each of which produces a homogeneous commodity using a constant returns-to-scale production function:

$$y_{it} = k_{it}^m l_{it}^n A_t, \tag{8.4}$$

where $m + n = 1$ and $A_t > 0$. Each firm takes the aggregate productivity shock A_t as given. However, A_t is determined in practice by the activity of other families:

$$A_t = \left[\int_i k_{it}^m l_{it}^n \, di \right]^\theta. \tag{8.5}$$

I will assume that there is no growth in this example, although growth can easily be added by using labor-augmenting technical progress. Substituting from 8.5 into 8.4 and assuming that all firms use the same capital and labor leads to an expression for the social production function:

$$y_t = k_t^\mu l_t^v, \quad \mu = m(1 + \theta), \quad v = n(1 + \theta). \tag{8.6}$$

Firms rent labor and capital in competitive factor markets, which implies that in equilibrium

$$n = \frac{\omega_t l_t}{y_t}, \tag{8.7}$$

$$m = \frac{r_t k_t}{y_t}, \tag{8.8}$$

where ω_t is the wage rate and r_t is the rental rate, both measured in terms of the consumption good. Factor shares in national income, m and n, will differ from the social marginal products, μ and v, due to the existence of externalities in production.

8.3.3 Solving the Consumer's Problem

Since we assume that all households and all firms are identical, I will drop the subscript i from this point on, when describing the solution to the household problem. To understand how nonseparable preferences may alter the indeterminacy conditions, lets define a variable λ_t that represents the marginal utility of consumption:

$$\lambda_t \equiv c_t^{-\sigma} V(l_t)^{1-\sigma}. \tag{8.9}$$

Using this definition, we can write the first-order condition to the maximizing problem 8.3, for the choice of labor, as follows:

$$\omega_t \lambda_t = -c_t^{1-\sigma} \frac{V'(l_t)}{V(l_t)^\sigma}. \tag{8.10}$$

Substituting 8.9 into 8.10 and using the fact that the wage equals the marginal product of labor leads to the static condition

$$n\frac{y_t}{l_t} = \omega_t = -c_t \frac{V'(l_t)}{V(l_t)}, \tag{8.11}$$

which is the requirement that the negative of the ratio of the marginal disutility of labor supply to the marginal utility of consumption should be equated to the real wage.

A second optimality condition, referred to as the stochastic Euler equation, takes the form

$$\lambda_t = E_t\beta\left[\lambda_{t+1}\left(1-\delta+m\frac{y_{t+1}}{k_{t+1}}\right)\right], \tag{8.12}$$

where I have used the firm's optimizing condition 8.8 in equation 8.12 to write the rental rate as a function of output and capital.

8.3.4 Equations That Characterize Equilibrium

Armed with our definition of λ_t, one can write the equations that define equilibrium in this model, as follows:

$$\lambda_t \equiv c_t^{-\sigma} V(l_t)^{1-\sigma}, \tag{8.13}$$

$$y_t = k_t^\mu l_t^\nu, \tag{8.14}$$

$$n\frac{y_t}{l_t} = -c_t \frac{V'(l_t)}{V(l_t)}, \tag{8.15}$$

$$k_{t+1} = k_t(1-\delta) + y_t - c_t, \tag{8.16}$$

$$\lambda_t = E_t\beta\left[\lambda_{t+1}\left(1-\delta+m\frac{y_{t+1}}{k_{t+1}}\right)\right]. \tag{8.17}$$

Equation 8.13 is key to understanding the difference between the cases of separable and nonseparable preferences. In the case in which preferences are separable, the marginal utility of consumption, λ_t, is the inverse of consumption. In this case equation 8.17 can be written as an equation in consumption that also contains the variables y_{t+1} and k_{t+1}. By solving 8.14 and 8.15 for y_t and l_t as functions of c_t and k_t, one can find a dynamical system in c_t and k_t that describes equilibrium. The main result in Benhabib and Farmer [17] is that a necessary and sufficient condition for indeterminacy when there are externalities in capital and labor is that the labor demand and labor supply curves should cross with the "wrong slopes." Bennett and Farmer show that a similar condition holds in the case of nonseparable preferences provided that one amends ones definition of labor supply.

The nonseparable case is different because 8.13 can no longer be solved for c_t. Instead, the dynamics of the system must be modeled as a system in the two variables k_t and λ_t, where λ_t is the marginal utility of consumption. Given some weak assumptions about the properties of the function $V(\ )$, it is relatively easy to establish that the model has a unique steady state in which l_t is equal to some value we will call l^*. Define the parameters

$$\psi = \left(\frac{-l^* V'(l^*)}{V(l^*)} \right), \tag{8.18}$$

$$\gamma = \frac{l^* h'(l^*)}{h(l^*)}, \quad \text{where} \quad h(l) \equiv -\frac{V'(l)}{V(l)}, \tag{8.19}$$

to represent the curvature of the utility function in the neighborhood of the steady state. Using this notation, it is helpful to distinguish the *constant consumption* labor supply curve from the *Frisch* labor supply curve. The former is labor supply as a function of the real wage, holding constant consumption. The latter is labor supply as a function of the real wage holding constant the marginal utility of consumption.[4]

When $\sigma = 1$, the utility function is logarithmic, and in this case the Frisch labor supply curve and the constant consumption labor supply curves are identical and given by

$$\log \omega_t = \log c_t + \gamma \log l_t,$$

and the labor demand curve is

$$\log \omega_t = \text{constant} + \mu \log k_t + (v - 1)\log l_t.$$

In this case the slope of the labor supply curve is γ, the slope of the labor demand curve is $v - 1$, and a necessary condition for indeterminacy is that the slope of the labor demand curve is larger than the slope of the labor supply curve. In the more general case where intertemporal substitution differs from one, the necessary condition for indeterminacy is that

$$v - 1 > \frac{(\sigma - 1)}{\sigma} \psi + \gamma.$$

In this case the Frisch labor supply curve and the constant consumption labor supply curve differ. The Frisch labor supply curve is

$$\log \omega_t = \text{constant} - \frac{1}{\sigma} \log \lambda_t + \left(\frac{(\sigma - 1)}{\sigma} \psi + \gamma \right) \log l_t, \qquad (8.20)$$

and the labor demand curve is

$$\log \omega_t = \text{constant} + \mu \log k_t + (v - 1) \log l_t. \qquad (8.21)$$

Notice that in general, the necessary condition for indeterminacy implies that the labor demand curve and the Frisch labor supply curve cross with the wrong slopes. Since the coefficient of $\log l_t$ in the Frisch labor supply curve depends on the sign of $(\sigma - 1)$, indeterminacy may occur in the more general model when the labor demand curve slopes down. This may occur, for example, if $\sigma < 1$ and $v - 1$ (the slope of labor demand) is negative but greater than $(\psi(\sigma - 1)/\sigma) + \gamma$ (the slope of Frisch labor supply). Note that in this case the Frisch labor supply curve would slope down also. If one substitutes for λ_t from equation 8.13 into equation 8.20, one obtains the constant consumption labor supply curve

$$\log \omega_t = \text{constant} + \log c_t + \gamma \log l_t, \qquad (8.22)$$

which is identical (up to a constant) to the separable case. Equation 8.22 slopes up for all $\gamma > 0$ (a necessary condition for both consumption and leisure to be normal goods). It follows that when the model is generalized to allow for differing degrees of intertemporal substitution, the labor demand curve and the constant consumption labor supply curve may return to their traditional slopes even when the steady state is indeterminate.

8.3.5 Example

Bennett and Farmer check for indeterminacy in a calibrated version of their model in which the discount rate is approximately 3%, capital's share is 0.3, and labor is infinitely elastic. In table 8.1 I reproduce the results from their paper in which they look at a case where utility is slightly different from the separable log case; specifically they let the intertemporal substitution parameter σ drop from 1 to 0.75. The Bennett-Farmer calibration is for a continuous time model in which the condition

Table 8.1
Roots of the model at the steady state for various values of returns to scale when $\sigma = 0.75$

Returns to scale	Root 1	Root 2	Dynamics
1	−2.1306	2.1956	Saddle path
1.01	−2.8655	3.0814	Saddle path
1.02	−7.8212	10.7812	Saddle path
1.03	−0.2535 + 3.316i	−0.2535 − 3.316i	Sink
1.04	−0.1464 + 2.2681i	−0.1464 − 2.2681i	Sink
1.05	−0.1136 + 1.8294i	−0.1136 − 1.8294i	Sink
1.06	−0.0977 + 1.5729i	−0.0977 − 1.5729i	Sink
1.07	−0.0883 + 1.3995i	−0.0883 − 1.3995i	Sink
1.08	−0.0821 + 1.2721i	−0.0821 − 1.2721i	Sink
1.09	−0.0776 + 1.1733i	−0.0776 − 1.1733i	Sink
1.1	−0.0744 + 1.0938i	−0.0744 − 1.0938i	Sink
1.2	−0.0617 + 0.7087i	−0.0617 − 0.7087i	Sink
1.3	−0.0581 + 0.5532i	−0.0581 − 0.5532i	Sink
1.4	−0.0565 + 0.4619i	−0.0565 − 0.4619i	Sink
1.5	−0.0555 + 0.3992i	−0.0555 − 0.3992i	Sink
1.6	−0.0548 + 0.3522i	−0.0548 − 0.3522i	Sink
1.7	−0.0544 + 0.3148i	−0.0544 − 0.3148i	Sink
1.8	−0.054 + 0.2839i	−0.054 − 0.2839i	Sink
1.9	−0.0538 + 0.2575i	−0.0538 − 0.2575i	Sink

for indeterminacy is that both roots of the dynamical system should be negative. Notice from the table that when $\sigma = 0.75$, indeterminacy occurs for returns to scale of 1.03 which is well within the empirically relevant range and accords with the point estimates of Basu and Fernald.

Although the two-sector model may be consistent with a low degree of returns to scale; this *does not* imply that it can be used to generate business cycles when driven purely by sunspots in the manner described by Farmer and Guo [49]. When labor demand and constant consumption labor supply curves cross with the conventional slopes, purely sunspot driven business cycles will cause consumption and employment to move countercyclically; in the data they are procyclical. We will return to this issue below when we discuss the two-sector model. At this point we note that the model with nonseparable utility does lead to the possibility that indeterminacy may provide an additional transmission mechanism for shocks originating in the real sector.

8.4   Two-Sector Models

A second route that has been explored in recent literature is that multi-sector technologies may contribute to indeterminacies. Here the mechanisms that generate indeterminacy are not the same as in the one-sector case, and a number of recent papers have established that indeterminacy can be obtained for parameter values that imply a much lower degree of increasing returns to scale than in the single-sector economy. The following model is based on the paper by Benhabib and Farmer [18].

8.4.1   Technology

To make comparison with the one-sector model as simple as possible, I will construct a two-sector model in which, in the absence of externalities, both sectors of the economy would produce with identical constant returns-to-scale technologies. Let there be a continuum of families indexed by $j \in [0, 1]$ and assume that each family operates a firm that produces both consumption goods c_{jt} and investment goods i_{jt} using the technologies:

$$c_{jt} = A_t(k_{jt}^c)^m (l_{jt}^c)^n, \tag{8.23}$$

$$i_{jt} = B_t(k_{jt}^i)^m (l_{jt}^i)^n. \tag{8.24}$$

where the symbols $k_{jt}^c, (k_{jt}^i)$ and $l_{jt}^c, (l_{jt}^i)$ represent the use of capital and labor by the jth family in the production of consumption (investment) goods. Each of these technologies is assumed to be subject to constant returns to scale

$$m + n = 1;$$

however, the technology parameters A_t and B_t that are taken as given by individual firms in the economy will in fact be a function of the use of resources in the consumption or investment sectors by other families in the economy. A_t and B_t are modeled by the expressions:

$$A_t = \left[\int_j (k_{jt}^c)^m (l_{jt}^c)^n \, dj \right]^\theta, \tag{8.25}$$

$$B_t = \left[\int_j (k_{jt}^i)^m (l_{jt}^i)^n \, dj \right]^\theta, \tag{8.26}$$

where the terms in square brackets indicate the average output of consumption goods (investment goods) by all other families. If we substitute the expressions from equations 8.25 and 8.26 into the private production technologies 8.23 and 8.24, we arrive at descriptions of the aggregate technology faced by society as a whole:

$$c_t = (k_t^c)^\mu (l_t^c)^v, \tag{8.27}$$

$$i_t = (k_t^i)^\mu (l_t^i)^v, \tag{8.28}$$

where the social marginal products μ and v add up to more than 1:

$$\mu + v = (m + n)(1 + \theta) > 0.$$

The terms c_t and i_t refer to the average economywide production of consumption and investment goods, and k_t^c, (k_t^i) and l_t^c, (l_t^i) represent economywide use of capital and labor in the consumption (investment) goods industries.

8.4.2 Production Possibilities Frontier

The two-sector model with identical technologies behaves (in the absence of externalities) exactly like a one-sector model. Each family allocates resources across the two product types to equate marginal products to factor prices. Since all families behave in the same way, the first-order conditions for profit maximization imply that the ratio of aggregate consumption to capital used in the production of consumption goods will equal the ratio of aggregate investment to capital used to produce investment goods. A similar condition is true for the use of labor in the two sectors:

$$m \frac{c_t}{k_t^c} = r_t = m \frac{i_t}{k_t^i}, \tag{8.29}$$

$$n \frac{c_t}{l_t^c} = \omega_t = n \frac{i_t}{l_t^i}. \tag{8.30}$$

By combining these equations, one can show that the fractions of aggregate labor and aggregate capital used in each sector must be the same:

$$\frac{k_t^c}{k_t} = \frac{l_t^c}{l_t} \equiv \lambda_t, \tag{8.31}$$

$$\frac{k_t^i}{k_t} = \frac{l_t^i}{l_t} \equiv (1 - \lambda_t). \tag{8.32}$$

Equations 8.31 and 8.32 tell the jth family how to allocate capital and labor between consumption and investment goods. Given that the family allocates resources optimally to the two sectors, we can write the production functions for consumption and investment goods in terms of its total use of capital and labor, k_{jt} and l_{jt}, and the fraction of resources used in the consumption goods sector, λ_{jt}:

$$c_{jt} = \lambda_{jt} A_t (k_{jt})^m (l_{jt})^n, \tag{8.33}$$

$$i_{jt} = (1 - \lambda_{jt}) B_t (k_{jt})^m (l_{jt})^n. \tag{8.34}$$

We can eliminate λ_{jt} between these equations to write the private production possibilities frontier (the production possibilities available to a single family in the economy):

$$c_{jt} + \frac{A_t}{B_t} i_{jt} = A_t (k_{jt})^m (l_{jt})^n, \tag{8.35}$$

which is linear with slope A_t / B_t.

The private production possibilities frontier describes the trade-off between the production of consumption goods and investment goods faced by a single family. As it transfers resources from the production of consumption goods to investment goods, the jth family will gain A_t / B_t investment goods for every consumption good that it gives up. The fact that the private ppf is linear follows from the assumption that factor intensities are equal in the two sectors.[5]

We can derive a similar relationship for the economy as a whole that we refer to as the social production possibilities frontier. This is obtained by adding up the ppf over all firms and recognizing that in the aggregate, A_t and B_t are determined by equations 8.25 and 8.26. The social analogs of 8.33 and 8.34 are given by

$$c_t = \lambda_t^{1+\theta} k_t^\mu l_t^\nu, \tag{8.36}$$

$$i_t = (1 - \lambda_t)^{1+\theta} k_t^\mu l_t^\nu. \tag{8.37}$$

Once again we can eliminate λ_t between these equations to write the social production possibilities frontier:

$$c_t^{1/(1+\theta)} + i_t^{1/(1+\theta)} = k_t^m l_t^n.$$

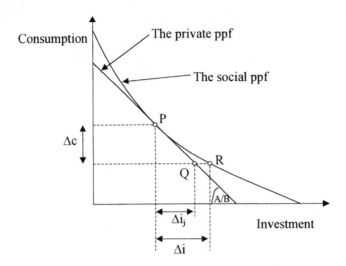

Figure 8.1
Production possibilities frontier

Figure 8.1 illustrates the difference between the private and social production possibilities frontiers. Consider an economy that is producing at point P. Suppose that a single family transfers resources from consumption to investment, reducing its production of consumption goods by Δc, but all other families in the economy keep producing at point P. The private production possibilities frontier indicates that the family will be able to increase its production of investment goods by Δi_j moving from point P to point Q. Now suppose that all families in the economy simultaneously reduce their production of consumption goods by Δc. In this case the social production possibilities frontier indicates that the jth family will be able to increase its production of investment goods by Δi moving from point P to point R. If all families act simultaneously, each family is able to produce more investment goods, for a given reduction in the production of consumption goods, because sector-specific externalities increase the productivity of the investment sector as social resources are transferred into it.

8.4.3 Behavior of the Representative Family

One can describe the behavior of a representative family in the two-sector economy with a maximization problem similar to that of the single-sector economy. Each family maximizes the utility function

$$U_j = \sum_{s=t}^{\infty} E_t \beta^{s-t} \left[\log(c_{jt}) - \frac{l_{jt}^{1+\chi}}{1+\chi} \right]$$

subject to the capital accumulation equation

$$c_{jt} + \frac{A_t}{B_t} [k_{jt+1} - (1-\delta)k_{jt}] \le A_t y_{jt}, \qquad t = 1, \dots \infty, \tag{8.38}$$

and the production function

$$y_{jt} \equiv (k_{jt})^m (l_{jt})^n. \tag{8.39}$$

The first-order conditions for a maximum to this problem include the Euler equation

$$\frac{A_t}{B_t} \frac{1}{c_{jt}} = \beta E_t \left[\frac{1}{c_{jt+1}} \left(\frac{A_t}{B_t} (1-\delta) + m A_t \frac{y_{jt+1}}{k_{jt+1}} \right) \right]. \tag{8.40}$$

This instructs the jth family how to allocate resources between periods and the labor equation

$$n \frac{y_{jt}}{l_{jt}} = c_{jt} l_{jt}^{\chi}, \tag{8.41}$$

instructs it how to allocate its time between work and leisure. Since the production possibilities frontier for the jth family is linear, these equations are identical to the solution to the single-sector model. The difference comes when we recognize the effects of sector specific externalities. By combining equations 8.33 and 8.34 with equations 8.36 and 8.37, we can find expressions for the values of the external effects in each sector in terms of the aggregate variables c_t and i_t:

$$A_t = c_t^{\theta/(1+\theta)},$$

$$B_t = i_t^{\theta/(1+\theta)}.$$

Combining these expressions with the first-order conditions for the individual family, we can find a set of equations that characterize an equilibrium in the two-sector model with sector specific externalities. These equations are laid out below:

$$k_{t+1} = (1-\delta)k_t + i_t, \tag{8.42}$$

$$c_t^{1/(1+\theta)} + i_t^{1/(1+\theta)} = y_t, \tag{8.43}$$

$$y_t = k_t^m l_t^n, \tag{8.44}$$

$$nc_t^{\theta/(1+\theta)} \frac{y_t}{l_t} = c_t l_t^\chi, \tag{8.45}$$

$$\frac{1}{i_t^{\theta/(1+\theta)} c_t^{1/(1+\theta)}} = \beta E_t \left[\frac{1}{i_{t+1}^{\theta/(1+\theta)} c_{t+1}^{1/(1+\theta)}} \left(1 - \delta + mi_{t+1}^{\theta/(1+\theta)} \frac{y_{t+1}}{k_{t+1}} \right) \right]. \tag{8.46}$$

Equation 8.42 is the capital accumulation equation, 8.43 is the social production possibilities frontier, 8.44 is the production function, 8.45 is the first-order condition for the allocation of time between work and leisure, and 8.46 is the Euler equation. Notice that when $\theta = 0$, these equations collapse to the system that describe the single-sector model. For $\theta > 0$, however, the equations reflect the fact that society gains by specializing either in consumption goods or in investment goods. For example, in equation 8.45, the term $c_t^{\theta/(1+\theta)}$ appears in the marginal product of labor, reflecting the fact that there is greater immediate benefit to working (in terms of additional consumption goods) if the economy is producing a product mix that is high in consumption goods.

8.4.4 Indeterminacy and the Two-Sector Model

Benhabib and Farmer investigate the conditions for indeterminacy to arise in the two-sector model when the rate of time preference is set at 0.95 and the shares of capital and labor are set at $m = 0.3$ and $n = 0.7$. For this calibration figure 8.2 indicates the region of the parameter space for which the model admits an indeterminate equilibrium in the continuous time version of the model studied by Benhabib and Farmer. Indeterminacy is more easily obtained when χ is low (labor supply is very elastic) and when θ is large (big sector specific externalities). For very elastic labor supply ($\chi = 0$), the model admits an indeterminate equilibrium when θ is as low as 0.064.

8.4.5 Procyclical Consumption

An obvious question is what are the characteristics of business cycles driven by purely sunspot shocks in the two-sector model? Here the results are less clear than in the one-sector model, since without technology shocks the model predicts that investment and employment will be procyclical but that consumption will be countercyclical. In any optimizing model there will be a first-order condition of the form

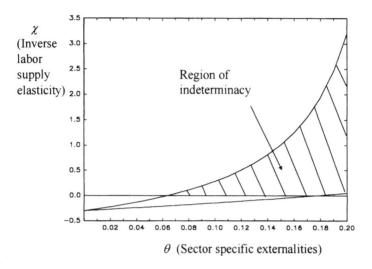

θ (Sector specific externalities)

Figure 8.2
Region of indeterminacy

$$U_c(c,l)MPL(l) = -U_l(c,l),$$

where $MPL(l)$ is the marginal product of labor and $U(c,l)$ is period utility as a function of consumption and labor. Suppose that employment increases spontaneously, as would be the case if "sunspots" were the dominant source of fluctuations. In this case the increase in l would decrease $MPL(l)$ and increase $-U_l(c,l)$, and equality would be restored only if c falls and $U_c(c,l)$ rises. In other words, sunspot fluctuations would cause consumption to be countercyclical. Benhabib and Farmer point out that there are three channels that might break this link.

1. The first possibility is that demand and/or Frisch labor supply curves have nonstandard slopes. If the marginal product of labor, MPL, is increasing in l, which gives an upward-sloping labor demand, or if $-U_l(c,l)$ is decreasing in l, which gives a downward-sloping labor supply, then an increase in l may be associated with an increase in consumption, and the first-order condition for labor could still hold. This is the route followed in one-sector models with strong increasing returns.

2. A second way to reintroduce procyclical consumption follows from work on monopolistic competition such as the papers by Rotemberg and Woodford [95, 96] or Gali [53, 54]. In this setting the relevant variable for

the first-order condition for labor is not *MPL* but *MPL* adjusted for a markup. If the markup is constant, the conclusions that follow from the first-order condition, are unchanged, but if the markup is countercyclical, then procyclical consumption can be rescued.

3. A third possibility is that the model is driven by both technology shocks and sunspots. In this case output may rise sufficiently to allow both investment, and consumption to increase in response to a positive shock, even though labor may move out of the production of consumption goods to the production of investment goods. Indeterminacy would still remain, so that given the capital stock and the realization of the technology shock, investment, and consumption would not be uniquely determined. In other words, even if one thinks that technology shocks provide the impulse to the business cycle, indeterminacy still has a considerable amount to add to the story by providing a plausible explanation of an endogenous propagation mechanism.

8.4.6 Calibrated Two-Sector Model

Benhabib and Farmer calibrate a discrete time version of their model, and they find that indeterminacy obtains under reasonable and standard parametrizations for an economy with mild externalities. They introduce sunspot and technology shocks and study the linearized dynamics around a steady state. In their discrete calibration they set the capital share, m, to 0.35, the labor share, n, to 0.65, the quarterly depreciation rate, δ, to 0.025, the quarterly discount factor, β, to 0.99, and the inverse elasticity of labor supply, χ, to 0, implying linear preferences in leisure. The externality parameter, θ, is set to 0.2 which gives returns to scale of 1.2, quite a bit higher than the value of 1.03 used in Bennett and Farmer but still well within the upper bounds of the recent estimates by Bartlesman, Caballero, and Lyons [11].

Figure 8.3 illustrates series on the deviations of output, consumption and investment from trend that are generated from a parameterized version of their model using the assumption that sunspot shocks and productivity shocks are correlated.

8.5 Concluding Remarks

Indeterminacy and self-fulfilling prophecies has become an important research agenda in the last five years. Early models based on one-sector

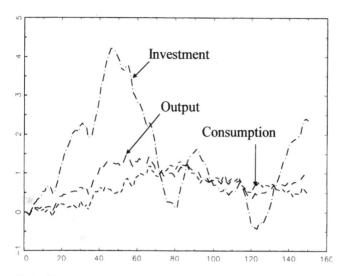

Figure 8.3
Simulated data from a two-sector model

economies with separable preferences require an unrealistically high degree of increasing returns to scale, but a newer generation of models seems more realistic. There are two main avenues that seem promising. One is stimulated by the question, Where does the Solow residual come from? A possible answer to this question is that a multisector model with indeterminate equilibria might have a representation as a one-sector model in which the technology shock absorbs the misspecification error. As agents shift resources between sectors the aggregate technology becomes more or less productive. A second avenue that remains to be explored more carefully is the question, What is the role of indeterminacy and self-fulfilling beliefs in monetary models. This is a topic that we will take up in Chapters 11 and 12.

8.6 Problems

1. Consider the utility function

$$U(C, L) = \frac{\{C \exp[-L^{1+\gamma}/(1+\gamma)]\}^{1-\sigma} - 1}{1 - \sigma}.$$

Prove that as $\sigma \to 1$,

$$U(C, L) \to \ln(C) - \frac{L^{1+\gamma}}{1+\gamma}.$$

2. Consider a two sector model in which

$$C = K_c^a L_c^{1-a}, \quad I = K_I^m L_I^{1-m},$$

where C and I are production of consumption goods and investment goods, $K_C(K_I)$ is usage of capital in the consumption (investment) sector, and $L_c(L_I)$ is use of labor. The economy has one unit of labor and one unit of capital, both inelastically supplied. Assume that the consumption goods sector and the investment goods sector are each competitive. Find an expression for the production possibilities frontier in this economy. (*Hint:* Let λ be the fraction of labor allocated to the consumption goods sector. Find expressions for C and I as functions of λ.) Prove that this frontier is linear if $a = m$.

3. A representative family solves the problem

$$\max U = \sum_{t=1}^{\infty} \beta^t E_t[U(C_t, L_t)]$$

such that

$$K_{t+1} = K_t(1 - \delta) + Y_t - C_t, \quad t = 1, \ldots, \infty, K_1 = \bar{K}_1.$$

$$Y_t = U_t K_t^a ((1+g)^t L_t)^{1-a},$$

$$U_t = U_{t-1}^\lambda e_t, \quad 0 < \lambda < 1,$$

$$E_{t-1}[e_t] = 1, \quad e_t \in [1 - \varepsilon, 1 + \varepsilon],$$

where K_t is capital, L_t is labor supply, C_t is consumption, Y_t is output, and a, g, ρ, and β are parameters. U_t is an autocorrelated productivity shock with autocorrelation parameter λ, and e is an i.i.d. innovation that has mean 1 and small bounded support. The period utility function is the same as in problem 1.

a. Write down a pair of first order conditions for the choice of K_{t+1} and L_t.

b. What is the transversality condition for this model?

c. What is meant by a balanced growth path?

d. Define the variables

$$k_t = \frac{K_t}{(1+g)^t}, \quad y_t = \frac{Y_t}{(1+g)^t}, \quad c_t = \frac{C_t}{(1+g)^t},$$

and show how to write the model and the first order conditions of the representative family in terms of these transformed variables.

e. Set $\{e_t\}_{t=1}^{\infty} = 1$, and provide an algorithm (indicate how you would write computer code) to find the values for the variables k, L, y, and c in a balanced growth path as functions of the parameters.

f. Is the equilibrium of this economy determinate or indeterminate? How do you know?

g. Find the Frisch labor supply curve for this model. Find the constant consumption labor supply curve. Can either or both of these curves slope down? If so, for what parameter values.

4. Adapt the model in problem 3 by allowing for externalities in production. Let θ represent the degree of externalities in production so that

$$Y_t = U_t K_t^{a(1+\theta)}((1+g)^t L_t)^{(1-a)(1+\theta)}.$$

a. Set $\sigma = 0.75$, $\beta = 0.95$, $a = 0.33$, $g = 0$, $\delta = 0.1$, $\gamma = 0$, and solve for the steady state of the nonstochastic model as a function of θ.

b. Define λ_t to be

$$\lambda_t = U_C(C_t, L_t),$$

and find a pair of linear difference equations in $\ln(\lambda_t)$ and $\ln(C_t)$ that characterize equilibria in the neighborhood of the steady state.

c. Write a computer program to calculate the roots of this difference equation for different values of θ. At what value of θ does the equilibrium become indeterminate?

d. Repeat the previous steps when $\sigma = 2$.

9 General Equilibrium Theory and Uncertainty

9.1 Introduction

In this chapter I am going to show how the finite general equilibrium model that was introduced in chapter 4 can be extended to handle uncertainty. This extension is important both for macroeconomics and for the modern theory of finance where it forms the basis for thinking about security pricing.

There are two ways of thinking about the general model under uncertainty. One of these ways is due to Debreu who pointed out in *The Theory of Value* that a commodity could be interpreted in a very broad sense that includes indexation to the state of nature in which it is delivered. The second formulation is due to Arrow who showed how the allocations that arise in a general equilibrium model with contingent commodities could be supported by a set of sequential securities markets. I will look at the relationship between Debreu's formulation and Arrow's formulation, and I will introduce an important concept in the finance literature, that of complete (or incomplete) markets.

9.2 Debreu's Formulation of the Problem

The basic insight of Debreu in chapter 7 of *Theory of Value* is that one can interpret a commodity as indexed by date, location, and state of nature. One can then think of an equilibrium as the outcome of a single market that occurs at the beginning of time in which agents trade commodities for future delivery based on the occurrence of future events. Under this interpretation an example of a commodity might be, apples in New York City on January 3, 1999, *if it rains*.

9.2.1 Preferences under Uncertainty

Simple Example Suppose that there are two dates, 1 and 2, two states of nature, α and β, and l basic commodities at each date. At date 1 agents meet and trade l commodities for delivery at date 1 and $2 \times l$ commodities for delivery at date 2. If $l = 2$, then there are six objects that are traded: apples at date 0, oranges at date 0, apples at date 1 if it is sunny, oranges at date 1 if it is sunny, apples at date 1 if it rains, and oranges at date 1 if it rains.

At date 1 assume that agents meet in a single centralized market and they trade the commodity vectors $x_1, x_2(\alpha)$ and $x_2(\beta)$ where the subscript denotes date of delivery and the index α, β denotes state of nature. Each of these vectors is an element of R_+^l. Under Debreu's formulation of the problem one defines a utility function $U : R_+^{3l} \mapsto R$:

$$U = U(x_1, x_2[\alpha], x_2[\beta]).$$

Debreu places no restrictions on the utility function of the ith agent, U, other than the standard continuity and monotonicity assumptions plus quasi-concavity. He proceeds to define an equilibrium in contingent commodities using the same framework developed for the case of equilibrium under perfect certainty. When date 2 arrives, either state α or state β occurs, and the trades that were contracted in date 1 are executed.

Uncertainty That Resolves through Time   In practice, it has become usual to place a lot more structure on utility functions when one applies general equilibrium theory to problems in which uncertainty evolves through time. For example, suppose that agents live for T periods and at date 1 they contract for a sequence of state-dependent commodities each of which is to be delivered if and only if a particular state of nature occurs. Consider an example in which there is a single commodity in each period, four periods and two states. Figure 9.1 summarizes the way in which uncertainty unfolds.

In each period there are two possible events, α and β. If there is a single commodity in each period, then there will be fifteen commodities in total; one at date 1, two at date 2, four at date 3, and eight at date 4. There are

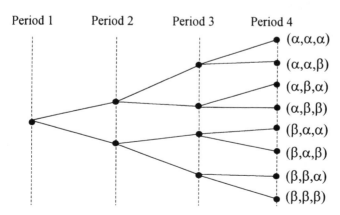

Period 1   Period 2   Period 3   Period 4

(α,α,α)

(α,α,β)

(α,β,α)

(α,β,β)

(β,α,α)

(β,α,β)

(β,β,α)

(β,β,β)

Figure 9.1
Evolution of uncertainty

eight possible states of nature contingent on date 1 information, but commodities may only be indexed by information that is available at the date at which uncertainty is resolved.

One typically places a lot more structure on utilities than that which is implied by continuity assumptions, monotonicity, and quasi-concavity. In particular, it has become common to make strong assumptions about the way in which probabilities enter the utility function. One would expect by a priori reasoning that commodities delivered in states with high probabilities of occurring are likely to be more desirable than commodities for delivery in states with low probabilities. This argument implies that probabilities should be included as arguments of the utility function. The way in which probabilities enter utility has been investigated in great depth in the theory of choice under uncertainty.

In the economics of uncertainty one typically assumes that the function U is linear in probabilities. This assumption can be justified with an axiomatic formulation that was first discussed by von Neumann and Morgenstern who introduced a set of assumptions about the way that rational agents might be expected to rank alternative probability distributions over income. The bottom line of their approach is that under some assumptions, rationality can be equated with the maximization of expected utility.

The original von Neumann-Morgenstern approach did not explicitly consider the evolution of uncertainty through time, and the original axioms were justified by appeals to their reasonableness in the context of timeless gambles. They also did not explicitly consider the possible multidimensional nature of choice. Both of these deficiencies have been rectified in subsequent work by defining utility functions over a space of intertemporal probability distributions. In this extension agents are thought to rank alternative lotteries. Instead of the outcome of a lottery being a single number that represents income, the outcome is a sequence of numbers that represents a stream of consumption commodities through time. This generalization seems quite reasonable, although one must be careful to check that the original axioms make sense when they are interpreted in the broader sense in which time plays a nontrivial role.

An example of one problem that may arise in the intertemporal context is connected with an axiom that is referred to in the literature as the reduction of compound lotteries. This axiom allows one to replace a compound gamble that involves a sequence of coin flips by a simpler gamble in which the same outcomes are achieved by a single randomizing device that delivers the same probability of any particular event. In the context of intertemporal problems, this axiom may not be as reasonable as it first appears, since a sequence of gambles may take place at different points in time. In this context the reduction axiom implies that agents are indifferent to the time at which uncertainty resolves.

As an example of behavior that seems to contradict the reduction axiom, consider the behavior of a couple who choose not to discover the sex of their unborn child in advance. Expected utility theory implies that the couple should wish to discover this information, since there is a planning advantage to knowing the sex of the child (e.g., whether to buy blue or pink diapers). The fact that in practice many couples choose not to know the sex of their unborn child suggests a direct preference for the late resolution of uncertainty, a behavior that is inconsistent with the standard implementation of expected utility theory. An example of an approach that generalizes the assumption of indifference to the timing of the resolution of uncertainty is the recent work by Epstein and Zin [44], Weil [113], and Farmer [45], all of whom build on earlier work by Kreps and Porteus [71] which is described below.

Expected and Nonexpected Utility Theories   The implication of expected utility theory for the theory of choice is that the utility function $U(x_1, x_2[\alpha], x_2[\beta])$ which was introduced in the two-period problem can be written in the form

$$U = \sum_{s=\alpha,\beta} \pi_s u(x_1, x_2[s]),$$

where π_s is the probability that state s will occur. The function u is referred to as a von Neumann-Morgenstern utility function.[1] Expected utility theory has a long history in economics, and it is still the most commonly encountered approach to choice under uncertainty. Expected utility theory is tractable, and it avoids the problem of time consistency, which is one of the major pitfalls that can arise if one abandons the approach.

The time consistency issue arises in Debreu's formulation of utility if one asks the question, Are individuals satisfied with the trades that they have made as uncertainty unfolds through time? If preferences are written in the very general form

$$U = U(x, \pi),$$

then one must recognize that the probabilities that enter utility will change as they are updated with the acquisition of new information. This implies that an agent who maximizes utility at date $s > t$ will face a different objective function from the one that he maximized at date t, and that in general there is no guarantee that the agent will be content with the trades that were negotiated at the earlier date. If the agent's choices *do* coincide at different dates, then his intertemporal preferences are said to be *time consistent*.

The most general form of intertemporal choice under uncertainty that still maintains the expected utility postulate at each date and that imposes an axiom of time consistency is defined by the following recursive structure introduced by Kreps and Porteus [71]:

$$U_t = w(x_t, E_t[U_{t+1}]), \tag{9.1}$$

$$U_T = u_T(x_T). \tag{9.2}$$

The terminal utility function u_T expresses the ith agents preferences for consumption defined over the commodity vector x_T given that all uncertainty has been resolved. Standing at date $T - 1$, one can then evaluate alternative combinations of probability distributions over x_T and certain allocations x_{T-1} using the utility functional U_{T-1}. This functional is defined recursively by combing the expected value of U_T with the allocation x_T using the *aggregator* function w. Von Neumann-Morgenstern preferences on the space of probability distributions over intertemporal consumption sequences are a special case of this recursive structure in which the aggregator function is linear in its second argument.[2] Although Kreps-Porteus agents are expected utility maximizers over one-step-ahead uncertainty, they are *not* expected utility maximizers in the broader sense of the choice of lifetime consumption sequences.

In macroeconomics one typically writes down preferences of the form

$$U_t = \sum_{s=t}^{T} \beta^{s-t} E_t u_s(x_s),$$

which can be derived from the specification in equation 9.1 using the aggregator function $w(x, y) = x + \beta y$.

9.2.2 Budget Constraints

Under Debreu's formulation of the problem of choice, agents trade in a single market and maximize utility subject to a single budget constraint. The prices that agents face incorporate the market assessment of the probability that any particular event will occur.

Suppose that there are T periods, n events, and l basic commodities in each period. The set of events that can be distinguished at any date will then be growing by the power of n in each period. At date 1 there will be l possible commodities that can be traded. At date 2 there will be $n \times l$ commodities (l in each state of nature); at date 3, $n^2 \times l$; and so on. We will need a notation to describe this unfolding of states.

Let the set of *event histories*, H_t, be defined recursively as follows: Let H_1 consist of the singleton event h_i that is known to have occurred, and let H_2 consist of the n possible events $\{s^1, s^2, \ldots, s^n\}$ that could occur in period 2. Denote this set by S and let $H_2 = \{H_1, S\}$. Now let H_t, for $3 \le t \le T$, be defined as $H_t = \{H_{t-1}, S\}$, and let $|H_t|$ be the number of elements in H_t. Using this notation, we may describe the budget constraint faced by the ith agent as follows:

$$p_1 \cdot (\omega_1 - x_1) + \sum_{t=2}^{t=T} \sum_{h_t=1}^{|H_t|} p_{h_t} \cdot (\omega_{h_t} - x_{h_t}) \ge 0, \tag{9.3}$$

where p_{h_t} is the price vector at date t of the bundle of l commodities x_{h_t}. The jth element of this price vector represents the number of units of account that must be given up in date 1 in order to guarantee delivery of commodity j at date t in event history h_t. The notation $\omega_{h_t}(x_{h_t})$ refers to the endowment vector (allocation) of the ith individual at date t in event history h_t.

In order to demonstrate the equivalence of Debreu's formulation of general equilibrium under uncertainty with the sequential markets approach of Arrow, we will need to ensure that preferences are time consistent. We will go a little further than this and assume that agents maximize an expected utility functional that is separable through time. By this assumption, each agent is assumed to solve the problem:

$$\max U = E_1 \sum_{s=1}^{T} u_s(x_s^i) \tag{9.4}$$

such that

$$p_1 \cdot (\omega_1 - x_1) + \sum_{t=2}^{t=T} \sum_{h_t=1}^{|H_t|} p_{h_t} \cdot (\omega_{h_t} - x_{h_t}) \geq 0, \tag{9.5}$$

where the expectation in equation 9.4 is computed by weighting the utility of the consumption bundle in event history h_t by the conditional probability that this history will occur. Given this structure, one can define aggregate excess demand functions that are continuous in the contingent commodity prices and that satisfy all of the assumptions necessary to guarantee existence of an equilibrium by the application of a fixed point argument.

9.3   Arrow's Formulation of the Problem

9.3.1   Trade in Financial Securities

The single-market approach of Debreu is attractive, since it places the theory of choice under uncertainty in the same framework as standard general equilibrium theory with nothing other than a reinterpretation of the basic assumptions and definitions. But it is not a completely satisfactory description of the real world of commerce partly because we do not observe all trade occurring in a single timeless market. Under some assumptions, however, one can show that an alternative set of institutions that is more in keeping with the real world is capable of replicating the allocations that occur in the contingent commodity equilibrium of Debreu.

The idea, originally due to Arrow [4], is that a sequence of securities markets may economize on information by reducing the number of objects that need to be traded. In the Debreu market there is an enormous amount of redundant trade, since most of the branches of the event tree will never occur. Arrow's idea was that agents need not worry about these future events, since the same allocations that occur in a Debreu equilibrium can be replicated by a sequence of trades in financial assets.

Since the appearance of Arrow's paper a number of different approaches have been followed in the literature on trade in sequences of financial markets. We are going to pick just one approach in which a security is defined as a vector b of which the jth element of b represents the number of units of account that will be received by the holder of the security if state j occurs.[3] For example, money is the security with the payoff vector:

$$b = \begin{bmatrix} 1 \\ 1 \\ \vdots \\ 1 \end{bmatrix}.$$

If we call the unit of account a dollar then this security pays off one dollar next period in every state of nature.

Suppose that there are two periods (1 and 2), two states of nature (α and β) and two commodities. Assume that agents have von Neumann-Morgenstern utility functions

$$U = \sum_{s=\alpha,\beta} \pi_s u(x_1, x_2[s]). \tag{9.6}$$

In Arrow's formulation of this problem there are two markets, one at date 1 and one at date 2. In the market at date 1 the ith agent faces the following budget constraint:

$$p_1 \cdot (\omega_1 - x_1) - \sum_{j=1}^{j=K} q^j y^j \geq 0. \tag{9.7}$$

The term q^j is the price and y^j is the quantity demanded or supplied of the jth security. We assume that there are K securities and we allow the agent to choose y^j to be positive or negative. If y^j is negative, then the agent is said to *short sell* security j.

In period 2 we assume that uncertainty is resolved and the agent faces one of two possibilities. His trading opportunities in period 2 will depend on the trades that he made in period 1, since each of the K securities may pay off different amounts in different states. There will therefore be a different budget constraint in each state of nature:

$$p_2[1] \cdot (\omega_2[1] - x_2[1]) + \sum_{j=1}^{K} y^j b^j[1] \geq 0, \tag{9.8}$$

$$p_2[1] \cdot (\omega_2[2] - x_2[2]) + \sum_{j=1}^{K} y^j b^j[2] \geq 0. \tag{9.9}$$

The term $b^j(s)$ represents the dollar payoff of security j in state s. In an economy with n states and two periods, there will be n budget constraints in period two, but only one of them will be relevant ex post.

9.3.2   Complete and Incomplete Markets

One may define a *payoff* matrix, B, for the securities that takes the form

$$B = \begin{bmatrix} b^1(1) & \cdots & b^K(1) \\ \vdots & \ddots & \vdots \\ b^1(n) & \cdots & b^K(n) \end{bmatrix}.$$

The payoff matrix is an array of numbers that is primitive to the economy. It serves to define the *market structure*. An important example of a market structure is the case originally defined by Arrow in which there exists a set of n securities with the payoff matrix

$$\begin{bmatrix} 1 & \cdots & 0 \\ \vdots & \ddots & \vdots \\ 0 & \cdots & 1 \end{bmatrix}.$$

In this case the securities have become known as "Arrow securities." The jth Arrow Security pays off one unit of account if state j occurs, and nothing otherwise. If a general payoff matrix B has full row rank, then the economy is said to possess *complete markets*. The case of a complete set of Arrow securities is a special case of market completeness. More generally, complete markets requires that there be at least as many securities as states of nature. But this is not enough. It must also be possible for the consumer to transfer income between states by trading in securities. If, for example, there are as many securities as states of nature, but the payoff matrix is singular, the market structure is said to be incomplete. In this case at least one security is redundant in the sense that its payoff matrix can be replicated by buying or selling a linear combination of the remaining ones.

The importance of a complete market structure is that it allows one to write the sequential choice problem of the individual in the form of a constrained maximization problem subject to a *single* budget constraint. This is most easily demonstrated by example. Let there be two states of nature, two commodities, two periods, and two Arrow securities. In this case the sequential budget constraints are of the form

$$p_1 \cdot (\omega_1 - x_1) + q^1 y^1 + q^2 y^2 \geq 0 \tag{9.10}$$

in period 1, and

$$p_2[1] \cdot (\omega_2[1] - x_2[1]) + y^1[1] \geq 0, \tag{9.11}$$

$$p_2[2] \cdot (\omega_2[2] - x_2[2]) + y^2[2] \geq 0, \tag{9.12}$$

in period 2. By substituting for y^1 and y^2 from inequalities 9.11 and 9.12 into inequality 9.10, one obtains the following single life cycle constraint:

$$p_1 \cdot (\omega_1 - x_1) + q^1 p_2[1] \cdot (\omega_2[1] - x_2[1]) + q^2 p_2[2] \cdot (\omega_2[2] - x_2[2]) \geq 0. \tag{9.13}$$

The monotonicity of the objective function implies that the inequalities 9.11 and 9.12 will hold with equality at an optimum which serves to define the composition of the agent's portfolio $\{y^1, y^2\}$ between the two securities.

The equivalence of Arrow's formulation of the problem and Debreu's formulation follows from two facts. (1) If agents have von Neumann-Morgenstern utilities then their choices will be time consistent. (2) If markets are complete, then the budgets sets are equivalent under the two alternative formulations, and the Debreu contingent commodities prices are equal to the Arrow spot prices weighted by the price in period 1 of the appropriate Arrow security.

Arrow's formulation has spurred a vast literature in financial economics in which it forms the basis for thinking about the pricing of securities. In this literature one typically assumes that the market structure is complete, and one proceeds to calculate the value of an arbitrary security as a linear combination of the prices of some basis of fundamental securities that spans the space of payoffs. For example, suppose that there are three states. In state 1 the firm is bankrupt and has zero value. In states 2 and 3 it is solvent. Debt is then the security with the payoff vector

$$b = \begin{bmatrix} 0 \\ 1 \\ 1 \end{bmatrix}.$$

This security could be constructed from a set of three Arrow securities by holding equal amounts of securities 2 and 3 and none of security 1.

9.3.3   Multiple Budget Constraints and Incomplete Markets

Cass and Shell [33] have drawn an important distinction between incomplete markets and *incomplete participation* in markets. This distinction arises naturally in overlapping generations economies in which in agents are unable to trade in securities markets that open before they are born. Under the Cass-Shell definitions, markets are incomplete if the payoff matrix B has less than full row rank (a special case is when there are fewer Arrow securities than states of nature), and incomplete participation occurs if some agents are barred from trading in the securities markets. In this book we will be more concerned with the case of incomplete participation, although, for the sake of completeness, we briefly describe the research agenda that has evolved in the area of incomplete markets.

The starting point of the incomplete markets literature is the idea that it may be costly to set up a market. For this reason one starts with the assumption that the payoff matrix B may have less than full row rank, and one proceeds to examine the implications of this assumption for general equilibrium theory. The main results in the literature center around the possible nonexistence of equilibrium, the nonoptimality of equilibrium, and the dimension of the equilibrium manifold. This last point refers to the fact that there may be a high-dimensional manifold of equilibria in models with incomplete markets. Roughly speaking, this multiplicity arises because, in an economy with incomplete markets, agents face multiple budget constraints.

Consider the two-state, two-period example with one or more commodities in each period. With a complete set of securities the problem faced by an individual in this economy has the following structure:

$$\max_{y^{\alpha}, y^{\beta}, x(\alpha), x(\beta)} \sum_{s=\alpha,\beta} \pi_s u(x_1, x_2[s]) \tag{9.14}$$

such that

$$p_1 \cdot (\omega_1 - x_1) - q^{\alpha} y^{\alpha} - q^{\beta} y^{\beta} \geq 0, \tag{9.15}$$

$$p_2[\alpha] \cdot (\omega_2[\alpha] - x_2[\alpha]) + y^{\alpha} \geq 0, \tag{9.16}$$

$$p_2[\beta] \cdot (\omega_2[\beta] - x_2[\beta]) + y^{\beta} \geq 0. \tag{9.17}$$

These multiple constraints may be combined to yield

$$p_1 \cdot (\omega_1 - x_1) + q^\alpha p_2[\alpha] \cdot (\omega_2[\alpha] - x_2[\alpha]) + q^\beta p_2[\beta] \cdot [\omega_2[\beta] - x_2[\beta]) \geq 0.$$
$$(9.18)$$

In the case of incomplete markets things are different. Suppose that there is a single security that pays off one unit of account in each state. In this case the budget constraints take the form

$$p_1 \cdot (\omega_1 - x_1) - qy \geq 0, \tag{9.19}$$

$$p_2[\alpha] \cdot (\omega_2[\alpha] - x_2[\alpha]) + y \geq 0, \tag{9.20}$$

$$p_2[\beta] \cdot [\omega_2[\beta] - x_2[\beta]) + y \geq 0, \tag{9.21}$$

where y is the quantity purchased (or sold) of the single security and q is its price. In this case one can no longer substitute the two constraints from period 2 back into the single constraint in period 1, since there are not enough securities to transfer income between states. It is, however, possible to reduce the number of constraints from three to two by using equation 9.19 to eliminate y from 9.20 and 9.21. When there is one security and two states the agent faces two independent constraints of the form

$$p_1 \cdot (\omega_1 - x_1) + p_2[\alpha] \cdot (\omega_2[\alpha] - x_2[\alpha]) \geq 0, \tag{9.22}$$

$$p_1 \cdot (\omega_1 - x_1) + p_2[\beta] \cdot (\omega_2[\beta] - x_2[\beta]) \geq 0. \tag{9.23}$$

In standard general equilibrium theory in which demand functions are derived from utility maximization subject to a single constraint, there is a dependency that arises among the demand equations that arises from the Walras law of markets. In models in which the market structure is artificially restricted, there will as many dependencies as budget constraints; that is, there are multiple versions of Walras's law. The upshot of all of this is that there are not enough independent equations to determine prices and in economies with incomplete markets there may be many equilibria.[4]

9.4 Infinite Horizon Economies with Uncertainty

9.4.1 Asset Pricing in Lucas Tree Economies

The main application of general equilibrium theory and uncertainty to macroeconomics has taken place in the context of simple representative

agent economies in which choice is typically represented in the context of
sequential markets. One of the most influential papers in this field is the
work of Lucas [76] on asset pricing. The economy studied by Lucas is
populated by a large number of identical agents each of whom maximizes
expected utility

$$\max U = \sum_{t=1} E_1 \beta^{t-1} u(c_t), \tag{9.24}$$

where c_t is consumption, β is the discount factor, and E_1 is the expectation
operator conditional on date 1 information. Output in the economy consists entirely of fruit that falls effortlessly from a stock of trees which is
fixed in number. These trees cannot be reproduced, and each tree yields a
stochastic dividend stream of the perishable consumption commodity in
each period. Agents know the probability distribution of the dividend
stream; their economic activity in each period consists of trading shares
where a share represents a claim to the future stream of dividends.

   To fit this structure into the general equilibrium framework, we will
assume that the dividend stream takes realizations in each period that are
elements of a finite set

$$d_t \in \{d_1, d_2, \ldots, d_s, \ldots, d_n\}$$

and that state s occurs with probability π_s. In every period the consumer
faces a budget constraint of the form

$$S_t P_t = S_{t-1} P_t + d_t S_{t-1} - c_t, \tag{9.25}$$

where S_t is the number of shares that he buys in period t, P_t is the price of
shares in terms of the consumption commodity, and d_t is the dividend per
share that pays off on shares acquired in period $t - 1$.

   Asset pricing papers that use this model typically make a further assumption: that the market structure is complete. In economies with many
agents each of whom has different attitudes toward risk, the complete
markets assumption would require one to specify a complete set of
securities. These could be Arrow securities, or they could be some other
set of more complicated securities as long as the payoff matrix has full
rank. By assuming that there is a single type of agent, however, one is able
to considerably simplify this problem, since by assumption there is no
other agent in the economy with whom to trade insurance. In this chapter
I will show how to introduce a complete set of securities, since this is the

general case, and then I will proceed to illustrate how the representative agent assumption is used to simplify security pricing.

9.4.2 Digression on Market Structure

In this section we will look at the machinery that is necessary to describe equilibrium in an Arrow-Debreu economy with uncertainty when there are heterogeneous agents. Since this gets rather notation intensive, the reader might want to skip ahead to section 9.4.3 and return to this section on later reading.

Since the horizon of the economy is infinite, the model will have an infinite number of states. As in the finite model the number of state-dependent commodities in every period is growing with the power of n, the number of primitive states. In order to complete the market structure, however, agents do not need to trade an infinite number of securities in every period. As with the finite economy, we may define the set of *event histories* as follows:

$$S = \{s_1, \ldots, s_n\},$$

$$H_2 = S,$$

$$H_t = \{H_{t-1}, S\}, \qquad t = 3, \ldots, \infty.$$

The set of histories H_1 is the singleton $\{i\}$ where i is the known event that occurred. Consider the following set of constraints faced by a representative agent in an endowment economy with a complete set of Arrow securities and l commodities in every period:

$$\sum_{j=1}^{n} q_{h_t}^j y_{h_t}^j \le y_{h_{t-1}}^i + p_{h_t} \cdot [\omega_{h_t} - c_{h_t}], \qquad i = 1, \ldots, n, t = 1, \ldots, \infty. \quad (9.26)$$

The term $y_{h_t}^j$ represents the quantity of Arrow security j that the agent purchases in event history h_t. At every date there are n possible budget constraints, one for each primitive state. The constraint that occurs in state i allows the agent allocate his wealth between consumption and saving where wealth consists of his endowment ω_{h_t} plus $y_{h_{t-1}}^i$, the payoff at date t from his holdings of security i which may be positive or negative. His savings are represented by a portfolio of n Arrow securities where the jth security will payoff one unit of account in period $t+1$ if and only if state j occurs. Notice that since event history $h_t \equiv \{h_{t-1}, i\}$, the agents allocation and his endowment as well as market prices may also fluctuate across realizations of the primitive state at date t even though we do not explicitly index these variables by i.

The consumer who makes plans at date t must take account of the actions that he expects to take in all future periods. In particular, he must put aside sufficient financial resources to meet his needs in all possible future event histories. Just as with the infinite economy under certainty, it is possible to define a set of present value prices that represents relative prices in event history h_τ expressed in period 1 units of account. More explicitly define

$$Q_{h_1}^{h_1} \equiv p_{h_1}, \tag{9.27}$$

$$Q_{h_1}^{h_s} \equiv p_{h_s} \prod_{v=2}^{s} q_{h_{v-1}}^{h_v}, \qquad s \geq 2. \tag{9.28}$$

The notation $q_{h_{v-1}}^{h_v}$ refers to the price of a one-step-ahead security that is purchased at date $v-1$ in history h_{v-1} and that pays off one unit of account at date v if event history h_v occurs, and nothing otherwise. There are exactly n of these securities issued in each date v, since every event history h_v has n possible continuations in period $v+1$.

Using this notation, we can consolidate the budget constraints from periods 1 to τ for all possible histories:

$$\sum_{t=1}^{\tau} \sum_{h_t=1}^{|H_t|} Q_{h_1}^{h_t} \cdot (\omega_{h_t} - x_{h_t}) - \sum_{h_{\tau+1}=1}^{|H_{\tau+1}|} Q_{h_1}^{h_{\tau+1}} y^{h_{\tau+1}} \geq 0. \tag{9.29}$$

Notice that the number of commodities per period is equal to $|H_t|$ which is growing by a multiple of n each period.

In order to complete the reduction of the set of constraints to a single life cycle constraint, one must be able to restrict the ability of the consumer to borrow. Sometimes the following assumption is referred to as "no Ponzi schemes" in reference to the case of a banker from Boston who used new deposits to keep paying off depositors while he absconded with the bulk of the bank's assets. In the absence of such an assumption, individuals would be able to borrow infinite amounts against the future and never pay off their debts:

ASSUMPTION 9.1

$$\lim_{\tau \to \infty} \sum_{h_{\tau+1}=1}^{|H_{\tau+1}|} Q_{h_\tau}^{h_{\tau+1}} y^{h_{\tau+1}} \geq 0.$$ (9.30)

We also need a condition that restricts the domain on which prices are defined in order for the infinite horizon problem to have a well defined solution:

ASSUMPTION 9.2

$$\lim_{\tau \to \infty} \sum_{t=1}^{\tau} \sum_{h_t=1}^{|H_t|} Q_{h_1}^{h_t} \cdot \omega_{h_t} < \infty.$$ (9.31)

When there is no uncertainty, the price of a one-step-ahead security is the inverse of the gross rate of return on a one period bond. In this special case the restriction 9.31 amounts (roughly speaking) to the assumption that interest rates are greater than the rate of endowment growth, and it is a sufficient condition to guarantee that wealth is finite.

Assumptions 9.30 and 9.31 allow one to write the sequence of budget constraints 9.26 by a single life cycle budget constraint and to describe the agent's problem in the following terms:

$$\max U = E_1 \sum_{t=1}^{\infty} \beta^{t-1} u(c_t)$$ (9.32)

such that

$$\sum_{t=1}^{\infty} \sum_{h_t=1}^{|H_t|} Q_{h_1}^{h_t} \cdot (\omega_{h_t} - x_{h_t}) \geq 0.$$ (9.33)

This problem is identical to the problem under certainty that we studied in chapter 5 with the difference that the set of commodities is growing through time. As with the simpler problem under certainty, the agent's holdings of securities are defined by the fact that the period by period constraints must hold with equality at an optimum.

9.4.3   Asset Pricing in the Representative Agent Case

Most of the literature on macroeconomics and asset pricing does not concern itself with Arrow securities or life cycle budget constraints.

Instead, the agent's problem is typically represented in the following way:

$$\max U = \sum_{s=t} E_t \beta^{s-t} u(c_s) \tag{9.34}$$

such that

$$S_t P_t = S_{t-1} P_t + d_t S_{t-1} - c_t. \tag{9.35}$$

This looks a lot like a problem with incomplete markets, since the agent is assumed to be able to buy and sell a single security, the tree. In the representative agent economy, however, the specification of alternative assets becomes irrelevant, since these securities must necessarily remain in zero net supply in equilibrium. Suppose that we augment the consumer's budget constraint by allowing him to buy or sell some asset A that pays off $X_{t+1} A_t$ of the consumption commodity at date $t+1$ and costs q_t units of the consumption commodity at date t:

$$A_t q_t + S_t P_t = S_{t-1} P_t + X_t A_{t-1} + d_t S_{t-1} - c_t. \tag{9.36}$$

Here X_{t+1} is a random variable, and q_t represents its price. Pricing the assets A and S means that we must compute the sequence $\{q_t\}$ and $\{P_t\}$ that would hold in equilibrium.

Using the budget constraint at each period to express utilities in terms of asset portfolios, the objective function becomes

$$\max U = \sum_{s=t}^{\infty} E_t \beta^{s-t} u(S_{s-1} P_s + A_{s-1} + d_s S_{s-1} - A_s q_s + S_s P_s), \tag{9.37}$$

and the optimal quantities of the assets A and S must obey the first-order conditions

$$q_t u'(c_t) = \beta E_t [X_{t+1} u'(c_{t+1})], \tag{9.38}$$

$$P_t u'(c_t) = \beta E_t [(P_{t+1} + d_{t+1}) u'(c_{t+1})]. \tag{9.39}$$

In a complete markets economy with many agents, one would proceed to substitute the first-order conditions for the infinite sequence of assets holdings back into the life cycle budget constraint to arrive at a set of excess demand equations as functions of the Arrow-Debreu prices. These equations could then be aggregated across agents and set equal to zero to find an equilibrium price sequence.

In a representative agent economy matters are much simpler, since in equilibrium the consumption stream of the representative agent must equal the dividend stream of the tree. Since this dividend stream is assumed to have a known stochastic structure, the asset price P_t can be computed by iterating the functional equation

$$P_t = E_t \left[\beta \frac{(P_{t+1} + d_{t+1}) u'(d_{t+1})}{u'(d_t)} \right] \tag{9.40}$$

into the future. This procedure leads to the well-known result that the stock price of the firm is equal to the expected net present value of its expected future stream of dividends.

The process can also be applied to the arbitrary asset A, since

$$q_t = E_t \left[\beta \frac{X_{t+1} u'(d_{t+1})}{u'(d_t)} \right]. \tag{9.41}$$

It follows that an arbitrary random variable is priced according to it's covariance with the representative agent's marginal utility of consumption. This procedure also explains why, in the case of a representative agent, one does not need to specify a complete set of asset markets. Since the assets are necessarily in zero net supply, the relevant first-order conditions do nothing other than determine the price of the security that is just sufficient to cause the agent to want neither to buy nor to sell. In the case of heterogeneous agents, the procedure breaks down because the agent's consumption is no longer equal to the exogenous dividend: there may be insurance trades across agents.

9.5 Concluding Remarks

The basic point of this chapter has been to demonstrate how uncertainty can be incorporated into the general equilibrium framework. It has also introduced the idea of market completeness and provided a simple application of general equilibrium theory to the case of asset pricing.

Most of the applications of uncertainty to macroeconomics have taken place in the context of complete markets, and they have been conducted under the assumption of a representative agent. The kinds of results that one generates in this context are close analogues of the results of finite general equilibrium theory. The equilibria are finite in number, and they are generically determinate. This follows directly by the same argument that was used in chapter 5. I will be concerned with these results because they form an important benchmark, but as with the case of general equilibrium theory under certainty, I do not believe that the results of the benchmark case are useful descriptions of the world in which we live.

The same kinds of departures from the basic model that I applied to the certainty case can also be shown to hold in economies with uncertainty. For example, by introducing an infinite set of agents *and* an infinite set of commodities, one can demonstrate that equilibria may no longer be determinate. They may also not be Pareto optimal, since interest rates may be "too low." There is also another more interesting class of suboptimalities that can occur in stochastic economies, and it is this class that we shall be concerned with in the following chapter. Basically the idea is that fluctuations in economic activity may arise as a result of waves of pessimism or optimism on the part of economic agents. Since agents would generally prefer to smooth their consumption streams, these paths will not be Pareto optimal, and the theory of why they occur offers the potential of forming the foundation for a theory of stabilization policy.

9.6 Problems

1. What is meant by the present value price of a state-dependent commodity?

2. A model has two periods and three states of nature in period 2. There exist three securities with payoff matrix

$$\begin{bmatrix} 1 & 2 & 3 \\ 1 & 1 & 1 \\ 3 & 5 & 7 \end{bmatrix}$$

where rows denote states and columns denote securities.

a. Are markets complete or incomplete?

b. Suppose instead that the payoff matrix is given by

$$\begin{bmatrix} 1 & 2 & 3 \\ 1 & 1 & 1 \\ 0.5 & 1 & 1.5 \end{bmatrix}.$$

Are markets complete or incomplete? Explain.

3. What assumptions are required for Arrow's formulation of equilibrium with uncertainty to be equivalent to Debreu's formulation?

4. Suppose that households live for n periods. In each period the household maximizes the utility function

$$U = E_s \left[\left(\sum_{t=s}^{n} c_t^\lambda \right)^{1/\lambda} \right], \qquad s = 1, \ldots, n-1.$$

a. Prove that unless $\lambda = 1$, the household's plans for consumption at future dates will be different for different values of s.

b. Would Debreu's and Arrow's formulation of equilibrium be the same if agents maximized a utility function of this form? Explain your answer.

5. Suppose that a person lives for 70 years and that there are two basic events in each year of his life. Assume that in the period of his birth, this person trades complete contingent commodities and that there is a single commodity in each period of life, indexed to the state of nature. How many contingent commodities will enter his utility function?

6. Consider a model with three periods and two states in periods 2 and 3. If Z_t^i is the price at date t of a security that pays one dollar at period $t+1$, if state i occurs, find an expression for the relative price of a period 1 dollar and a period 3 dollar (delivered for sure) in terms of the sequence of securities prices $\{Z_1^1, Z_1^2, Z_2^1, Z_2^2\}$.

10 Sunspots

10.1 Introduction

In the 1970s macroeconomics underwent a revolution in the treatment of expectations. In the context of general equilibrium theory under uncertainty, this revolution amounted to the assumption that agents know the value of the Arrow-Debreu prices that will prevail in all future states of nature. The combination of the market-clearing assumption with rational expectations has become known as the rational expectations approach to macroeconomics. What it amounts to is the wholesale adoption of the Arrow-Debreu program as a research agenda for macroeconomics.

When rational expectations was introduced into economics, it was seen as a way of endogenizing beliefs. If one identifies the state of nature with a particular *fundamental* configuration of preferences, endowments, and technology and if prices are determined in an Arrow-Debreu equilibrium, then rational expectations would seem to suggest that beliefs must be pinned down by fundamentals. If this were true, then there could be no role in general equilibrium models for the view of business cycles that became popular after the publication of Keynes's *General Theory* in which the pessimistic beliefs of investors may itself depress the level of economic activity.

In this chapter we are going to describe two strands of literature that explore the implications of the idea that extraneous beliefs may influence economic activity. The first strand evolved from an important paper by David Cass and Karl Shell [33], and it spawned a large and growing literature in the microeconomics of general equilibrium theory. The second strand evolved from a paper by Costas Azariadis [7], and it has generated an equally large literature that applies the sunspot idea to macroeconomics.

The basic idea of the Cass-Shell paper is that small departures from the Arrow-Debreu assumptions can lead to economies in which equilibria may display the property that agents' allocations are different across different states of nature, *even though nothing fundamental has changed.* Cass and Shell refer to an equilibrium with this property as an equilibrium where *sunspots matter*.[1] In the context of the applied general equilibrium program as a research agenda for macroeconomics, the sunspot theorem of Cass and Shell has profound implications, since it permits the possibility that sunspots ("animal spirits" in Keynes's words) are quite consistent with the existence of a rational expectations equilibrium. This in turn has implications for welfare: If agents are risk averse, then they would prefer to eliminate fluctuations, and sunspot equilibria may, in some environments, be eliminated by the correct design of government policies.

10.2   Do Sunspots Matter?

10.2.1   Complete and Incomplete Participation

In this section we are going to describe the structure of a simple example that formed the basis for Cass and Shell's paper, "Do Sunspots Matter?" This example serves to introduce the basic concepts and to allow us to describe a second type of failure of the welfare theorems that can occur in overlapping generations economies in addition to the failure that occurs in deterministic models as a result of inefficient growth paths.

The idea of sunspots hinges on the distinction between *intrinsic* and *extrinsic* uncertainty. Intrinsic uncertainty is anything that affects preferences, endowments, or technologies. Extrinsic uncertainty is anything that doesn't. For example, if there are two states of nature that differ because in one state technology is more productive than in the other, then that is referred to as intrinsic uncertainty. If, on the other hand, the two states differ because in one state the unit of account is called a dollar and the other it is called a zloty, then that is referred to as extrinsic uncertainty.

A second important distinction is between economies in which there is *complete participation* and economies in which there is *incomplete participation*. To see this distinction more carefully, take a look at figure 10.1 which describes the timing of events. The Cass-Shell economy is a simple two-period world in which some of the agents (G_1) are born in period 1 and some of them (G_2) are born in period 2. All uncertainty is resolved *between* the two periods. Since generation 2 households are unable to

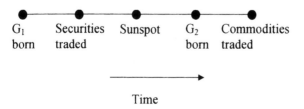

Figure 10.1
Timing of events

participate in the insurance market that opens before they are born, this is a structure in which incompleteness arises very naturally as a result of the timing of births and deaths. Cass and Shell refer to this as incomplete participation.[2]

10.2.2 Setting up the Environment

We will look at a formulation of the environment in which agents trade contingent commodities (the Debreu formulation), although one may equally well formulate the model as one in which agents trade a complete set of Arrow securities. Cass and Shell use both approaches and show that they are equivalent. The securities market model is more realistic in the sense that we observe empirical analogs of financial securities. The contingent commodities formulation is useful, however, since it is closer to standard general equilibrium theory.

Although there are two dates, we will only allow commodities at date 2. Define the following two vectors of contingent commodities:

$$x_h(\alpha) = \{x_h^1(\alpha), x_h^2(\alpha)\},$$

$$x_h(\beta) = \{x_h^1(\beta), x_h^2(\beta)\}.$$

The superscript refers to commodity, the subscript indexes households, and there are two states of nature, α and β. The notation $x_h^i(s)$ refers to the consumption of commodity i by household h in state s.

If one interprets the model as one in which trade is accomplished through the institution of securities markets, then the sequence of events is as follows: First a securities market opens, and agents in generation 1 trade securities that are contingent on the realization of a sunspot. The assumption of complete markets requires that there be exactly two Arrow securities, one that pays off one unit of account if state α occurs and one that pays off one unit of account if state β occurs. When the securities market closes, all of the uncertainty in the model is resolved and agents find out whether the sunspot has, or has not, occurred. Finally, generation 2 is born and trades take place in commodities.

In the contingent commodities interpretation of the model the initial market is one in which agents trade claims to the four distinct commodities: $\{x_\alpha^1, x_\alpha^2, x_\beta^1, x_\beta^2\}$. Generation 2 may be present in this contingent commodities market, but it is not allowed to trade across states of nature. This second representation is fictitious in the sense that we are allowing agents to be present in a market that opens in meta-time and we are representing the generational structure by restrictions on the trades that agents are able to make.

The following equations describe the problem that is solved by a member of generation 1 in the contingent commodities market:

$$\max U = \sum_{s=\alpha,\beta} \pi_s u_h(x_h(s)), \qquad h \in G_1, \tag{10.1}$$

such that

$$p \cdot x_h \leq p \cdot \omega_h, \tag{10.2}$$

where

$$x_h = \{x_h^1(\alpha), x_h^2(\alpha), x_h^1(\beta), x_h^2(\beta)\},$$

is the 4 vector that describes the allocation of individual h and

$$p = \{p^1(\alpha), p^2(\alpha), p^1(\beta), p^2(\beta)\},$$

is the 4 vector of contingent commodities prices.

The market participation restriction is captured by requiring that a household that is a member of generation 2 should face two distinct problems:

$$\max U = u_h(x_h(\alpha)), \qquad h \in G_2, \tag{10.3}$$

such that

$$p(\alpha) \cdot x_h(\alpha) \leq p(\alpha) \cdot \omega_h(\alpha) \tag{10.4}$$

if state α occurs, and

$$\max U = u_h(x_h(\beta)), \qquad h \in G_2, \tag{10.5}$$

such that

$$p(\beta) \cdot x_h(\beta) \leq p(\beta) \cdot \omega_h(\beta) \tag{10.6}$$

if state β occurs.[3] The notation $x_h(i)$ for $i = \{\alpha, \beta\}$ represents the two-vector $\{x_h^1(i), x_h^2(i)\}$, and $p(i)$ is the corresponding two vector of commodities prices in state i.

Cass and Shell impose standard restrictions on the utility functions u_h: In particular, they assume that u_h, the von Neumann-Morgenstern utility, is strictly concave. This assumption means that agents would strictly prefer a smooth consumption profile across states of nature from one that fluctuates but has the same mean. In a standard model of uncertainty, an equilibrium will typically be associated with some fluctuation of realized utilities across states of nature, since there will be a certain amount of undiversifiable risk that stems from the existence of intrinsic uncertainty. For example, the endowments ω_h may differ across states in a systematic way across households. The following assumption rules out this possibility:

ASSUMPTION 10.1   *All uncertainty is extrinsic; that is,*

$$\omega_h(\alpha) = \omega_h(\beta)$$

for $h \in G_1 \cup G_2$.

Since we have not allowed for the possibility that utility functions may be different across states, all intrinsic uncertainty in the economy must be captured by endowment fluctuations. By explicitly ruling out endowment uncertainty, we are setting up a very stark example of an economy in which any fluctuations that arise must be attributed to some other source. This suggests the following definition:

DEFINITION 10.1   *Sunspots matter if there is an equilibrium in which*

$$x_h(\alpha) \neq x_h(\beta).$$

10.2.3   Sunspot Theorems

Description of the Main Idea   Given the definition of sunspots, Cass and Shell go on to demonstrate three basic results.

PROPOSITION 10.1   *If $G_2 \equiv \varnothing$, (unrestricted participation), then sunspots do not matter.*

PROPOSITION 10.2   *Sunspot equilibria are Pareto inefficient.*

PROPOSITION 10.3   *If $G_2 \neq \varnothing$, there may exist equilibria in which sunspots matter.*

The first two of these propositions rest on the fact that if there is unrestricted participation, the economy is a standard, finite, Arrow-Debreu economy. Since agents are assumed to be risk averse, they would strictly prefer to receive the mean of $x_h(\alpha)$ and $x_h(\beta)$ in both states to the random allocation $x_h(\alpha)$ with probability π_α and $x_h(\beta)$ with probability π_β. Since there is no intrinsic uncertainty, the safe allocation is attainable. The sunspot allocation cannot therefore be Pareto optimal. It follows directly from the first welfare theorem that the sunspot allocation cannot be a competitive equilibrium; that is; sunspots do not matter.

The third proposition is demonstrated by constructing an example in which the economy with complete participation has three equilibria. Which equilibrium prevails is not explained in the context of standard general equilibrium theory, but whichever equilibrium is observed will necessarily have equal allocations across states in light of propositions 10.1 and 10.2.

When there is incomplete participation, then another set of possibilities arises. It becomes possible to construct an equilibrium in which the allocations across alternative states are different by randomizing across the allocations of the separate equilibria in the complete participation case. These randomized allocations cannot be ruled out by the Pareto criterion because some of the agents who would benefit from a reallocation are unable to participate in the insurance market. We will construct a specific example of an economy in which sunspots matter in the next section. The main implication of the proposition is that the idea of animal spirits is entirely consistent with the assumptions of rational expectations and market clearing.

Connection between Sunspots and Determinacy   In the earlier chapters we emphasized the idea that general equilibrium models often have indeterminate equilibria. Although there is no direct connection between indeterminacy and sunspots, it turns out that, in practice, models with indeterminate steady states are good examples of economies in which sunspots matter. The reason follows from the method that Cass and Shell use to construct a sunspot equilibrium; that is, they randomize over the equilibria of an economy in which there exist multiple equilibria if all agents are allowed to participate in the insurance market. It turns out, in practice, that models with indeterminate equilibria also have many sunspot equilibria for the reason that there are now many equilibria over which one can conduct this randomization exercise.

The first paper to study sunspots in a macroeconomic model is due to Azariadis [7] who used a simple overlapping generations model to demonstrate the existence of equilibria indexed by beliefs. Azariadis and Guesnerie went on to show that in this simple model there is a connection between sunspots and cycles in the sense that beliefs can matter if and only if there is an equilibrium with an endogenous cycle. The Azariadis example spawned a number of subsequent papers which explored alternative models, and in the following section we are going to look at one such model where sunspots matter. Our example exploits the existence of an indeterminate steady state to construct an economy where so-called animal spirits can cause independent fluctuations in employment.

10.3 Example of a Macroeconomic Model Where Sunspots Matter

10.3.1 Description of the Environment

Our first example of a sunspot economy is an overlapping generations model that is adapted from a paper of mine with Michael Woodford [50].

The model is one in which agents live for two periods. They work only when young and consume in old age. Each agent solves the following problem:

$$\max U = E_t \left[c_{t+1} - \frac{n_t^2}{2} \mid \Omega_t \right] \tag{10.7}$$

such that

$$y_t = n_t, \tag{10.8}$$

$$M_t \le p_t y_t, \tag{10.9}$$

$$M_t \ge p_{t+1} c_{t+1}, \tag{10.10}$$

where the two budget constraints 10.9 and 10.10 can be consolidated into the following single life cycle constraint:

$$p_{t+1} c_{t+1} - p_t n_t \le 0. \tag{10.11}$$

The term M_t is the stock of money, p_t is the price of the consumption commodity in terms of money, y_t is the quantity of output produced by the young agent in period t, and n_t is labor that he uses to produce this output by the constant returns technology described in equation 10.8.

We assume that there is a single agent in each generation and that the entire nominal stock of money, M_t, turns over each period. In this environment the young agent works and produces output that he sells to the old agent in return for real balances M_t/p_t. These real balances are the only possible source of saving.

Notice that this is a model in which there is no intrinsic uncertainty, although, as we will see below, there may be equilibria in which *extrinsic uncertainty* is important. In an equilibrium where extrinsic uncertainty matters, the price at date $t + 1$ may be random, even though nothing fundamental is changing. If this happens we will assume that the expectation, conditional on the information set Ω_t, is taken with respect to the actual distribution of future prices.

Putting together the above constraints, we may write the problem of an agent born in period t as

$$\max E_t \left[c_{t+1} - \frac{n_t^2}{2} \mid \Omega_t \right] \tag{10.12}$$

such that

$$p_{t+1} c_{t+1} - p_t n_t \leq 0, \tag{10.13}$$

which has the following closed form solution:

$$n_t = E_t \left(\frac{p_t}{p_{t+1}} \right). \tag{10.14}$$

This behavioral equation presents a very simple example of a mechanism that has become known as the *intertemporal substitution* mechanism for explaining employment fluctuations. Some version of intertemporal substitution is the driving force behind most equilibrium explanations of economic fluctuations. In the simple overlapping generations model in which money is the only means of transferring resources through time, the term p_t/p_{t+1} *is* the real rate of interest between periods. Employment increases if the expected real rate of return goes up because agents perceive a favorable shift in the terms of trade between today and tomorrow. Since labor supply occurs today and consumption occurs tomorrow, this shift results in more output. Although the model is very simple in the sense that our agents do not consume and work in the same period, more complicated models rely on the same mechanism.

As with all overlapping generations models, we must say something about the problem faced by the initial generation. We assume that the agent that represents this generation is endowed with an initial stock of money, M_0, and that he makes the trivial decision

$$c_1 = \frac{M_0}{p_1}. \tag{10.15}$$

To close the model, we need to model the behavior of the government, and we must specify the market-clearing condition, which we write as

$$y_t = n_t = c_t + g, \tag{10.16}$$

where g represents the quantity of commodities that are purchased each period, by the government, for a purpose that does not yield utility to the consumer.[4] We will assume that the government's policy is to set g equal to a constant and to print exactly enough money in every period to finance it:

$$M_t = M_{t-1} + gp_t. \tag{10.17}$$

Rearranging the budget constraint of the government we have

$$\frac{p_{t-1}}{p_t} = \frac{(M_t/p_t) - g}{M_{t-1}/p_{t-1}}. \tag{10.18}$$

But from the consumer's problem we know that real balances turn over every period in exchange for the output of the young:

$$\frac{M_t}{p_t} = n_t. \tag{10.19}$$

By substituting equations 10.18 and 10.19 into the behavioral equation 10.14, one obtains the following nonlinear functional equation which must satisfied by any sequence of probability distributions over employment in a rational expectations equilibrium:

$$n_t^2 = E_t[n_{t+1} - g]. \tag{10.20}$$

The initial condition of the economy must satisfy

$$n_1 = \frac{M_1}{p_1}, \tag{10.21}$$

where $M_1 = M_0 + gp_1$.

The functional equation 10.20 summarizes the content of the theory of rational expectations equilibrium. An equilibrium can be represented by a sequence of probability distributions over employment that satisfies this equation. Since real balances are equal to employment and to output, this equation also summarizes the behavior of these two variables. In the following section we are going to investigate the properties of a number of different types of equilibria that can occur.

10.3.2 Set of Equilibria

The model that we have described is a standard version of the overlapping generations model with one slight modification represented by the choice of government policy. In the standard model there are two steady states, one in which money has value and one in which it does not. The effect of allowing for positive government spending is to introduce a second steady state in which money has value. Notice that as g shrinks down to zero, the lower steady state eventually disappears and the upper steady state increases to the monetary steady state of the standard model in which $n = 1$. Since, in our example, $n_t = M_t/p_t = p_t/p_{t+1}$, and since the inverse inflation factor p_t/p_{t+1} *is* the real rate of return, this upper steady state, in the case of no government spending, is associated with a zero real rate of interest.

The first kind of equilibria that we will look at are nonstochastic. There are two types of these: stationary equilibria in which n_t is constant through time and nonstationary equilibria in which output and employment are changing every period even though the fundamentals remain fixed. In figure 10.2, I have drawn a picture of the solutions to the nonstochastic difference equation $n_t^2 = n_{t+1} - g$. Inspection of this figure reveals that there are exactly two stationary equilibria, depicted as $\underline{n}$ and $\bar{n}$, which are given by the roots of the quadratic $n^2 = n - g$. There are also

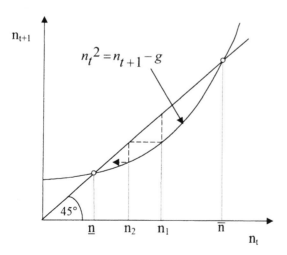

Figure 10.2
Set of nonstochastic equilibria

many nonstationary equilibria in this economy which are represented by sequences that begin with values of n_1 in the open interval $(0, \bar{n})$, all of which converge to the lower steady state in which $n = \underline{n}$. One such equilibrium is represented by the sequence that begins at n_1 in figure 10.2.

So much for the nonstochastic equilibria, but these are not the only possible candidates. Indeed, although our economy contains no fundamental uncertainty, it may be possible for prices and quantities to fluctuate randomly merely because agents come to believe that this will be so. As an example of one such equilibrium, suppose that employment follows the stochastic process

$$n_{t+1} = n_t^2 + g + u_{t+1}, \tag{10.22}$$

where u_{t+1} is an arbitrary stochastic process with a conditional mean of zero and a "small" support on the interval $[-a, b]$. This process defines a sequence of probability distributions over the random variable n_t. By substituting the proposed equilibrium back into the functional equation 10.20, one can verify that this sequence of probability distributions satisfies all of the requirements of a rational expectations equilibrium. Since there are infinitely many stochastic processes with these properties, we have shown that this model contains infinitely many rational expectations equilibria in which extrinsic uncertainty can affect allocations.

Figure 10.3 demonstrates what is happening in the stochastic equilibria in this model. The assumption that the distribution of sunspot uncertainty has a small finite support, $[-a, b]$ implies that the curves $n_t^2 + g - a$ and $n_t^2 + g + b$ both intersect the 45-degree line twice. The points $\underline{n}_a$ and $\underline{n}_b$ represent the two lower intersections of these curves. If the economy begins at any point $n_1 \in (0, \bar{n}_b)$, the economy will move toward the interval $(\underline{n}_a, \underline{n}_b)$ with probability 1, since all possible realizations of the sunspot uncertainty cause it to move in this direction.

The stochastic process $n_{t+1} = n_t^2 + g + u_{t+1}$ is an example of a Markov process. At any date t, u_{t+1} is a random variable and n_t is known. Since n_{t+1} is a function of a random variable, it is itself random, and its conditional probability distribution can be derived from the distribution of u_{t+1}. By computing this distribution at every point in time, one can compute a sequence of conditional probability distributions from the process $n^2 + g + u$. Under some relatively mild regularity conditions, one can show that this sequence of probability distributions converges to an invariant distribution with support $[a, b]$.[5]

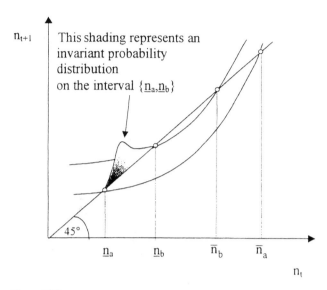

Figure 10.3
Set of stochastic equilibria

The basic idea that we have used to construct sunspot equilibria works by randomizing across the nonstationary equilibria of a general equilibrium model that has an indeterminate steady state. Since there are many such equilibria in the perfect foresight model, it is relatively easy to find sunspot equilibria in the rational expectations case. But, although the equilibria of the underlying model are nonstationary, the sunspot equilibria that use this construction all converge to stationary distributions. This is an important point because it has direct bearing on an argument that is often used to justify the rational expectations assumption, that agents will eventually learn about their environment. If equilibria are nonstationary, it is hard to understand how agents might come to have the beliefs that support them. But stationary sunspot equilibria are another matter, and they would seem to have at least as much claim to consistency with rational choice as equilibria that depend on fundamentals alone.

Since the stochastic equilibria that we have constructed are rational expectations equilibria, the probability distribution of realized prices must be equal to the probability distribution of beliefs about future prices. It follows that one possible interpretation of sunspot equilibria is that they are supported by self-fulfilling beliefs about the future. In the following section we will provide support to this interpretation of sunspots by showing how any particular equilibrium may come to be supported by a rule that agents use to forecast prices.

10.3.3   Supporting Sunspot Equilibria with Beliefs

The analysis of the previous section does not explain how any particular rational expectations equilibrium might come into being. In this section we will show that every rational expectations equilibrium can be supported by a mechanistic rule that is used by agents as a way of forecasting the future. This rule constitutes the agent's belief.

It does not seem to be controversial to argue that agents use rules of thumb in deciding how to behave. The rational expectations revolution does not deny this possibility. It argues that *however* agents forecast the future in a stationary environment, their rules must be consistent with the observed probability distribution of prices. In practice, when there is a unique rational expectations equilibrium, this argument uniquely determines the forecast function that agents must use in terms of the fundamentals of the model. In a model with multiple rational expectations equilibria, there is no such argument that restricts beliefs; rather, there are many sets of beliefs that are consistent with equilibrium. This should not disturb us any more than the observation that there are many sets of preferences that are consistent with the assumption of rational behavior.

Suppose, for example, that a sociologist were looking at the Arrow-Debreu model for the first time. Such an individual might legitimately point out that the assumption of fixed preferences is ludicrous. He would ask whether anyone really believed that an infant is born with the ability to distinguish between a good and a bad bottle of wine. The sociologist's criticisms do not make us run away and read introductory sociology texts, nor should they, since the general equilibrium model is a useful way of organizing our observations of the world. An economist might point out that the assumption of exogenous tastes does not have to hold exactly and that the model will still be useful if tastes are only slowly changing, or if the factors that cause tastes to change can be thought of as independent of the macroeconomic variables that are of interest to the modeler.

I will argue that exactly the same arguments that one might use to defend the assumption of fixed preferences can be applied to the assumption that beliefs are primitives of the model. In models where there are multiple rational expectations equilibria, we should think of the *belief function* as a primitive construct that tells us how agents predict the future. The rational expectations assumption, in this class of models, is a consistency principle that restricts the class of belief functions that are admissible to the modeler, and it plays the same role in models with multiple equilibria that the assumption of transitivity plays in the theory of rational choice. Since every belief function has a unique implication for the time series behavior of the data, this assumption does not pose any new philosophical problems. The econometrician can, in principle, estimate the parameters of beliefs just as he can in principle estimate the parameters of the utility function.[6] As an example of a set of rational belief functions for the above model, suppose that agents forecast prices using the following belief function:[7]

$$\frac{p_t}{p_{t+1}} = \left(\frac{p_{t-1}}{p_t}\right)\left(\frac{p_{t-1}}{p_t} - (u_t - \bar{u})\right) + g + (u_{t+1} - \bar{u}), \tag{10.23}$$

where u_{t+1} and u_t are independently distributed sunspot variables with mean $\bar{u}$ that have no relevance for economic activity other than that agents believe them to affect prices. Using the fact that agents use this forecast rule, it follows that the actual price level in period t will be found by equating the demand and the supply of money. The demand for money, using the forecast rule 10.23 and the behavioral rule 10.14 is given by the following expression:

$$\frac{M_t}{p_t} = E_t\left(\frac{p_t}{p_{t+1}} \mid \Omega_t\right) = \left(\frac{p_{t-1}}{p_t}\right)\left(\frac{p_{t-1}}{p_t} - (u_t - \bar{u})\right) + g. \tag{10.24}$$

Agents believe that prices are stochastic and that they will fluctuate in period $t + 1$ by an amount that depends on the difference of u_{t+1} from its mean, but in forming their best guess of the expected factor of deflation, the term $(u_{t+1} - \bar{u})$ is eliminated by the expectations operator. Agents also believe that the current observed value of the sunspot will influence the price ratio between periods t and $t + 1$, and they take this into account when deciding how much labor to supply in period t. This accounts for the presence of the term $(u_t - \bar{u})$ in the demand for money equation, 10.24.

The supply of money is given by the money supply rule which I have written in terms of real balances in equation 10.25:

$$\frac{M_t}{p_t} = \left(\frac{M_{t-1}}{p_{t-1}}\right)\left(\frac{p_{t-1}}{p_t}\right) + g. \tag{10.25}$$

Equating the right-hand sides of equations 10.24 and 10.25, one obtains the following expression that describes equilibrium in period t:

$$\left(\frac{p_{t-1}}{p_t}\right)\left(\frac{p_{t-1}}{p_t} - (u_t - \bar{u})\right) + g = \left(\frac{M_{t-1}}{p_{t-1}}\right)\left(\frac{p_{t-1}}{p_t}\right) + g. \tag{10.26}$$

First notice that we can subtract g from both sides of this equation and that the term (p_{t-1}/p_t) can be canceled to leave the equality

$$\left(\frac{p_{t-1}}{p_t} - (u_t - \bar{u})\right) = \left(\frac{M_{t-1}}{p_{t-1}}\right). \tag{10.27}$$

But, if agents in period $t - 1$ formed their expectations using the same rule that we have assumed for period t, then the stock of real balances in period $t - 1$ must be given by the expression

$$\frac{M_{t-1}}{p_{t-1}} = \left(\frac{p_{t-2}}{p_{t-1}}\right)\left(\frac{p_{t-2}}{p_{t-1}} - (u_{t-1} - \bar{u})\right) + g, \tag{10.28}$$

which is just the expression that we obtained for the demand for money lagged one period. Finally, by substituting this expression back into 10.27, one obtains the equation determines the price level in period t given that agents forecast with the belief function described in 10.23:

$$\frac{p_{t-1}}{p_t} = \left(\frac{p_{t-2}}{p_{t-1}}\right)\left(\frac{p_{t-2}}{p_{t-1}} - (u_{t-1} - \bar{u})\right) + g + (u_t - \bar{u}). \tag{10.29}$$

Equation 10.29 confirms that this belief function is self-fulfilling in the sense that if agents used this rule to forecast prices in periods $t - 1$ and if agents continue to use the rule in period t, then the rule will turn out to be correct. Since the sunspot process is arbitrary, there are many belief functions that could support rational expectations equilibria of this kind. Furthermore, since all of these are described by Markov processes that converge to a bounded interval, all of them can be described by invariant probability distributions, that is, as *stationary* rational expectations equilibria.

I like to think of the sunspot as the predictions for the economy of the *Wall Street Journal*. What our analysis suggests is that these predictions can be self-fulfilling in some types of economies if agents believe in them.

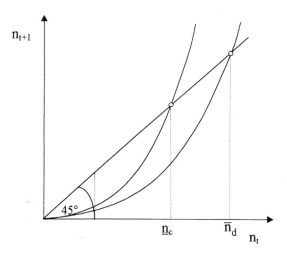

Figure 10.4
Constant money growth model

10.3.4   Sunspots, Bubbles, and Regular Equilibria

In this section I would like to try to reconcile the results that I have discussed with some of the literature that uses the rational expectations assumption. There is a large literature that uses a model very similar to the one that I have discussed above to generate some very standard kinds of results in monetary theory. The main feature that I have added, which makes my model a little different from many of the examples in the literature, is the assumption that the government chooses its level of expenditure and lets the supply of money be endogenously determined. As an alternative to this assumption, suppose that the money stock is expanded each period at rate μ_t:

$$M_t = \mu_t M_{t-1}. \tag{10.30}$$

In this case the functional equation that must be satisfied by rational expectations equilibria takes the form

$$n_t^2 = E_t\left[\frac{1}{\mu_{t+1}} n_{t+1}\right]. \tag{10.31}$$

Let us assume that the money growth process is stochastic by letting $\{\mu_t\}$ be a stochastic process with support $[c, d]$ and expected value equal to one.

Suppose that one were to try to construct a sunspot equilibrium in this economy by writing a process of the form

$$n_{t+1} = \mu_{t+1} n_t^2 + u_{t+1}, \tag{10.32}$$

where u_{t+1} has support $[-a, b]$. In the case of a policy of constant government spending, I showed that this technique would generate a sequence of probability distributions that converge to a bounded interval provided that the initial value was close enough to $\underline{n}$. In the constant money growth economy, however, this process would not be successful, since the sequence of probability distributions over n_t that is generated by this Markov process will converge to zero or infinity depending on the value of the initial condition.

The probability distribution $n_t = 0$ with probability one *is* a rational expectations equilibrium. But it is not a monetary rational expectations equilibrium, since the value of money associated with it is zero. Equilibria of this type are usually ruled out by assumption.

There is another type of rational expectations equilibrium in this economy that can be calculated by iterating the functional equation 10.32 into the future and taking the limit as $t \to \infty$. The fact that an equilibrium of this kind exists can be established by using a fixed point argument in the space of probability distributions. In our example this equilibrium can also be solved explicitly, and if the μ_t sequence is independently distributed through time, it is given by the expression[8]

$$n_t = E_t[\mu_{t+1}]. \tag{10.33}$$

Notice that the unique stationary rational expectations equilibrium in this economy is one in which output is fixed for all time and fluctuations in the quantity of money are taken up by fluctuations in prices. This follows from the observation that $n_t = M_t/p_t$. Since n_t is constant in equilibrium, and since M_t fluctuates, prices must move one for one with the money supply.

There is a considerable literature in the area of finance that has followed up on the possibility that models in this class contain other equilibria that are nonstationary. For example, equilibria in which

$$n_{t+1} = \frac{1}{\mu_{t+1}} n_t^2 \tag{10.34}$$

for initial conditions $n_1 \leq c$ can be used to generate sequences of probability distributions over n_t that satisfy equation 10.31, but they are not stationary. These equilibria have the property that prices "explode" to infinity, and for this reason they are often referred to as bubbles. A great deal of effort has gone into testing the proposition that the actual movement of stock prices may contain a bubble of this type, but almost no attention has been devoted to stationary sunspot equilibria.

Perhaps the most important reason for the profession's neglect of stationary sunspot equilibria is that until recently there have been very few models of the economy in which one can take the idea seriously.[9] Most work in the area has been conducted in the context of a two-period overlapping generations model in which the period of the model is difficult to reconcile with the observed transactions frequency. The natural frequency of a two-period model is of the order of half a lifetime, but we do not observe economies in which agents trade every thirty-five years: in practice they trade much more frequently. Although the work of Kehoe and Levine [64] suggests that economies with more realistic periods may display similar phenomena, there are considerable technical difficulties that one encounters in constructing workable versions of stochastic overlapping generations economies.

10.4   Concluding Remarks

This chapter has covered a relatively large amount of material in a relatively short space. The basic theme has been that general equilibrium economies may display sunspot fluctuations even when all possible insurance markets are open. The connection of this idea to indeterminacy is that models with indeterminate steady states are good candidates for belief-driven equilibria to occur, since they allow one to construct *stationary* sunspot equilibria that can be supported by forecast rules that are fully rational. The example that I presented in this chapter is of historical interest since it was one of the first examples of a model in which results of this kind were shown to occur. But it is not the only class of models in which "sunspots matter," and more recently there has been a good deal of work that attempts to find models that are more realistic in the sense that they might help us to understand business cycle phenomena. One such model is the work that I discussed in chapter 7 which explores externalities in a real business cycle economy. In chapter 12 I will introduce a second example that deals with a monetary economy and uses idea that noncompetitive elements may help us to understand some features of a monetary economy.

10.5   Problems

1. Answer the following questions:

a. Briefly explain what Cass and Shell mean when they say that "sunspots matter."

b. What is the difference between incomplete markets and incomplete participation in markets?

c. Why can't sunspots matter when there are complete markets and complete participation?

d. Explain what is meant by indeterminacy. Is indeterminacy the same thing as sunspots? If not, how are the concepts different?

2. Consider a simple overlapping generations model in which agents work when young and consume when old. The preferences of an agent of generation t are given by

$$U_t = \frac{(c_{t+1})^{1-\rho}}{1-\rho} - n_t, \qquad \rho > 0,$$

where n_t is labor supply when young and c_{t+1} is consumption when old. The world begins at date 1, and the initial old generation consumes and is endowed with a single unit of fiat money. Labor can be transformed into the consumption good using the technology

$$c_t = y_t = n_t.$$

There is no population growth, and money is in fixed supply.

a. Is this a Samuelson or a classical economy in the terminology of David Gale? Explain your answer.

b. Write down the life cycle budget constraint of an agent of generation t assuming money is the only store of wealth.

c. Define a competitive equilibrium for this economy.

d. What is meant by a sunspot equilibrium. Can this model display stationary sunspot equilibria? If so, for what values of ρ do these equilibria exist?

3. If sunspots matter, does it still make sense to estimate models of the economy. Can we still use these models to predict? Explain.

4. Suppose that the equilibria of an economic model can be described by solutions to the following functional equation:

$$y_t = a + bE_t[y_{t+1} + x_{t+1}]$$

where y_t is an endogenous variable and x_t is an exogenous variable. x_t is an i.i.d. random variable with a uniform probability distribution on the interval $[-1, 1]$.

a. State conditions on the parameters of the model that guarantee the existence of a unique stationary rational expectations equilibrium. In the case that equilibrium is unique, find a function $f(\ )$ such that $y_t = f(x_t)$ characterizes a rational expectations equilibrium.

b. Repeat your answer to part a under the assumption that x_{t+1} is $AR(1)$ with autocorrelation parameter ρ.

c. Under what conditions will there exist multiple stationary rational expectations equilibrium? How is this possibility related to the existence of sunspots. Characterize one of the possible set of rational expectations equilibria in the case where equilibrium is nonunique.

11 Macroeconomic Models of Money

11.1 Introduction

It is not possible to give a comprehensive account of monetary theory in a book of this size, and I am not even going to try. However, since monetary theory is such an important part of macroeconomics, I will attempt a brief introduction to some of the ways that theorists have attempted to incorporate money into simple general equilibrium models of the macroeconomy.

There are two puzzles that form the core of monetary theory. The first of these is the question of why a piece of paper that has no intrinsic value can come to be exchanged for commodities that yield utility. The second issue is why apparently identical pieces of paper that have identical risk characteristics can trade at different prices. The first issue is the question of why the price of money in terms of commodities is positive, and the second is the question of why the money rate of interest is positive.

11.1.1 Rate-of-Return Dominance and Legal Restrictions Theory

Although the overlapping generations model gives a partial answer to the first question of monetary theory, it has little or nothing to say about the second. It is this second issue, of *rate-of-return dominance*, that many economists take to be the central question of monetary theory. To place the issue in context, think of what happens in the weekly treasury bill auction that is conducted by the Federal Reserve board. A three-month treasury bill is a piece of paper that represents a promise to repay a fixed number of dollars in three months time. Let us suppose, to keep ideas concrete, that we are thinking of buying a one hundred thousand dollar treasury bill. Let us be a little more imaginative and think of an economy in which one hundred thousand dollar bank notes are also circulating. You may object that hundred thousand dollar bank notes do not exist in the United States, and this is true, but bear with me for the sake of argument because I hope to persuade you that the answer to the return dominance puzzle cannot lie in the issue of divisibility.

How much would I be prepared to pay for a one hundred thousand dollar treasury bill? That clearly depends on the rate of interest that I get from other financial instruments which we will take to be 10% per year or 2.5% per quarter. Well now the answer is clear, I would offer no more than $1/(1 + .025) \times 100,000 = \$97,561$ for the promise to repay $100,000 in three months, since then I would be earning the market rate of 2.5% on my investment. Why is this puzzling? Consider what I am buying: a piece of paper backed by the United States government; consider what I am giving up to get it: a piece of paper backed by the United States government. So why do treasury bills sell at a discount?

The superficial answer is that dollar bills circulate as a medium of exchange but treasury bills do not. Hence the banknote is useful to me in the three months between now and the time at which the treasury bill will be redeemed. Why is it useful? Because the government will exchange it at no cost for 100,000 small pieces of paper that other agents will willingly accept in exchange. But this leads to a real puzzle—why won't the government chop up the treasury bill into smaller pieces. This argument was laid out by John Bryant and Neil Wallace [27], and its logical conclusion is that it is inefficient to finance deficits with government debt; they should all be monetized!

Neil Wallace's answer [112] to rate-of-return dominance has become known as legal restrictions theory. He argues that in a frictionless world, without legal interference from government, private agents would be able to intermediate between money and treasury bills by creating their own banknotes. If treasury bills sell at a discount, then Roger Farmer could set up the REAF bank. The REAF bank would issue convenient dollar-sized pieces of paper, each of which would be backed by the reputation of Roger Farmer.[1] These notes would get into circulation when the REAF bank offered them to a private individual in return for a treasury bill, and the treasury bill would be held in the vaults of the REAF bank as backing for the notes. The activity of issuing currency is profitable to the REAF bank as long as treasury bills sell at a discount. Here is how it works: On January 1st the bank buys a treasury bill for 97,561 REAF notes, and on March 1st it sells the treasury bill back for $100,000. The holders of 97,561 REAF notes come back and reclaim U.S. dollars, and the REAF bank keeps the $2,439 profit.

The kind of activity that we described above does not occur mainly because governments prohibit the private issue of banknotes. Legal restrictions theory claims that it is *only* because of legal prohibitions of one kind or another that the rate of interest on short-term government debt is anything other than zero.

11.1.2   Some Quick Fixes to Rate-of-Return Dominance

A possible answer to the rate-of-return puzzle, and one that we will pursue here, is that money is what money is. According to this explanation the reasons why treasury bills sell at a discount are to be found in psychology and not in economics. Support for this view can be found in episodes like the Susan B. Anthony dollar, a coin that was discontinued because it was unpopular with the public. Or reports from prisoner-of-war camps that certain brands of cigarettes are circulated in exchange, but not others.

Once one has identified an object that is widely acceptable in exchange, there are a number of ways of capturing exchange value that can be grafted onto general equilibrium theory. The pioneer of these approaches was Don Patinkin in his book *Money Interest and Prices* [89]. Patinkin developed the argument that the *real* value of cash balances should be thought of both as a productive asset (money in the production function) and as a utility yielding durable goods like a refrigerator. This approach became known as money in the utility function, or MIU. The argument is based on the idea that agents can economize on transactions costs by holding money, since cash is widely acceptable in exchange, it is portable and divisible, and its value is universally understood.

More recently there has been a move toward models in which money is held because one assumes that agents must hold *cash in advance*, or CIA. The advocates of the cash-in-advance approach claim that it is superior to the technique of including real cash balances as an argument of the utility function, since it is important to completely specify the *economic environment*. Proponents of MIU, on the other hand, claim that the CIA approach is an inflexible version of MIU, inflexible since, in its crudest form, cash-in-advance forces the velocity of circulation to be equal to unity. This is a consequence of fixing the period between transactions and requiring *all* transactions to go through cash. My own view is that including real balances in the production function or in the utility function is not a sin of any greater magnitude than the assumption of the existence of an aggregate Cobb-Douglas production function. Both approaches are convenient shortcuts that sweep a lot of assumptions under the rug. Both approaches need to be used with care.

11.2   Models of Money

I am going to begin this section by expanding the representative agent model of exchange that was discussed in chapter 5. I will retain the infinite horizon model in which a finite number of families meets each period in a market for the purpose of trade, although all of the issues that I will talk about arise both in the infinite horizon model and in overlapping generations economies. Think of the environment as that of a small agricultural community, and suppose that every Saturday the families meet in the local market town to trade their produce. As a way of transferring purchasing power between periods, we may suppose that these families can borrow and lend to each other and that borrowing and lending involves the promise to repay with interest. My first task is to explain why rate-of-return dominance is an issue.

We normally think of the exchanges that take place in the market place as mediated by cash. For example, a trader may bring some eggs to market but he may need to purchase shoes. To accomplish this transaction, the trader will sell his eggs for cash and proceed to the cobbler. If the value of the shoes that he purchases is less than the value of the eggs that he sells, then he will try to buy a bond from another family that needs more cash this week than the value of its produce. Buying a bond makes sense, since, when he returns to the market the following Saturday, the trader's purchasing power will be greater by the value of the interest earned on his loan than if he had held on to the cash. The problem with this way of thinking about exchange is that the cash that finances the alternative timing of purchases and sales is like a hot potato. Everyone needs cash to smooth their payment patterns but no one wants to hold on to cash at the end of the day. By including money in the utility function, or money in the production function, an economic model explains why agents hold an asset, money, that is dominated in rate of return by a bond.[2]

11.2.1 Budget Sets: The Opportunity Cost of Holding Money

In this section we are going to formalize the idea that holding cash is costly by developing the idea of a single budget constraint and showing that the opportunity cost of holding cash, when bonds are an alternative, is equal to the money (or the nominal) rate of interest. A point that can be confusing when one first meets the idea is that the nominal rate, rather than the real rate, is the cost of holding *real cash balances*. Why isn't it real rates that matter? The alternative to holding cash is a bond that is denominated in dollars. If prices are expected to rise, then anticipated inflation will devalue the cash that is held for whatever purpose, *but it will devalue the bond by the same amount.*

If a family wants to save some of the cash from its sale of produce on one Saturday, it may buy a bond from another family who will promise to repay R_t dollars next week for every dollar borrowed today. R_t is called the money (or the nominal) interest factor, and it is related to the more familiar concept of the interest rate by the identity

$$R_t \equiv (1 + r_t),$$

where r_t is the interest rate on money borrowed in period t that must be repaid in period $t + 1$. Let us use the symbol m_t to represent the money that is held by a representative family between period t and period $t + 1$, and let b_t be the dollar denominated stock of one-period bonds purchased in period t for redemption in period $t + 1$. Each of these bonds costs one dollar in period t and pays off R_t dollars in period $t + 1$. Let us further work with an economy in which there is a single final commodity that is produced with the technology

$$y_t = l_t,$$

where y_t is the quantity of output produced by the representative family and l_t is the number of hours of labor that are used to produce this output.

At each market meeting we can write down the budget constraint that will be faced by the representative family:

$$m_t + b_t \leq m_{t-1} + b_{t-1}(1 + r_{t-1})$$
$$+ w_t l_t - p_t c_t + x_t, \qquad t = 2, \ldots, \qquad (11.1)$$

Since we will need to be careful about what can happen in the very first period, we will write down this constraint separately:

$$m_1 + b_1 \leq m_0 + b_0(1 + r_0) + w_1(\bar{l} - l_1) - p_1 c_1 + x_1. \qquad (11.2)$$

These constraints need some explanation. In period t of the model, our representative family is holding m_{t-1} units of money, b_{t-1} units of bonds, and it is endowed with $\bar{l}$ hours of leisure time per week. Some of this time, l_t is sold to a firm, and in return the family receives w_t dollars per hour. Since we will want to be able to talk about an economy in which the quantity of money may be increasing over time, we must introduce a method for injecting money into the economy. This is the role of the term x_t which represents a transfer payment (or a lump-sum tax if it is negative) that is paid to every household on Saturday. The family takes its income from working, $w_t l_t$, its assets, $m_{t-1}(1 + r_{t-1})b_{t-1}$, and any transfers, x_t, that it receives from the government to the market place. It buys c_t consumption commodities that cost p_t dollars, and it re-balances its portfolio of assets by deciding how much of its wealth to hold in the form of cash, m_t, and how much to lend to other families or to the government, b_t, between period t and period $t + 1$.

Using equation 11.1, we may write a compound constraint that must hold over the first T periods of the agents life, just as we did in the case of the economy without money:

$$b_0(1 + r_0) + m_0(1 + r_0) + \sum_{s=1}^{T} Q_1^s[w_s l_s + x_s - p_s c_s - r_{s-1}m_{s-1}]$$

$$- Q_1^T(b_{T+1} + m_{T+1}) \geq 0. \tag{11.3}$$

To arrive at equation 11.3, I have used 11.1 to write m_1 in terms of the other variables and substituted this expression into 11.2. This leaves an expression with an m_2 in it. But m_2 can be removed by a similar substitution. Repeating this process T times leads to 11.3.[3] The terms Q_1^s are defined in the same way as in chapter 5, as the period 1 price of a period s dollar:

$$Q_1^s \equiv \frac{1}{\Pi_{v=1}^{s-1}(1 + r_v)}.$$

Now that I have defined the terms I am going to put together all of the budget constraints that are faced by the family over its entire infinite existence. This involves taking limits in equation 11.3, and just as we did in chapter 5 we must make some assumptions to make sure that the limits make sense.

ASSUMPTION 11.1

$$H_0 \equiv \lim_{T \to \infty} \sum_{s=1}^{T} Q_1^s(w_s \bar{l} + x_s)$$

exists and is finite.

ASSUMPTION 11.2

$$\lim_{T \to \infty} Q_1^T[b_{T+1} + m_{T+1}] \geq 0.$$

The first of these assumptions is a statement that the definition of *human wealth*, the present value (after taxes and transfers) of the family's time, is well defined at present value prices $\{Q_1^s\}_{s=1}^{\infty}$ and wages $\{w_s\}_{s=1}^{\infty}$. The second assumption bounds the rate at which the debts of the family can grow. If both assumptions hold, then it makes sense to take the limit of 11.3 as $T \to \infty$

$$\sum_{s=1}^{\infty} Q_1^s[p_s c_s + w_s(\bar{l} - l_s) + r_{s-1} m_{s-1}] \le (b_0 + m_0)(1 + r_0) + H_0. \qquad (11.4)$$

The left-hand side of this constraint represents the sum of expenditures on consumption, leisure, and the services of holding money valued at present value prices. The right-hand side is the sum of financial wealth and human wealth. This budget inequality is written in terms of nominal period 1 dollars, but one could easily divide all of the terms by the price of consumption at date 1 to obtain an expression in real terms. This way of writing the constraint looks like this:

$$\sum_{s=1}^{\infty} Q_1^s \frac{p_s}{p_1} \left[c_s + \frac{w_s}{p_s}(\bar{l} - l_s) + r_{s-1} \frac{m_{s-1}}{p_s} \right] \le \left(\frac{b_0 + m_0}{p_1} \right)(1 + r_0) + \frac{H_0}{p_1}.$$

Take a look at the term in square brackets on the left of this inequality. The consumption commodity is the numéraire, which means that the price of consumption is defined to be one. The price of leisure is the real wage, w_s/p_s. But the real value of the family's cash balances at the opening of trade on Saturday is equal to the money that it brought into the period m_{s-1} valued at today's prices p_s, and the cost of holding these *real cash balances* m_{s-1}/p_s is the *nominal* rate of interest that the family gave up by choosing not to invest all of its wealth in bonds at date $s - 1$. This is the idea that I alluded to at the outset: The *nominal* rate of interest is the appropriate price for measuring the cost of holding *real* cash balances.

11.2.2 Objective Functions: Cash in Advance and Its Relationship to Money in the Utility Function

If holding cash is costly, then the representative family must have some motive for choosing to forego interest. The money-in-the-utility-function approach has been explored in some detail in a paper by Brock [24] who studies a pure exchange economy with no production. In our framework the no production assumption implies that

$y_t = l_t = \bar{l}.$

In Brock's formulation consumers care about the value of their money balances after they have finished trades for the day, since he assumes that the representative agent maximizes the function

$$\max \sum_{s=1}^{\infty} \beta^{s-1} u\left(c_s, \frac{m_s}{p_s}\right) \tag{11.5}$$

subject to the constraint 11.4. In order to be able to directly compare the money-in-the-utility-function model with the cash-in-advance approach, I will modify Brock's utility function and assume that consumers maximize

$$\max \sum_{s=1}^{\infty} \beta^{s-1} u\left(c_s, \frac{m_{s-1}}{p_s}\right), \tag{11.6}$$

where

$$u(x, y) \equiv (x^{\rho} + y^{\rho})^{1/\rho}. \tag{11.7}$$

The difference between equations 11.5 and 11.6 is that one model assumes that agents care about the value of their money balances at the close of trade and the other model assumes that agents care about the value of their cash balances at the beginning of trade.[4] The beginning-of-period model is more interesting for our purposes, since, as $\rho \to -\infty$, it behaves like a cash-in-advance economy. When $\rho = -\infty$, the utility function 11.7 is Leontief, that is, real money balances and the consumption commodity become perfect complements and they behave like left and right shoes. A family gets *no* utility from consumption unless it holds an exactly equal quantity of money. A family with this utility function will choose to hold exactly enough cash to exactly purchase its desired level of consumption.

For comparison, one of the nicest formulations of the cash-in-advance model appears in a paper by Wilson [114]. Wilson's work allows for variable labor supply, and he models the need for cash by assuming that agents solve the problem

$$\max \sum_{s=1}^{\infty} \beta^{s-1} u(c_s, l_s),$$

subject to the budget constraint 11.4 and the sequence of *cash-in-advance* constraints,

$$c_t \leq \frac{m_{t-1}}{p_t}, \qquad t = 1, \ldots .$$

If one were to impose a fixed labor supply on Wilson's model, namely $l_t = \bar{l}$ for all t, then Wilson's model could be derived from our modified version of Brock's framework by choosing the Leontief specification of utility. It is this sense in which the money in the utility function is more general than cash in advance.

11.3 Dynamics of a Cash-in-Advance Model

11.3.1 Different Types of Monetary Policy

In this part of the chapter I am going to write down a consolidated budget constraint for the government sector; it is consolidated because I will put together the budget constraints of the treasury and of the Federal Reserve system. A complete statement of the regime that is followed by the central government involves a plan that dictates how much will be spent on goods and services, on transfers to the public and of the portion of this expenditure that will be financed by taxes. Any such plan necessarily defines a sequence of government borrowing $\{b_t\}_{t=1}^{\infty}$ which represents the debt that must be floated in each period to finance any deficit or surplus that accrues from government spending and taxation. A plan that sets these quantities is called a *fiscal policy*.

Given a sequence of government borrowing requirements, the consolidated government sector must make a second decision that involves the choice of the fraction of the government's debt that should be raised by borrowing directly from the public and the fraction that should be raised by borrowing from the central bank. When the central bank buys debt on the open market, this debt is replaced by money, and the fraction of the debt that is owned by the central bank is said to be *monetized*.

In the United States the central bank is relatively independent of political influence from the legislative branches of government, and the decision over *monetary policy* is taken by the open market committee of the Federal Reserve system. For much of its history, the open market committee of the Fed has paid a great deal of attention to the interest rate on short term debt. The Fed operates by targeting this rate, influencing it through the open market purchase and sale of treasury bills and other short-term government securities. A policy in this class will be referred to as one of *interest rate control.* An alternative class of monetary policies that was tried briefly between 1979 and 1982 is one in which the Fed directly targets the rate of growth of a monetary aggregate; a policy in this class is called a *fixed money growth rule.*

11.3.2 Government's Budget Constraints

The sequence of constraints faced by the central government is similar to the sequence of market constraints faced by a representative household. In the first period the government is assumed to begin with initial stocks of debt and money:

$$b_0 = \bar{b}_0, \quad m_0 = \bar{m}_0,$$

and to choose a transfer or tax to households of an amount x_1. This transfer, or tax, can be financed either through borrowing or through increasing the stock of money. The government's budget constraint in period 1 of the model looks like this:

$$m_1 + b_1 \geq \bar{m}_0 + \bar{b}_0(1 + r_0) + x_1.$$

The right-hand side of this inequality represents ways in which the government can spend money. First, it may retire the existing supply of money, $\bar{m}_0$. If this sounds odd, then you should think of the stock of the money as a debt that the government owes to the public. If the money supply remains constant, then the government is essentially rolling over this stock of noninterest-bearing debt. Second, the government may pay off the principal and interest on it's outstanding debt; this is the term $\bar{b}_0(1 + r_0)$. Finally, the government may make a transfer to the public of an amount x_1. These three ways of spending money must be financed either through issuing new money, m_1, or through issuing new debt, b_1.

In period 2 and later, the government faces a similar constraint which I will write as

$$m_t + b_t \geq m_{t-1} + b_{t-1}(1 + r_t) + x_t, \qquad t = 2, \ldots.$$

Consolidating the first T periods, one may write a compound constraint:

$$\bar{m}_0(1 + r_0) + \bar{b}_0(1 + r_0) + \sum_{s=1}^{T} Q_1^s[x_s - r_{s-1}m_{s-1}] - Q_1^s[b_{T+1} + m_{T+1}] \leq 0.$$

$$(11.8)$$

To get to this compound constraint, I have used the same substitutions that I applied to the households constraints in the previous section. Think of the terms $\{x_s\}_{s=1}^{T}$, $\bar{m}_0$, and $\bar{b}_0(1 + r_0)$ as ways in which the government can spend money over the first T periods of the model.[5] Think of m_{T+1}, b_{T+1} and $\{r_{s-1}m_{s-1}\}_{s=1}^{T}$ as sources of funds that can be used to pay for each of these expenditures. The terms $\{x_s\}$ are straightforward; they represent direct transfers to households. The term $\bar{m}_0$ is the initial stock of money which is a debt to the public. Just like any other debt, this debt could be paid off. Similarly $\bar{b}_0(1 + r_0)$ is the principal and interest on the government's debt which could also be paid off. How can the government finance these expenditures? First, it can borrow from the future; this is the term b_{T+1}. Second, it can print money; this is similar to borrowing from the future with the exception that the borrowing is interest free. Third, it can rely on *seignorage revenues* that come from money creation; this seignorage revenue is represented by the terms $\{r_{s-1}m_{s-1}\}_{s=1}^{T}$. Where do these seignorage revenues come from? They are taxes on the holders of money, each of whom is losing the purchasing power $r_{s-1}m_{s-1}$ in each period $s - 1$ by holding cash instead of bonds.

Just as with the representative household we are going to take the limit of this compound constraint as we let the horizon of the agent tend to infinity. To make sure that this limit is well defined, we will need to make an assumption that is the analogue of assumption 11.2 which we placed on the households.

ASSUMPTION 11.3

$$\lim_{T \to \infty} Q_1^T(b_{T+1} + m_{T+1}) \geq 0.$$

Armed with assumption 11.3 we may take the limit of 11.8 as $T \to \infty$ to yield the single budget constraint:

$$b_0(1 + r_0) + m_0(1 + r_0) + \sum_{s=1}^{\infty} Q_1^s(x_s - r_{s-1}m_{s-1}) \leq 0,$$

which we can also write, using consumption as the numéraire, as

$$\frac{b_0}{p_1}(1 + r_0) + \frac{m_0}{p_1}(1 + r_0) + \sum_{s=1}^{\infty} Q_1^s \frac{p_s}{p_1}\left(\frac{x_s}{p_s} - r_{s-1}\frac{m_{s-1}}{p_s}\right) \leq 0.$$

This inequality is often referred to in the literature as *the* government budget constraint. A couple of special cases are helpful to understand the limitations that it places on alternative policy regimes. First note that in an economy with no money, the net present value of tax revenues must be at least as great as the initial government debt:

$$\sum_{s=1}^{\infty} Q_1^s \frac{x_s}{p_1} \leq -\frac{b_0}{p_1}(1 + r_0).$$

The terms $\{x_s\}$ must be negative, (i.e., x_s must be taxes rather than a transfers), and the net present value of these taxes must exactly offset the debt. When there is money in the economy, this is no longer true because the government is earning seignorage revenues.

11.3.3 Typology of Policy Regimes

Before we can talk about the types of equilibria that can occur in a simple monetary economy, we will need to be precise about the policy options that are available to the government. Rather than provide a model of how governments operate, I will take the actions of the government to be outside of the scope of the model and just describe the feasible options. A *government policy* is a sequence of transfers or taxes $\{x_s\}_1^{\infty}$, a sequence of levels of government debt $\{b_s\}_{s=1}^{\infty}$, a sequence of money stocks $\{m_s\}_{s=1}^{\infty}$, and a sequence of interest rates $\{r_s\}_{s=1}^{\infty}$ that satisfies the constraint

$$\frac{b_0}{p_1}(1 + r_0) + \frac{m_0}{p_1}(1 + r_0) + \sum_{s=1}^{\infty} Q_1^s \frac{p_s}{p_1}\left(\frac{x_s}{p_s} - r_{s-1}\frac{m_{s-1}}{p_s}\right) \leq 0.$$

Since the government will operate in a system of private markets only two of these four policy options are independent of each other. This suggests the following definition:

A **fiscal policy** is a choice of

F1   *either* $\{x_s\}_{s=1}^{\infty}$

F2   *or* $\{b_s\}_{s=1}^{\infty}$.

A **monetary policy** is a choice of

M1   *either* $\{m_s\}_{s=1}^{\infty}$

M2   *or* $\{r_s\}_{s=1}^{\infty}$.

In the real world it is probably more realistic to think of governments as picking a sequence of expenditures, in our model a sequence of taxes or transfers, and floating enough debt to pay for these flows. This would correspond to a policy of picking $\{x_s\}_{s=1}^{\infty}$. In the world of theoretical economics papers, it has become quite common to examine what happens if the government holds constant the stock of debt across periods, that is, a policy of fixing $\{b_s\}_{s=1}^{\infty}$. This fixed debt policy is much easier to analyze than a fixed flow policy, and in this chapter I will follow this route as a way of concentrating on the effects of different monetary regimes.

Similarly, in the real world, central banks typically try to control interest rates by manipulating the outstanding stock of money. A fiscal monetary mix of F1 and M2 corresponds most closely to what has been observed for much of this century. A mix of F1 and M1 was tried briefly between 1979 and 1982, but it was abandoned after it led to wildly erratic interest rate fluctuations. Since this chapter is about monetary policy and I would like to isolate the effects of the differences between policy M1 and M2, I am going to try to simplify the interactions of monetary and fiscal policy by looking at two artificial combinations, that is, F2, M1 and F2, M2. Neither of these policy mixes, as far as I am aware, has ever been tried in practice, since we have never seen governments that maintain a fixed outstanding level of debt. However, since the device of examining a fixed debt policy makes the monetary side of the models much easier to understand, we are going to study these policy mixes purely as an expository device.

11.4 Equilibrium under Interest Rate Control

11.4.1 Policy Mix A: Fixed Interest Rates and Zero Debt

In this section I am going to study the equilibria of a simple cash-in-advance economy when the central bank follows the policy of fixing the rate of interest and when the government picks its fiscal policy in each period by choosing to maintain a fixed stock of debt. To further simplify the fiscal side of the model, I am going to set the stock of debt equal to zero. Since there is no debt outstanding, the government's budget constraint simplifies to

$$m_t = m_{t-1} + x_t, \qquad t = 1, \ldots, \tag{11.9}$$

where we have written the constraint as an equality under the assumption that the government chooses not to throw away resources. The constraints 11.9 serve to determine the sequence $\{x_s\}_{s=1}^{\infty}$ for any given path of the money supply. Under the policy of interest rate control, I will assume that the central bank chooses some target, $\bar{r}$, and that it engages in open market operations in every period by purchasing or selling private debt in exchange for money. This policy fixes the opportunity cost of holding money,

$$r_t = \bar{r},$$

and leads to an endogenous demand for money, m_t, which is determined by the requirements of private agents balancing their portfolios . Since the fiscal authorities choose to maintain a zero stock of outstanding debt, they must react to the open market operations of the central bank by returning the value of any private debt purchased by the bank to the public, in the form of a transfer. Alternatively, if the bank must sell private debt in order to maintain its interest rate goals, then the treasury is committed to taxing the public by exactly enough to finance the banks operations.

   Using Wilson's version of a cash-in-advance economy, we may write the problem of a private agent as follows:

$$\max \sum_{t=1}^{\infty} \beta^{t-1}[u(c_t) + v(1 - l_t)], \tag{11.10}$$

such that

$$\frac{m_0}{p_1}(1 + r_0) + \sum_{t=1}^{\infty} Q_1^t \frac{p_t}{p_1}\left(l_t - c_t + \frac{x_t}{p_t} - r_{t-1}\frac{m_{t-1}}{p_t}\right) \geq 0 \tag{11.11}$$

and

$$c_t \leq \frac{m_{t-1}}{p_t}. \tag{11.12}$$

Notice that we have assumed that utility is separable in consumption and leisure and that we have normalized the endowment of leisure $\bar{l}$ to 1. We have also made use of the fact that leisure can be transformed into the consumption good one for one to set the real wage, w_t/p_t, identically equal to one. To solve this problem formally, one must write down a Lagrangian and find the Kuhn-Tucker conditions

$$\max \mathscr{L} = \sum_{t=1}^{\infty} \beta^{t-1}\{u(c_t) + v(1 - l_t)\}$$

$$+ \lambda \left\{ \begin{array}{c} \left(\dfrac{m_0}{p_1} - c_1\right)(1 + \psi_1) + l_1 + \dfrac{x_1}{p_1} \\[2mm] + \displaystyle\sum_{t=2}^{\infty} Q_1^t \dfrac{p_t}{p_1}\left[l_t - c_t - r_{t-1}\dfrac{m_{t-1}}{p_t} + \dfrac{x_t}{p_t} + \psi_t\left(\dfrac{m_{t-1}}{pt} - c_t\right)\right] \end{array} \right\}.$$

$$(11.13)$$

I have separated the decision that is made by the family in the first period, since the cash-in-advance constraint may or may not bind. One cannot assume that the cash held by the family is exactly enough, in this period, to purchase its desired consumption. If the family is holding too much cash, then it will dispose of the excess by buying bonds. If it is holding too little, then it will be constrained, in period 1, to purchase fewer consumption commodities than it would otherwise find optimal. This difference between period 1 and subsequent periods is reflected in the first-order conditions which I discuss below.

Notice that in all periods other than the first, the cash-in-advance constraint has altered the relative price of consumption and leisure. This change in relative prices occurs because the family must now hold cash, thereby forgoing the interest of r_{t-1}, to make its period t purchases. The first-order conditions for the family's maximization problem are laid out below:

$$u'(c_1) = \lambda(1 + \psi_1), \tag{11.14}$$

$$\psi_1 \geq 0, \quad \frac{m_0}{p_1} - c_1 \geq 0, \quad \psi_1\left(\frac{m_0}{p_1} - c_1\right) = 0, \tag{11.15}$$

$$\psi_t = r_{t-1}, \quad t = 2, \ldots, \tag{11.16}$$

$$\beta^{t-1} u'(c_t) = \lambda Q_1^t \frac{p_t}{p_1}(1 + \psi_t), \quad t = 2, \ldots, \tag{11.17}$$

$$\beta^{t-1} v'(1 - l_t) = \lambda Q_1^t \frac{p_t}{p_1}, \quad t = 1, \ldots. \tag{11.18}$$

Armed with this set of first-order conditions, we can proceed to define an equilibrium for the monetary economy when the government implements policy mix A:

An equilibrium for policy mix A when $r_t = \bar{r}$ and $\{b_t = 0\}_{t=1}^{\infty}$ is as follows:

1. A consumption plan $\{c_t\}_{t=1}^{\infty}$
2. A labor supply plan $\{l_t\}_{t=1}^{\infty}$
3. A portfolio plan $\{m_t\}_{t=1}^{\infty}$
4. A price sequence $\{p_t\}_{t=1}^{\infty}$
5. A sequence of transfers or taxes $\{x_t\}_{t=1}^{\infty}$

such that:

1. The first-order conditions 11.14 to 11.18 hold
2. $c_t = l_t$ for all t
3. $c_t = m_{t-1}/p_t$ for $t = 2, \ldots$
4. $x_t = m_t - m_{t-1}$

11.4.2   Equilibrium of the Real Economy under Interest Rate Control

The fixed interest rate regime is rather simple to analyze and suggests an important role for the central bank in determining the level of economic activity. This role follows from taking the ratio of the first-order conditions 11.17 and 11.18, using 11.16:

$$\frac{u'(c_t)}{v'(1 - l_t)} = (1 + \bar{r}).$$

Putting this equation together with the market-clearing condition, $l_t = c_t$, leads to the conclusion that the Federal Reserve Board has the power, in this economy, to determine the level of economic activity by setting *nominal* interest rates:

$$\frac{u'(l*)}{v'(1 - l*)} = (1 + \bar{r}). \tag{11.19}$$

An example of this model is depicted in figure 11.1 which is drawn for the special case in which the functions u and v are logarithmic. In this case the left-hand side of equation 11.19 is relatively easy to draw, since it is given by the function

$$\frac{u'(\cdot)}{v'(\cdot)} \equiv \frac{1 - l^*}{l^*}.$$

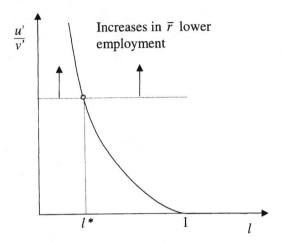

Figure 11.1
Power of interest rate control in a simple cash-in-advance economy

11.4.3 Equilibrium Rates of Change of Nominal Variables under Interest Rate Control

I have assumed that the central bank picks the interest rate and that it enforces its choice by making open market purchases and sales of private debt. I have also assumed that the central authorities choose to set the level of government debt equal to 0 in every period. It follows that the real value of money, m_{t-1}/p_t, must be endogenously determined. What determines m_{t-1} and p_t? First, observe that the first-order condition 11.17 must hold at every point in time. Taking the ratio of this condition at two adjacent dates leads to the equation

$$\frac{u'(c_t)}{\beta u'(c_{t+1})} = \frac{Q_1^t}{Q_1^{t+1}} \frac{p_t}{p_{t+1}} \frac{(1+\bar{r})}{(1+\bar{r})}, \tag{11.20}$$

where c_t is fixed equal to l^* from the real side of the economy and

$$\frac{Q_1^t}{Q_1^{t+1}} = (1+\bar{r})$$

from the definition of Q_1^t. It follows that 11.20 can be written in the form

$$\frac{p_{t+1}}{p_t} = (1+\bar{r})\beta$$

and that the inflation rate in equilibrium is equal to the interest factor weighted by the discount rate. In this economy, high interest rates lower output and increase inflation. One can also use the cash-in-advance constraint

$$\frac{m_{t-1}}{p_t} = c_t = l^*$$

to show that the money growth rate is equal to the inflation rate:

$$\frac{m_t}{m_{t-1}} = \frac{p_{t+1} l^*}{p_t l^*} = (1 + \bar{r})\beta.$$

The endogenous value of the transfer is given by

$$x_t = m_t - m_{t-1} = m_{t-1}(1 - [1 + \bar{r}]\beta).$$

11.4.4   Indeterminacy of the Nominal Scale of the Economy under Interest Rate Control

We have almost, but not quite, got enough information to completely determine the equilibrium prices. What is missing is a description of what happens in the first period of the economy in which the Kuhn-Tucker conditions

$$u'(c_1) = \lambda(1 + \psi_1), \tag{11.21}$$

$$\psi_1 \geq 0, \quad \frac{m_0}{p_1} - c_1 \geq 0, \quad \psi_1\left(\frac{m_0}{p_1} - c_1\right) = 0, \tag{11.22}$$

must hold. But since the agents in our model care about the real value of money balances and since the monetary authority picks the rate of interest and not the nominal quantity of money, there is no force pinning nominal magnitudes. Normally one would try to solve for p_1 by requiring the budget identity of the consumer to hold with equality. But under interest rate control, this constraint will hold identically for any initial price level.

The family's budget constraint is given by

$$\frac{m_0}{p_1}(1 + \bar{r}) + \sum_{t=1}^{\infty} Q_1^t \frac{p_t}{p_1}\left(l_t - c_t + x_t - \bar{r}\frac{m_{t-1}}{p_t}\right) = 0$$

By the assumption of market clearing, $l_t = c_t = l^*$, and the definition of Q_1^t, this equality implies that

$$\frac{m_0}{p_1}(1 + \bar{r}) + \frac{x_1}{p_1} - \bar{r}\frac{m_0}{p_1} + \left(\frac{1}{1 + \bar{r}}\right)\left(\frac{x_2}{p_1} - \bar{r}\frac{m_1}{p_1}\right)$$

$$+ \left(\frac{1}{1 + \bar{r}}\right)\left(\frac{1}{1 + \bar{r}}\right)\left(\frac{x_3}{p_1} - \bar{r}\frac{m_2}{p_1}\right) + \cdots = 0. \qquad (11.23)$$

But the sequence $\{x_t\}_{t=1}^{\infty}$ is determined according to the rule

$$x_t = m_t - m_{t-1},$$

which implies that the constraint 11.23 will hold identically. In a non-degenerate problem, the equality of the budget constraint could be used to solve for the value of the multiplier λ. But, under interest rate control, the price level in the first period *and the value of output and consumption in the first period* are not uniquely determined. For any given initial price level, $\hat{p}_1$, there is a level of consumption demand given by

$$\hat{c}_1 = \frac{m_0}{\hat{p}_1},$$

and there are values of ψ_1,

$$1 + \psi_1 = \frac{u'(\hat{c}_1)}{v'(1 - \hat{c}_1)},$$

and λ,

$$\lambda = v'(1 - \hat{c}_1),$$

that are consistent with this price.

11.4.5   Economics of Indeterminacy under Interest Rate Control

Under interest rate control, indeterminacy only affects the real economy in the first period. However, this distinction between the first period and all subsequent periods is really an artifact of the perfect foresight assumption. It is worth thinking about this distinction, since it leads us to ask what enforces perfect foresight. Why is indeterminacy reasonable in the first period but not in others?

By beginning the world in period 1, we are not asking where the initial level of money balances, m_0, came from. Suppose that we were to expand the model by adding a new period at the beginning of time, period 0. Now let us ask the question, What possible events might have occurred in period 0, given that we require that these events are consistent with what we observe in period 1? The answer to this question is that there are many possible period 1 prices, each of which is consistent with observing that agents are holding the money balances m_0. These different prices are each consistent with a period zero that is a properly specified expansion of the model to include a new initial period; they differ only in the rate of interest that agents faced in period 0. Different initial rates of interest would cause agents to hold different levels of *real balances* m_0/p_1, and since we do not observe the period zero interest rate, we cannot infer which is the *true* equilibrium.

Although the perfect foresight model has indeterminate quantities in period 1, in all other periods of the model the real side of the economy is well specified. One is entitled to wonder what is so special about period 1? The answer is that in all other periods of the model, the price level is pinned down by the *assumption* that agents have perfect foresight of the future. But there is nothing in the mechanics of the model that explains how this expectation is enforced. Once we have admitted this question, we must realize that our distinction between the first period of the model and all subsequent periods is an artificial assumption which was based on an unspecified mechanism that forces the expectations of agents to be correct.

11.5 Equilibrium under a Fixed Money Growth Rate Rule

A good deal of the literature on monetary economics does not study policies in which the interest rate is fixed by the central bank. Instead, it is often assumed that the stock of money is set to grow at some fixed rate. In this section I am going to show that the cash-in-advance economy, under a fixed money growth rate rule, leads to a first-order difference equation that describes equilibrium sequences. Furthermore this equation behaves very much like a simple two-period overlapping generations model. There will typically exist two stationary equilibria, one in which money has value and one in which it does not. The monetary equilibrium may, or may not be determinate, and one may construct examples of simple economies in which there may be many equilibria that are driven by self-fulfilling beliefs. It is therefore possible to interpret the equilibria of over-lapping generations economies as generated by long-lived agents who are cash constrained.[6]

11.5.1 Policy Mix B: Fixed Money Growth Rate and Zero Debt

An equilibrium for policy mix B when $M_t = \mu M_{t-1}$ and $\{b_t = 0\}_{t=1}^{\infty}$ is as follows:

1. A consumption plan $\{c_t\}_{t=1}^{\infty}$
2. A labor supply plan $\{l_t\}_{t=1}^{\infty}$
3. An interest rate sequence $\{r_t\}_{t=1}^{\infty}$
4. A price sequence $\{p_t\}_{t=1}^{\infty}$
5. A sequence of transfers or taxes $\{x_t\}_{t=1}^{\infty}$

such that:

1. The first-order conditions 11.14 to 11.18 hold
2. $c_t = l_t$ for all t
3. $c_t = m_{t-1}/p_t$ for $t = 2, \ldots$
4. $x_t = m_t - m_{t-1}$

11.5.2 Equilibrium of the Real Economy with a Fixed Money Growth Rate

In the economy with a fixed money growth rule, the interest rate is free to be determined by the requirement that the demand and supply of money should be equated in equilibrium. By taking the ratio of the first-order conditions 11.17 and 11.18, it follows that

$$\frac{u'(c_t)}{v'(1-l_t)} = (1 + r_{t-1}). \tag{11.24}$$

Similarly, by taking the ratio of 11.17 at two adjacent dates, one arrives at an expression that links consumption between periods:

$$\frac{u'(c_t)}{\beta u'(c_{t+1})} = \frac{Q_1^t}{Q_1^{t+1}} \frac{p_t}{p_{t+1}} (1 + r_{t-1}). \tag{11.25}$$

The first of these expressions, 11.24, equates the marginal rate of substitution between consumption and leisure to the relative price of these two commodities. This relative price is equal to the interest factor because of the assumption that cash is needed to buy consumption goods; but it is not needed to buy labor. The second expression, 11.25, equates the agent's marginal rate of substitution between consumption at different dates to the intertemporal relative price. Since

$$\frac{Q_1^t}{Q_1^{t+1}} = (1 + r_t),$$

these two marginal conditions may be combined in the following way:

$$\beta u'(c_{t+1}) = \frac{p_{t+1}}{p_t(1 + r_t)} v'(1 - l_t). \tag{11.26}$$

To close the model, one would like to eliminate p_t, p_{t+1}, and c_{t+1} from this difference equation and arrive at a description of equilibrium sequences that involves a single state variable. To achieve the necessary reduction, note that in equilibrium

$$p_{t+1}c_{t+1} = m_t,$$

since the cash-in-advance constraint will bind in any optimal program. Using this condition, one may write 11.26 as

$$\beta u'(c_{t+1}) = \frac{m_t}{c_{t+1}} \frac{c_t}{m_{t-1}} v'(1 - l_t),$$

and since $m_t/m_{t-1} = \mu$ when the government follows a fixed money growth rule and since $l_t = c_t$ from the market-clearing assumption,

$$\beta l_{t+1} u'(l_{t+1}) = \mu l_t v'(1 - l_t),$$

is the difference equation that we were seeking.

11.5.3 Example of Indeterminate Equilibria in a Simple Economy

In figure 11.2, I have drawn a picture of the difference equation that describes equilibrium sequences $\{l_t\}_{t=1}^{\infty}$ for the example where

$$u(c_t) = \frac{c_t^{1-\rho}}{1 - \rho}$$

and

$$v(1 - l_t) = 1 - l_t.$$

In this example the difference equation that describes equilibrium sequences takes the form

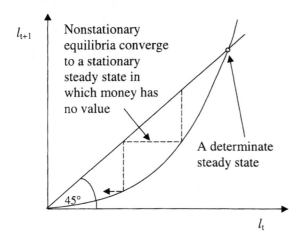

Figure 11.2
Example of possible equilibria in a simple economy under a fixed money growth rule

$$\beta l_{t+1}^{1-\rho} = \mu l_t,$$

or

$$l_{t+1} = \left(\frac{\mu l_t}{\beta}\right)^{1/(1-\rho)}.$$

When ρ is between zero and one, this example has a single determinate stationary equilibrium at $l^* = (\beta/\mu)^{1/\rho}$. Notice that this economy also has nonstationary equilibria that are associated with initial levels of output l_1 in the interval $(0, l^*)$. These nonstationary equilibria are associated with initial price levels given by the equality

$$p_1 = \frac{m_0}{l_1}.$$

When the parameter ρ is increased above 1, the nonstationary equilibria start to cycle around the steady state l^*. When ρ is greater than 2, these cycles converge; that is, the steady state equilibrium, $l_t = l^*$, is indeterminate. I have drawn a picture of this case in figure 11.3 which depicts a nonstationary equilibrium that cycles into the stationary equilibrium at l^*.

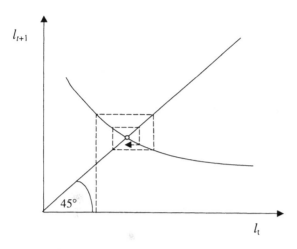

Figure 11.3
Example of an indeterminate steady state in a simple economy under a fixed money growth rule

11.6   Concluding Remarks

What is one to make of the simple examples of monetary economies that I have discussed in this chapter? One point that I want to stress is that the so-called problem of indeterminacy which is known to characterize simple overlapping generations models is also prevalent in infinite horizon economies with a cash-in-advance constraint. Although this fact is relatively widely known among monetary economists, it is not often discussed, and most research in the area imposes relatively strong assumptions on preferences that are sufficient to guarantee the existence of a unique *stationary* determinate monetary steady state. In the context of the simple example that we explored in this chapter, one might, for example, impose the assumption $\rho < 1$.

In the final chapter of this book I am going to explore some quantitative theoretical work in monetary theory that draws inferences about the magnitudes of some of the key parameters of a monetary economy by drawing on studies of the demand for money in the United States in the last century. I will explain why researchers in the field have inferred from their studies that although indeterminacy can occur in simple *theoretical* models, it is unlikely to be *empirically* relevant, since it requires one to make unreasonable assumptions about the importance of money. I will point out, in this closing chapter, why I believe that these arguments are mistaken, and I will summarize some of my own recent research in the area. It is my hope that I may persuade the reader that the research agenda that recognizes the possibility of self-fulfilling prophecies is an exciting agenda and that it offers the possibility of understanding a number of puzzles that are otherwise hard to understand within an equilibrium approach to macroeconomics.

11.7 Problems

1. What is meant by "legal restrictions theory"? Is this a better theory of money than money in the utility function? If so, why? If not, why not?

2. What properties separate money from other commodities? Does the overlapping generations model capture all of these properties? If not, which property or properties are missing?

3. Consider a cash-in-advance economy in which the representative agent has preferences

$$U = \sum_{t=1}^{\infty} \beta^{t-1} \left[\frac{c_t^{1-\rho}}{1-\rho} - \frac{l_t^{1+\gamma}}{1+\gamma} \right], \qquad \gamma > 0, \quad \rho > 0,$$

such that

$$b_t + m_t = b_{t-1}(1 + r_{t-1}) + m_{t-1} - p_t c_t + w_t l_t, \quad t = 1, \dots, \infty, \quad m_0 = \bar{m}_0,$$

$$c_t \le \frac{m_{t-1}}{p_t}, \qquad t = 1, \dots, \infty.$$

where m is money, b is bonds, w and p represent the money wage and the price level, c is consumption, and l is labor supply. There is also a technology that transforms one unit of labor into one unit of the consumption good.

a. Assume that monretary policy fixes the nominal supply of money. Find a difference equation in $z_t = m_{t-1}/p_t$ that characterizes equilibrium sequences of real balances.

b. Prove that there is a unique stationary equilibrium in which money has value.

c. For what values of γ and ρ is the steady state monetary equilibrium indeterminate?

4. This problem concerns an economy with a representative family that lives forever. The family produces a single nonstorable commodity using the technology

$$Y_t = m_t^\gamma,$$

where

$$M_t = \frac{M_{t-1}}{P_t}$$

is beginning of period real money balances. The family maximizes discounted utility of future consumption:

$$U = \sum_{t=1}^{\infty} \beta^{t-1} \frac{(C_t)^{1-\theta}}{1-\theta}, \qquad \theta \geq 0, \quad 0 \leq \beta < 1.$$

It can store wealth as money or as government debt, B, and the period budget constraint is given by

$$M_t + B_t = M_{t-1} + (1 + r_{t-1})B_{t-1} + X_t + P_t(Y_t - C_t), \qquad t = 1, 2 \ldots, \infty,$$

where X_t is a lump-sum transfer from the government.

a. What additional assumption do you need to make about the constraints on choice if this family's maximizing problem is to be well defined? (*Hint*: What would stop the family from continually borrowing from the future?)

b. What is the "transversality condition"? How does this condition differ from your answer to part a.

c. Find two intertemporal first-order conditions: one for the choice of money and one for the choice of debt by substituting for C_t in the utility function from the period budget constraint and maximizing utility with respect to M and B.

d. Suppose that the government operates a monetary policy by picking the money rate of interest and setting it equal to a constant each period. Using your answer to part c show that this economy will have a unique equilibrium value for real balances and output. Find these steady state values of Y and m.

e. Suppose that the government chooses the fiscal policy $B_t = 0$ in every period and that growth in the supply of money is governed by the rule

$$M_t = \mu M_{t-1}.$$

(*Note*: The government prints money and distributes it to families as a lump-sum transfer.) Show that the difference equation in real balances that characterizes competitive equilibrium sequences is given by the expression

$$(m_{t-1})^{1-\gamma\theta} = \frac{\beta}{\mu}(m_t)^{1-\gamma\theta}[1 + \gamma(m_t)^{\gamma-1}]. \qquad (11.27)$$

Show each step in your reasoning to arrive at this expression.

f. Find the unique steady state value of real balances.

g. Let z be the natural logarithm of m. Derive a linear difference equation in z that approximates the behavior of equation 11.27 around the steady state.

h. For what values of the parameters of the model will there be multiple perfect foresight equilibria?

12 Applied Monetary Theory

12.1 Introduction

In chapter 11, I introduced some of the issues that arise in monetary theory, and I compared cash-in-advance economies with infinite horizon models in which one assumes that real balances yield utility. One of the themes of this chapter, in line with the theme of this book, was that models of money *may* contain indeterminate steady states. The *possibility* of indeterminacy in monetary economies has been known for a long time. But the dominant view among those who work with applied models of monetary economies is that indeterminacy is a theoretical curiosity that doesn't describe the world in which we live. In this chapter I am going to explain why this view is widely held, and I am going to explain an alternative interpretation of the data which allows one to explain a set of facts that would otherwise be puzzling for equilibrium theory.[1]

Equilibrium models of monetary economies encounter a number of difficulties when one tries to use such models to explain some of the simple facts that characterize the behavior of money and output in the United States. Roughly speaking, those researchers who have tried to explain monetary facts with equilibrium theory have had to face the reality that prices do not respond rapidly to new information. This is the fact that Keynesians seize upon to justify the assumption that prices do not adjust instantaneously to equate demand and supply. I am going to show, in this chapter, that equilibrium models are fully consistent with prices that are slow to adjust to new information if one is prepared to use equilibrium models in which there may be indeterminate equilibria.

It is worth stressing at the outset of this chapter that the work described below is preliminary, and although I believe it to contain the right flavor that one would look for in an equilibrium explanation of sticky prices, there are significant leaps of faith in the theorizing. Not the least of these is that the explanation that I will present relies on the assumption that money has an important external effect on production, but this external effect is not developed carefully from first principles. In the summary at the end of this chapter I will return to this issue, and I will point out the direction in which I think some progress could be made on integrating the equilibrium approach to monetary theory with the models of real business cycles that I discussed earlier in the book.

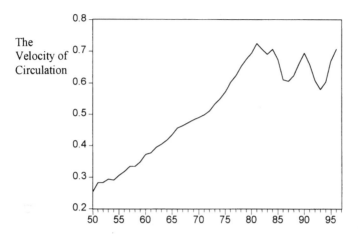

Figure 12.1
Behavior of $M1$ velocity in the United States

12.2 Monetary Facts: What There Is to Explain

Most work on monetary theory begins with some version of the quantity
equation which defines the velocity of circulation as

$$v = \frac{Y}{M},$$

where Y is the money value of GNP and M is a measure of the stock of
money. When M is chosen to be $M1$, the velocity of circulation has been
five on average over the postwar period. Since we are measuring GNP in
units of dollars per year, the fact that velocity has averaged five means
that Americans have held approximately 1/5 of a year or a little over two
months of income in the form of liquid assets, on average, over the past
forty years. But as figure 12.1 shows, velocity has been very far from
constant over this period; it has been trending up with an average rate of
growth of nearly 4% per year, and as figure 12.2 shows, the departures
of velocity from this trend are themselves highly persistent. The residual
series that arises from regressing velocity on a constant and on a trend is
highly autocorrelated, and it is better described by a random walk than by
a stationary statistical model that returns to trend.[2] A second fact that I
wish to draw attention to is that the cost of holding money, relative to
assets that yield a higher rate of interest, is quite small. In the postwar

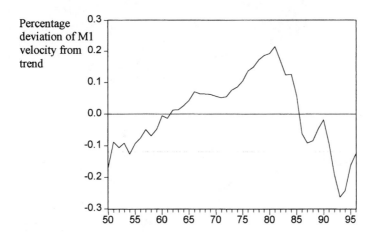

Percentage deviation of M1 velocity from trend

Figure 12.2
Deviations of $M1$ velocity from trend

U.S. data the interest cost of holding money as a percentage of GNP has been between one-half and two for most of the postwar period, although it has fluctuated quite widely within this band. In figure 12.3, I have drawn a picture of this quantity, which can be expressed as the interest rate divided by the velocity of circulation

$$\frac{iM}{Y} \equiv \frac{i}{v}.$$

The basic idea that I am going to put across in this chapter is that a good deal of work on the importance of money in the economy has inferred that money must be relatively unimportant because the opportunity cost of holding money is small. In a competitive model agents equate the marginal product with the marginal cost of holding real balances. I will show that the assumption that money is relatively unimportant has led researchers to build competitive equilibrium models in which the correlation between money and income is explained as an endogenous expansion of the money supply in response to real productivity shocks. But models with this property have a hard time capturing the impulse response of prices to money that I document below.

A *set* of facts that has been studied extensively by Chris Sims [106] is concerned with the relationship between four time series at different leads and lags. The time series that Sims has studied most closely are real U.S.

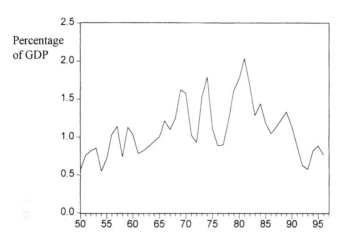

Figure 12.3
Opportunity cost of holding money

GNP, the price level, the interest rate on short-term securities, and a measure of the stock of money. To study how data behaves, Sims suggests using pictures of the *impulse response functions*. To calculate impulse responses, one would run a regression of the form

$$y_t = A_1 y_{t-1} + A_2 y_{t-2} + b + ct + u_t,$$

where y_t is a vector of the four time series. This means that each series would be regressed on a number of lags of itself (we use two lags as an example) and of every other series, on a constant and on a trend. To interpret impulse response functions, suppose that the estimated coefficients, $\hat{A}_1$, $\hat{A}_2$, $\hat{b}$, and $\hat{c}$ are correct; that is, suppose that we know the "true model." This true model has a deterministic part, $A_1 y_{t-1} + A_2 y_{t-2} + b + ct$, and a stochastic part, u_t. The time series that we observe in each period are determined by the superposition of these two parts, and impulse response functions are estimates of how the actual variables would return to their steady state growth paths if the system were displaced from this path and if the deterministic dynamics were then to be allowed to run their course.

I want to draw attention to one feature of impulse response functions from the Sims style VARs. This feature has been seized on by opponents of the equilibrium program in economics who argue that equilibrium theories are not consistent with so-called sticky prices. In the upper panel of figure 12.4, I have reproduced the response of the price to a money shock, and in the lower panel I have drawn what I have called the theoretical impulse response to a money shock in a regular model. Let me explain what I mean by this. Recall that a regular model is one in which the equilibrium is locally unique. The local uniqueness property means that the path that returns to the steady state is a saddle path, and if there is a disturbance to one of the initial conditions, say the stock of money, the price level must jump to the saddle path to maintain the convergence property that defines a rational expectations equilibrium. This is just a complicated way of saying that in regular models prices move around a lot to clear markets. I have been a bit loose in drawing figure 12.4, since I have failed to tell you exactly which model was supposed to produce this theoretical impulse response. It is not hard to do this, and Chris Sims has produced an example of a model that has this *regular* response pattern in a recent paper in the *American Journal of Agricultural Economics* [105].

I am going to argue that the response of prices to money shocks that characterizes the data is *not* hard to duplicate in equilibrium models provided that we are prepared to accept that money is much more important than one might infer from the assumption that it acts *like* a private input to the production process. I will show that if we allow for the possibility that money might have important social effects that are not taken account of by private agents, the impulse response of prices to money that is reflected in the data can be modeled as an *equilibrium* response in a model in which beliefs can independently influence outcomes. In terms of the arguments that I have made in this book, if money is important, then the steady state of a monetary economy may be indeterminate. In this case it is possible for prices to respond slowly, just like the picture of the responses that characterize the actual data.

12.3 Simple Monetary Model: Using Equilibrium Theory to Explain the Facts

I cited three stylized facts in the previous section of this chapter. Velocity is nonstationary, money is cheap, and prices are sticky. Ideally I would like to capture all of them in the model that I am going to lay out in this section, but accounting for the nonstationarity of velocity introduces more complications than I wish to deal with. The most reasonable way of dealing with nonstationary velocity is to recognize that the financial

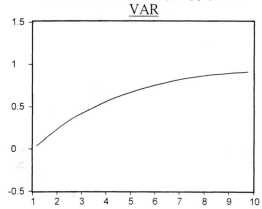

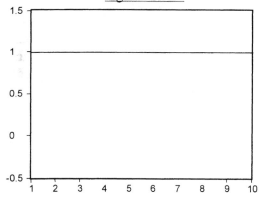

Figure 12.4
Response of the price level to a money shock

services industry has undergone significant technical innovation over the last fifty years. This argument suggests that one should include a productivity disturbance in the exchange technology to capture improvements in the methods that are available for paying for commodities. It is not difficult to follow this approach, but it makes the model much less elegant, and I am going to sidestep the issue of nonstationary velocity in this chapter by dealing with a purely perfect foresight economy with no financial innovation.

The second two facts that I cited involve the dynamic response of prices to money and the relative cost of holding money. It is these two facts that I am going to concentrate on, and the thrust of my argument is that most economists who have studied the data have concluded that money is relatively cheap and therefore it must be relatively unimportant. My argument is couched in terms of a model in which I think of the real value of cash balances as a productive asset like a machine or a factory. But the idea is more general than this, and it could equally well be couched in a model with money in the utility function or in a flexible version of the cash-in-advance model.

12.3.1   Modeling the Exchange Process

To study monetary exchange, I am going to model an economy that consists of a number of identical families each of whom lives forever. Each household receives a flow of commodities, like manna from heaven, but the household is unable to consume its own endowment. It must take its commodities and combine them with exchange services that are assumed to flow from holdings of cash. By combining its endowment with cash, the household produces a commodity that can be exchanged with the commodities similarly produced by other identical households in the economy.

To motivate the exchange technology that I will use here, I am going to tell a story. This story is developed from the idea of a sequential market that John Hicks described in *Value and Capital*. The economy contains a large number of identical families, and each Saturday these families come together in the local market town for the purpose of trade. In the simplest version of Hicks's trading day, all exchange takes place through an anonymous market that does not require the use of money. In reality, exchange is not accomplished by barter, and the family that comes to market to buy eggs and to sell butter will, at some time during the day, be holding onto cash from the sale of one commodity that has not yet been spent on another. It will also be true that the typical family will bring some cash to market to initiate trade even though it forgoes interest by doing so.

Suppose that one of the families places a low weight on the benefits of cash. This hypothetical family can still carry out all of the exchanges it needs to *as long as everyone else holds cash*. It needs simply to plan to sell its endowment of butter *before* it purchases its allocation of eggs. But the family's cashless trading strategy will only be successful if at least one other family in the economy holds cash. This argument suggests that if the process of exchange requires the use of money, there may be an externality that comes from the benefit to the individual agent from the cash that is brought to market by all of the other families.

12.3.2 Formalizing the Exchange Technology

Ideally one would like to develop a model of exchange based on the story that I introduced in the previous section. I am going to take a shortcut, and I am going to write down a function that summarizes some of the properties that one might expect to emerge from a more formal approach. This is not quite as satisfactory as a model that is based on a full account of who does what when—but it is a good deal more tractable. I am going to summarize the idea, that money economizes on transaction costs, by thinking of the value of the endowment to the individual as enhanced by his holdings of cash. But to capture the idea that agents may take advantage of the cash that is brought to market by other agents, I am going to include an *exchange externality* in the private agent's exchange technology. Specifically I will assume that the value of the agents endowment is given by an exchange technology

$$y = \hat{\phi}\left(e, z; \frac{\bar{z}}{\bar{y}}\right),$$

where e is the endowment that the agent brings to market and z is the agent's real balances. I will assume that $\hat{\phi}$ is increasing in z and e and that it is linearly homogeneous in e and z. These two arguments capture the part of the exchange process that is purely private. The third argument of the function $\hat{\phi}$ captures the idea of an externality in exchange; I have assumed that the private agent will benefit in his own transaction plans from the cash that is brought to market by other agents. Since this cash will also be financing the transactions of other agents, I have modeled the externality as a function of *the ratio* of average cash balances in the market to the average volume of trade, $\bar{y}$. This argument rests on the idea that externalities should be invariant to the scale of the economy so that an agent should derive the same trading externalities if he resides in England, an economy of fifty-five million people, as an agent who resides in America, an economy that is five times the size. The key feature of the argument is that an increase in the stock of money, holding everything else constant, will increase the social output. The effect of an increase in money comes through two channels, the private effect which increases y by increasing z and the external effect which increases y by increasing $\bar{z}$.

Before closing this section, I want to introduce two pieces of notation that help me to use fewer symbols when I write down the properties of an equilibrium. First, since the endowment of the agent, e, enters the problem parametrically, I will suppress it from the notation by defining $\phi(z; \bar{z}/\bar{y})$ as

$$y = \phi\left(z, \frac{\bar{z}}{\bar{y}}\right) \equiv \hat{\phi}\left(e, z; \frac{\bar{z}}{\bar{y}}\right).$$

Second, for much of the analysis that follows, I will want to be able to describe the average output of society as a function of the average money holdings *in an equilibrium*. The qualification *in an equilibrium* means that everybody will be holding the same money balances and the output of the representative family will be equal to the average output of all families. The function that we are looking for is implicitly defined by the equation

$$y = \phi\left(z, \frac{z}{y}\right)$$

which I will write explicitly as[3]

$$y = \Phi(z).$$

12.3.3 How to Describe an Equilibrium

This section gets a bit notation intensive, but the basic idea is quite simple. I am going to write down a problem that is solved by the agents in a fictitious economy, and I am going to solve this problem. Then I will assume that agents are in a perfect foresight equilibrium; I will impose a market-clearing assumption and out will pop the following equation:

$$g(z_t) = \frac{\beta}{\mu} g(z_{t+1}) h(z_{t+1}) \tag{12.1}$$

If you are willing to take this equation on faith, then you can skip ahead to the next section where I will tell you more about what it means. To preview this discussion, z_t represents the real value of money balances, and an equilibrium in this economy is a sequence of values for z_t that satisfies 12.1.

The problem that is faced by one of the families in our economy can be written like this:

$$\max \sum_{t=1}^{\infty} \beta^{t-1} u(y_t)$$

such that

$$\frac{m_t + b_t}{p_t} \leq \frac{m_{t-1} + b_{t-1} R_{t-1}}{p_t} + \hat{\phi}\left(e; z_t; \frac{\bar{z}_t}{\bar{y}_t}\right) + x_t - y_t, \qquad t = 1, \ldots,$$

where

$$z_t \equiv \frac{m_{t-1} + x_t}{p_t}, \qquad \bar{z}_t \equiv \frac{\bar{m}_{t-1} + \bar{x}_t}{p_t},$$

and

$$m_0 = \bar{m}_0, \qquad b_0 = \bar{b}_0 = 0.$$

The term m_t is the money that the household carries into period $t + 1$; b_t represents its holdings of bonds, and a bar over a variable denotes the economywide average. The term y_t is output, e is the agent's endowment, p_t is the price of the commodity in terms of money, and x_t represents a lump-sum transfer that is received by each household at the beginning of the period.

A couple of things about this problem might look a bit unfamiliar. First, we are not going to break up GNP into consumption goods and investment goods. This means that the function $u(y_t)$ must capture the utility to society of the resources y_t *to whatever use they are put.* Second, we are assuming that the representative agent needs to hold cash balances,

$$z_t = \frac{m_{t-1} + x_t}{p_t}, \tag{12.2}$$

before it can sell its endowment, e. You should think of e as an intermediate input that must be exchanged with the input of another agent before it can be consumed.[4] The solution to the agent's decision problem must satisfy a difference equation which looks like this:

$$\frac{u'(y_t)}{p_t} = \beta \frac{u'(y_{t+1})}{p_{t+1}} \left[1 + \phi_1 \left(z_t; \frac{\bar{z}_t}{\bar{y}_t} \right) \right],$$
(12.3)

where ϕ_1 is the derivative of ϕ with respect to its first argument.[5] The key to understanding what is meant by an equilibrium in this economy is to recognize that when we impose the market-clearing equations, 12.3 can be reduced to a difference equation in a single state variable, real balances.

To get to this equation, we must first make an assumption about the policy that is followed by the government. We will follow much of the literature in this regard and assume that bonds are in zero net supply and that the monetary authority follows a constant money growth rule,

$$m_t = \mu m_{t-1}.$$
(12.4)

Together these assumptions imply that the transfer x_t is endogenous and given by the budget constraint

$$x_t = m_t - m_{t-1}.$$

Now we use the policy rule 12.4 and the definition 12.2 to define the intertemporal price ratio in terms of z_t:

$$\frac{p_t}{p_{t+1}} = \frac{z_{t+1}}{\mu z_t}.$$

The final step is to use the market-clearing equation

$$y_t = \phi \left(z_t; \frac{\bar{z}_t}{\bar{y}_t} \right)$$

and the definition of intertemporal prices to describe equilibrium sequences of real balances as solutions to the equation,

$$g(z_t) = \frac{\beta}{\mu} g(z_{t+1}) h(z_{t+1}),$$
(12.5)

where

$g(z) \equiv zu'(\Phi[z])$,

$h(z) \equiv 1 + \phi_1\left(z; \dfrac{z}{\Phi[z]}\right)$,

Both of these definitions use the fact that *in equilibrium* the real balances held by the representative agent will equal the average real balances by all agents and that the output of all agents will equal the average social output $\bar{y}$:

$$z_t = \bar{z}_t, \quad y_t = \bar{y}_t = \Phi(z_t). \tag{12.6}$$

Equation 12.5 is the point where we began at the outset of this section, and in the next section I am going to use this equation to try to say something about the quantitative implications of 12.5 for the behavior of money and prices in the U.S. economy.

12.4   How Do Equilibria Behave?

12.4.1   Choosing Functional Forms

Now we are going to engage in an exercise in *quantitative theory*. This means that we will make assumptions about the functions $u(\cdot)$ and $\phi(\cdot)$, and we will ask about the properties of the time series that would be observed by an econometrician who studied data generated by an artificial economy that was a more elaborate version of the simple perfect foresight model that I have laid out above. Although I am cheating a little, I have not laid out the stochastic model with growth, for example, I am confident that it can be done because an exercise exactly like this has been conducted in a doctoral dissertation by Kenneth Matheny [83].

I am going to pick functional forms for $u(\cdot)$ and $\phi(\cdot)$ that are relatively simple but allow the elasticities of substitution between output at different periods, and between money and the intermediate good at a point in time, to be different from one. Specifically let the function $u(\cdot)$ be given by

$$u = \frac{y^{1-\rho}}{1 - \rho},$$

and let the function $\phi(\cdot)$ be given by

$$\phi = (1+z^{\lambda})^{1/\lambda}\left(\frac{\bar{z}}{\bar{y}}\right)^{\theta}. \tag{12.7}$$

The function $y^{1-p}/1-p$ has been widely used in empirical work to describe the utility derived by a representative agent from consumption in a given period. Estimates of p in this context are found by checking the covariance of consumption growth with asset returns, and they range between one, for which the function is logarithmic, and four.[6]

The function

$$(e^{\lambda}+z^{\lambda})^{1/\lambda}$$

is a constant-elasticity-of-substitution (CES) production function for which the elasticity of substitution between the intermediate input, e, and money, z, is given by

$$\frac{1-\lambda}{\lambda}.$$

To arrive at the parameterization 12.7, I have modified this constant elasticity function by allowing the technology to be shifted by the externality

$$\left(\frac{\bar{z}}{\bar{y}}\right)^{\theta},$$

where the importance of the externality at the margin is measured by the parameter θ. This way of describing the technology implies that the social output function Φ is given by

$$\Phi = (1+z^{\lambda})^{1/\lambda(1+\theta)}\bar{z}^{\theta/(1+\theta)}.$$

12.4.2 What Do Equilibria Look Like?

Given the functional forms that we are working with, it is relatively easy to show that the difference equation 12.5 which describes equilibrium sequences has a unique steady state. It is given by

$$h(\hat{z}) = \frac{\mu}{\beta}.$$

The obvious question to ask is whether there are any sequences of real balances, other than the constant sequence $\{z_t = \hat{z}\}_{t=1}^{\infty}$, that also constitute

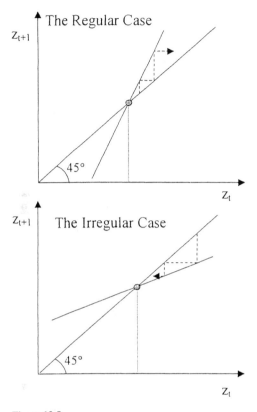

Figure 12.5
Regular and irregular models

equilibria. This question is the same thing as asking whether the slope of the difference equation

$$\tilde{z}_{t+1} = \frac{a}{a+b}\tilde{z}_t \tag{12.8}$$

is greater or less than one in absolute value. This equation is the linearized version of 12.5 around the steady state $\hat{z}$ where the parameters a and b and the variable $\tilde{z}_t$ are defined as

$$a \equiv \frac{\hat{z}}{g}\frac{\partial g}{\partial z}, \quad b \equiv \frac{\hat{z}}{h}\frac{\partial h}{\partial z}, \quad \tilde{z}_t \equiv \frac{z_t - \hat{z}}{\hat{z}}.$$

In figure 12.5, I have depicted possible behavior of this theoretical model for different values of a and b. The upper panel depicts the regular case in which $a/(a+b)$ is positive and greater than one, and the lower panel is the irregular case when $a/(a+b)$ is positive and less than one.

How could we get an idea of the relative magnitudes of a and b? The parameter b measures the elasticity of the marginal benefit of holding money. For the exchange technology that we have chosen, this function is decreasing in z, and it is given by the function

$$1 + (1 + z^{-\lambda})^{1/\lambda(1+\theta)}.$$

The parameter b is the elasticity of this function evaluated at $\hat{z}$, and for this functional form, b will always be negative.[7] If a is positive, and if b is between zero and minus one, the slope of the difference equation that describes equilibrium sequences will be greater than one. This is the regular case that corresponds to the models that have recently been studied by applied researchers in monetary economics.[8] But if a is negative, the slope of the difference equation 12.8 may be between zero and one. The existence of other equilibria in this economy therefore comes down to whether a is less than one.

The parameter a can be decomposed as

$$a = \frac{1}{u'[\Phi(\hat{z})]} \frac{\partial(\hat{z}u'[\Phi(\hat{z})])}{\partial z} \equiv 1 + \left(\frac{\Phi(\hat{z})u''(\hat{z})}{u'(\hat{z})}\right)\left(\frac{\hat{z}\Phi'(\hat{z})}{\Phi(\hat{z})}\right),$$

where, for our choice of functional forms,

$$\frac{\Phi(\hat{z})u''(\hat{z})}{u'(\hat{z})} = -\rho$$

is the intertemporal elasticity of substitution in utility and

$$\frac{\hat{z}\Phi'(\hat{z})}{\Phi(\hat{z})}$$

can be decomposed into two parts, a private effect of money and a social effect. This decomposition is given as

$$\frac{\hat{z}\Phi'(\hat{z})}{\Phi(\hat{z})} = \left(\frac{1}{1+\theta}\right)\left(\frac{1}{1+\hat{z}^{\lambda}}\right) + \left(\frac{\theta}{1+\theta}\right).$$

Most researchers who work in monetary theory work with models with no externalities; that is, they impose the assumption that

$$\theta = 0.$$

They then turn to evidence on studies of the demand for money to calibrate the magnitude of

$$\left(\frac{1}{1+\hat{z}^\lambda}\right).$$

Evidence for the value of this parameter comes from observing that

$$\phi_1\left(\hat{z};\frac{\hat{z}}{\Phi[\hat{z}]}\right) = \frac{\mu}{\beta} - 1 = i;$$

or in other words, the marginal product of money will be set equal to its opportunity cost. In terms of elasticities,

$$\frac{\hat{z}\phi_1(\hat{z};\hat{z}/\Phi[\hat{z}])}{\phi} = \left(\frac{1}{1+\hat{z}^\lambda}\right) = \frac{iz}{y} \simeq (0.05)\frac{1}{5} = 1\%.$$

The figure of 0.05 is the average interest rate on short-term securities, and 1/5 is the average of the velocity of circulation. This measurement exercise is a little like the way that real business cycle theorists calibrate the production technology. They argue that markets are competitive and therefore labor earns its marginal product. Labor's share of national income can be shown to be equal to its steady state marginal product; since labor's share has averaged 2/3 in U.S. data, it follows that the marginal product of labor is 2/3. Similarly, if markets are competitive, one can argue that the marginal product of money is equal to money's share of national income. In U.S. data only 1% of national income has been lost by firms and households holding money instead of interest bearing securities; it follows that money has been relatively cheap and that it must therefore be relatively unimportant. But, if there are no externalities in the exchange technology, then this exercise implies that the parameter a must be positive, since

$$a = 1 + \left(\frac{\Phi(\hat{z})u''(\hat{z})}{u'(\hat{z})}\right)\left(\frac{\hat{z}\Phi'(\hat{z})}{\Phi(\hat{z})}\right)$$

$$= 1 + (-\rho)\left(\frac{1}{1+\hat{z}^\lambda}\right)$$

$$= 1 + (-2)(0.01) \simeq 0.98,$$

where I have inserted a value of 2 for the intertemporal elasticity of substitution, a figure that many studies in asset pricing data have found plausible.

Suppose, on the other hand, that money is important because it has big external effects. For example, suppose that θ is of the order of 3.0 and ρ is around 2. If externalities are this important, then the social marginal product of money will be big:

$$\frac{\hat{z}\Phi'(\hat{z})}{\Phi(\hat{z})} = \left(\frac{1}{1+\theta}\right)\left(\frac{1}{1+\hat{z}^\lambda}\right) + \left(\frac{\theta}{1+\theta}\right) = \left(\frac{1}{4}\right)(0.01) + \left(\frac{3}{4}\right) \simeq 0.75,$$

and a will be given by

$$a = 1 + (-2)(0.75) = -0.5.$$

Since a negative value of a implies that the difference equation that describes equilibria may have an indeterminate steady state, it follows that large externalities may imply indeterminate equilibria.

12.4.3 Alternative Views of the Money-Income Correlation?

The issues that I have discussed in this chapter have played a central role in monetary theory for as long as economists have studied money. They come down to how one should interpret the high correlation between money and income that is observed in the data. Using the money-in-the-production-function approach, we can relate the data on money and income by the function

$$y_t = \Phi(e_t, z_t) \tag{12.9}$$

where this function is the social production function 12.6 in which I have put back the influence of fluctuations in the intermediate good, e_t. Taking a linear approximation to equation 12.9 around a steady state, we would expect to observe that fluctuations in y_t, e_t, and z_t were related by the function

$$y_t = \alpha + \beta e_t + \gamma z_t$$

where β and γ are the elasticities of the function Φ with respect to e_t and z_t and all variables are in logarithmic units. The first thing to observe is that all of these series appear to be stationary in differences, rather than in levels. If we ascribe this nonstationarity to the driving process e_t, and if this process is unobservable, the appropriate way to detrend the data is by taking differences. In figure 12.6, I have drawn of a picture of the growth in output and the growth in real balances. These series are positively correlated with a correlation coefficient of 0.2.

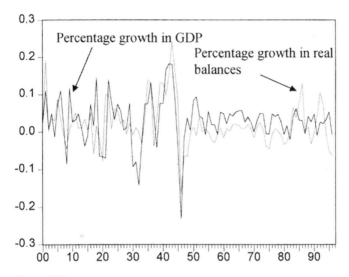

Figure 12.6
Correlation between money and income

In *regular* economic models y_t and z_t are correlated because both of these time series are driven by exogenous fluctuations in e_t. A high real shock increases output, and it causes real money balances to expand endogenously through a contemporaneous fall in prices. An alternative interpretation of the relationship is that fluctuations in z_t are caused by fluctuations in nominal money that increase z_t because prices are sticky. Advocates of this second view of the monetary transmission mechanism have typically argued that z_t causes an increase in e_t and that the transmission mechanism operates through a channel that involves disequilibrium in the labor market. The approach that I have suggested in this chapter is that increases in z_t directly increase y_t and that the channel operates through the external effects of money in the exchange technology.

12.4.4   What Does All of This Have to Do with Sticky Prices?

The two views of money and income, that real shocks cause money and output or that money causes output independently, have different implications for the intertemporal patterns that one would expect to observe in the relationships among money, income, the price level, and the interest rate. This is where the set of facts that Sims has documented may be brought to bear on the alternative theoretical explanations. In the first

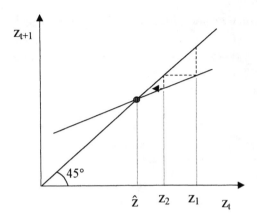

Figure 12.7
Sticky price equilibrium in a monetary equilibrium model

section of this chapter, I cited evidence that suggested that prices are slow to respond to new information. This evidence suggests that increases in the nominal quantity of money are associated, in the short run, with increases in output and in the long run with increases in prices. These facts are inconsistent with the endogenous money account which requires that prices should jump in response to an increase in money. This is where the idea of externalities in the exchange technology may be brought to bear in defense of an equilibrium explanation of the role of money. In figure 12.7, I have documented one of the possible responses to a monetary shock in a monetary model in which there is an irregular steady state. In this equilibrium an increase in the quantity of money is not met immediately by an increase in prices but by an increase in output. In the subsequent period real balances and output both begin to contract toward their long-run steady state as prices slowly increase to maintain long-run neutrality of money.

12.5 Concluding Remarks

This chapter brings me full circle, since it was with a simple model of an indeterminate equilibrium with which I opened the discussion in chapter 1. In the intervening chapters I have tried to expand on the idea that equilibrium theory is a much richer tool for understanding data than one might otherwise think, and I have done my best to dispel the notion that equilibrium models lead to particular normative conclusions. As a reader of this book you may or may not be sympathetic to an approach that argues that equilibria may be driven by sunspots. You may or may not be sympathetic to the idea of explaining sticky prices with models in which all markets clear. And you may or may not be sympathetic to the idea that governments have a role in managing the economy. But whatever side you take on a whole range of issues, both normative and positive, I hope to have persuaded you to be open to the idea that general equilibrium theory can provide us with a common language.

12.6 Problems

1. An econometrician estimates a vector autoregression for two variables x and y using one lag of each variable. The estimated VAR is

$$\begin{bmatrix} y_t \\ x_t \end{bmatrix} = \begin{bmatrix} 0.2 & 0 \\ 1 & 0.5 \end{bmatrix} \begin{bmatrix} y_{t-1} \\ x_{t-1} \end{bmatrix} + \begin{bmatrix} e_t \\ u_t \end{bmatrix}.$$

The variance covariance matrix of the shocks e_t and u_t is known to be diagonal. Write a computer program to, compute the impulse response functions out to ten periods for a shock to e_t. (*Hint*: Simulate the difference equation

$$\begin{bmatrix} y_t \\ x_t \end{bmatrix} = A^t \begin{bmatrix} 1 \\ 0 \end{bmatrix}, \qquad t = 1, 2, \ldots, 10,$$

where

$$A = \begin{bmatrix} 0.2 & 0 \\ 1 & 0.5 \end{bmatrix},$$

and plot the series $\{y_t\}_{t=1}^{10}, \{x_t\}_{t=1}^{10}$.)

2. This problem explores the idea that indeterminacy may arise in monetary models even without externalities if labor enters the utility function in a certain way. Suppose that an infinitely lived family chooses sequences of money, bonds, and labor supply to maximize the expression

$$\sum_{t=1}^{\infty} \beta^{t-1} U\left(C_t, \frac{M_t}{P_t}, L_t \right) \tag{12.10}$$

subject to the constraints described below in equations 12.11, 12.12, and 12.13, and the initial conditions:

$M_1 = \overline{M}, \quad B_1 = 0.$

The variable C_t is consumption, β is the discount factor, L_t is labor supply, M_t is money accumulated during period t and carried into period $t+1$, and P_t is the price of commodities.

Equation 12.11 represents the family's budget constraint in period t:

$$\frac{B_t}{P_t} + \frac{M_t}{P_t} = \frac{M_{t-1}}{P_t} + \frac{B_{t-1}(1 + i_{t-1})}{P_t}$$

$$+ Y_t - C_t + \frac{T_t}{P_t}, \qquad t = 1, 2 \ldots . \tag{12.11}$$

B_t is the quantity of nominal one period bonds that the family carries from period t to period $t+1$; these bonds pay interest at the nominal rate i_t. M_t is the money held between periods t and $t+1$. Y_t is output, and T_t is a nominal lump-sum transfer received from the government at the beginning of the period. In addition to the sequence of constraints, 12.11 which hold in every period, the family faces the borrowing limit

$$\lim_{s \to \infty} Q_t^s \left(\frac{B_s + M_s}{P_s} \right) \geq 0, \tag{12.12}$$

where Q_t^s is the period t value of a period s dollar. The production function is described by equation 12.13:

$$Y_t = L_t. \tag{12.13}$$

The policy followed by government is described in equations 12.14 and 12.15:

$$B_t = 0, \qquad t = 1, 2 \ldots , \tag{12.14}$$

$$M_t = \mu M_{t-1}, \qquad \mu > 1, \, t = 1, 2 \ldots . \tag{12.15}$$

The functional form of the period utility function $U(C, m, L)$ is given in equation 12.16:

$$U(C, m, L) = \frac{C^{1-\rho}}{1-\rho} - Lm^{1-\rho}, \qquad \rho > 1, \tag{12.16}$$

where m means real balances, M/P.

a. Give an expression that defines the period t value of a period s dollar in terms of the prices and interest rates between periods t and s.

b. Explain the role of the borrowing limit, inequality 12.12. What would be the solution to the problem if this inequality were absent?

c. Use the functional form in equation 12.16 to derive expressions for

i. the marginal utility of consumption

ii. the marginal disutility of work

iii. the marginal utility of real balances

d. Use equations 12.11 and 12.13 to write out the first two terms of the sum in equation 12.10 explicitly as a function of L, M, and B. (Eliminate C and Y.) Using the expression that you derive, find the first-order conditions that describe how the optimizing household will choose M, B, and L each period.

e. Prove that the following equation will hold in equilibrium:

$$\frac{U_m(C_t, M_t/P_t, L_t)}{U_C(C_t, M_t/P_t, L_t)} = i_t, \qquad (12.17)$$

where U_m and U_c are the derivatives of the utility function with respect to real balances and consumption. Your answer must show *all* of the steps by which you arrive at equation 12.17.

f. Define carefully what is meant by a competitive equilibrium in the context of this model. How many equilibria are there in the model? How does you answer depend on policy?

g. If you were to introduce extrinsic uncertainty into the model, is it possible that there might exist sunspot equilibria? Explain your answer.

h. Is indeterminacy of the equilibrium of a perfect foresight model a necessary condition to demonstrate the existence of sunspots? If so, explain why? If not, give a counterexample.

i. Explain how an indeterminate equilibrium in this model could be used to describe sticky prices.

Notes

Chapter 1

1. By "perfect markets" I mean that the assumptions of general equilibrium theory, described in chapter 4, can be assumed to hold.

2. I will be referring frequently to Arrow-Debreu economies throughout this book, although many economists have contributed to work on general equilibrium theory in the last couple of decades not least of whom is Lionel McKenzie [84]. Arrow and Debreu's *Econometrica* article [5] contains an early proof of existence of equilibrium, but a more comprehensive account of the general equilibrium framework can be found in Debreu's book [37]. There is an excellent survey by Gerard Debreu, of the literature on existence of equilibria, in the *Handbook of Mathematical Economics* [38].

3. For a view of Keynesian economics that takes a more traditional approach, see the collection of articles edited by Gregory Mankiw and David Romer [80].

4. A hyperbolic fixed point is one for which the Jacobian of the map f has no roots on the unit circle. In our case this just means that $|b|$ is not equal to one.

5. Since y_t can be a random variable, this statement is weakened to require boundedness only on sets that occur with positive probability.

Chapter 2

1. The study of chaotic dynamics has become popular in many disciplines over the last ten years. For an excellent survey of economic applications of complex dynamics, see the paper by Boldrin and Woodford [23] in the *Journal of Monetary Economics*.

2. More precisely, $\bar{y}^a$ and $\bar{y}^b$ are locally asymptotically stable. In the study of dynamics, there are several definitions of stability for nonlinear systems. Azariadis [9] has a good introduction to these concepts with economic examples.

3. A support of a random variable is a set of values **A** such that the probability that the variable will lie in **A** is equal to one. For example, a support of a normal variable is the entire real line. The support of the variable that is generated by throwing a die is the set $\{1, 2, 3, 4, 5, 6\}$. For a variable in an uncountable set, there could be multiple supports, since one could delete a set that has measure zero and still be left with a set that contains the random variable with probability one.

4. A number of authors are associated with the early work in this area, and the model dealt with in this book is often jointly named after Robert Solow and T. W. Swan. Swan's work [111] was coincident with Solow's.

5. The assumption of homogeneity of degree one is often referred to as constant returns to scale, since it implies that a doubling of all inputs will be associated with a doubling of output.

6. Solow's 1956 paper accounted for growth in output, in part, through growth in inputs. At this point in the text I am going to make the simplifying assumption that labor supplied to the market is constant and equal to one. In later sections I will discuss models in which labor supply grows through time and fluctuates over the business cycle. Even accounting for growth in labor and capital the value of GNP in the U.S. data shows a significant residual growth of around 0.5% per annum.

7. One often imposes the *Inada* conditions that $f'(0) = \infty$, and $f'(\infty) = 0$, to ensure the existence of an interior steady state. Recently, however, Rodi Manuelli and Larry Jones [81] have explored the idea that simple models may display sustained productivity growth, even if there is no exogenously growing productivity shock, A_t. The work of Manuelli and Jones relies on a violation of the second of these Inada conditions.

8. Except for the special case in which one of the roots of the system is on the unit circle. In the first-order model this special case occurs when the parameter a is exactly equal to one.

9. If you are unsure about this, you should draws a picture for the two cases where a is less than zero.

10. A Markov process is a sequence of probability distributions that governs the evolution of a (possibly vector-valued) random variable, y_t. The time homogeneous Markov property means that the probability distribution of y_{t+1} may depend on y_t but not on past realizations y_{t-s} for $s \geq 1$. In this book we are going to deal exclusively with a special case of a first-order Markov process which occurs when the variable x_t is drawn from a probability distribution with a *bounded support*.

11. There are at least two concepts, strong and weak convergence, that are used extensively in the literature. These alternative definitions use different concepts of what it means for one probability distribution to be close to another one. Stokey, Lucas, and Prescott [109] contains a good introduction to this issue with examples that are directed at economists.

12. The comment that I made regarding the nonstochastic model also applies to equation 2.15; there may be no interior solution unless one impose additional assumptions on f.

13. Notice that this decomposition is not unique since there is an arbitrary normalization involved in the choice of eigenvectors.

Chapter 3

1. This usage differs from the standard definition introduced by Blanchard and Kahn [20]. Blanchard and Kahn define a variable to be predetermined if it is a function only of variables that are known one period ahead. This definition is not very useful if one is interested in studying models with multiple rational expectations equilibria, since irregular models may have predetermined variables in the sense of Blanchard and Kahn even though these variables are not physically fixed in advance. This issue will be explored in more depth below, and it is discussed more fully in my paper [46].

2. The notation $O(x^2)$ means terms that are no bigger than x^2.

3. I am not going to cover the case where a root of A is exactly on the unit circle. A fixed point of the nonlinear model, which is associated with a Jacobian that has a unit root, is called *nonhyperbolic*. The dynamics of a nonlinear model are not well approximated by a linear model around a nonhyperbolic fixed point.

4. I have followed Hashem Pesaran's [90] usage in defining the terms regular and irregular. Hashem identifies the first usage of this term with an unpublished manuscript of Dennis Sargan [98].

5. If they are complex, then they will come in complex pairs, and the analogue of this statement is that the complex pair $a \pm bi$ may be inside or outside the unit circle.

6. The variable that enters the agent's budget constraint, in a discrete time model, is the interest *factor* rather than the interest rate. Since the interest factor is defined as one plus the interest rate and since $\log(1 + x)$ is approximately equal to x for small x, log linear models usually include interest rates in levels.

Chapter 4

1. This chapter is not designed to be a comprehensive account of general equilibrium theory; rather, it is an attempt to pick out those parts of the theory that are important for modern macroeconomics. I have drawn heavily on two sources. The first is Mas-Collels's excellent

book on general equilibrium theory [82] and the second is the survey article by Shafer and Sonnenschein [102] in the *Handbook of Mathematical Economics*. The classic reference for finite general equilibrium theory is *Theory of Value* [37]. The extension of general equilibrium ideas to the infinite-dimensional spaces that we deal with in macroeconomics is covered in an excellent article, "Valuation equilibrium and Pareto optimum," Debreu [39]. Although I am concentrating on the case of pure exchange, most of the ideas that I will discuss can be extended to economies with production.

2. Genericity is a mathematical property that formalizes the idea of "almost always." Technically a property is *generic* if the class of economies in which it happen is open and dense in the set of all economies.

3. The additional restrictions that apply to individual demand functions are summarized by the symmetry and negative definiteness of the matrix of price effects. For a deeper treatment of these issues, the interested reader should consult the survey by Shafer and Sonnenschein [102]. The idea, that only certain properties survive aggregation is formalized in the Debreu-Sonnenschein-Mantel theorem which we will return to briefly in section 4.5.3.

4. Notice that the definition of an allocation does not mention the idea of ownership—to be feasible, an allocation does not have to respect property rights. An equilibrium, on the other hand, is supposed to formalize the essence of the market mechanism. The idea of an equilibrium *does* respect property rights.

5. Notice that the intersection of the two excess demand functions doesn't mean anything economically because one function is in units of apples and the other is in units of oranges. But points where the intersection of these two functions crosses the simplex *are* interesting because these are equilibria.

6. More precisely, the intersection must be transversal. In the present context, transversal intersection places an additional restriction on the excess demand functions.

7. It is also possible for there to be an odd number of pieces that start above, and end below, the simplex. The number must be odd, since the boundary conditions may be used to show that f^1 must start on one side of f^2 and end on the other side of it.

8. See the chapter by Shafer and Sonnenschein [102] in the *Handbook of Mathematical Economics* for a more complete treatment and a list of references to the relevant literature.

Chapter 5

1. I have stressed the word *may* because not all of these economies have indeterminate steady states.

2. In higher-dimensional systems more complicated behavior is possible. The long-run behavior of the economy need not be described by a fixed point, but instead the economy may converge to a limit cycle or it may wander in some bounded region. See the work by Boldrin and Montrucchio [22].

3. Hicks's book *Value and Capital* (1939) appeared in print three years after the publication of Keynes's *General Theory* [65] and was overshadowed at the time.

4. It would be a good exercise to try to prove this result. Try writing down a simple general equilibrium economy in which two families have different discount rates. What will happen in this economy?

5. Recursive preferences were first defined by Koopmans [69] and have been studied by Epstein and Hynes [43] and Lucas and Stokey [78]. It is possible to generate many interesting results in economies with different infinite horizon agents. See Epstein and Hynes [43] for examples.

6. Mathematical economists have found a way around this problem by defining a criterion, the *overtaking criterion*, for describing how an infinitely lived agent would behave in this situation.

7. Make sure that you understand why this argument won't work if there is production. Is there an alternative assumption (like bounded utility) that you could impose on the production function?

8. It is also true that quasi-concavity of $\bar{u}_i$ implies that u_i must be concave. These facts are important in the economics of uncertainty when one deals with von Neumann-Morgenstern preferences. Arrow [4] contains a proof and applications in the uncertainty context.

9. The assumption is a little stronger than one requires, since it may be possible for equilibria to exist for economies in which this limit does not exist. For example, there are certain examples that one can construct in which interest rates cycle. To handle these cases, one needs to introduce something which is referred to as the *lim inf*. Stokey Lucas and Prescott [109] talk about these issues if you want to follow up on them, but you will not lose much of the economics of the issue if you ignore these special cases.

10. We have already met this idea in chapter 3 where we assumed that the Solow residual follows a first-order autoregressive process.

11. In addition to these equations, one also has an additional first-order condition for maximization known as the transversality condition. This is explained more fully in the appendix to this chapter.

12. These numbers are annual growth rates of consumption and GNP.

13. It is necessary to be little careful in interpreting the meaning of this result. Suppose, for example, that equation 5.30 has a stationary solution y such that $y = f(y)$. The determinacy of equilibria implies that in the neighborhood of y, there is a unique vector y_0 with the property that the sequence $\{y_t\}$, which is generated by iterating the map f from the initial condition y_0, constitutes an equilibrium. If it makes sense to linearize this system about y, that is, if the unique equilibrium converges back to the steady state y, then y must be a generalized saddle point and the equilibrium is found in the manner described in chapter 3. It is also possible, however, for equilibria never to converge to a stationary point, and in this case there is no hope of finding a linear representation of the model.

Chapter 6

1. Auerbach and Kotlikoff [6] have used a model of 55-period lives to analyze questions of optimal taxation.

2. Abel, Mankiw, Summers, and Zeckhauser [1] use a related criterion.

3. This is exactly the situation of fiat money in modern economies. The five-pound note in England, for example, still bears the inscription: "I promise to pay the bearer on demand the sum of five pounds." There was a time when a five-pound note could be presented to the Bank of England in exchange for gold, although the age of backed currencies has long passed. Today, if an individual takes a five-pound note to the bank and asks for five pounds, he will receive an identical piece of paper in exchange.

4. In economies with positive population growth, the golden rule can often be supported by a constant nominal stock of money that pays a zero nominal rate of return. In these economies the real interest factor is greater than one, since money and prices fall every period at the rate of population growth.

5. Recall that R_t is the interest *factor*, which is defined to be one plus the interest *rate*. We need the qualification "most" because the interest rate could be positive for a countably infinite number of periods and Malinvaud's criterion could still hold.

Chapter 7

1. The idea that externalities may be important dates back to a paper by Kenneth Arrow [3] who argued that the accumulation of capital involves a significant amount of learning by doing. Since learning is an interactive process, the higher the level of skill acquired elsewhere in the economy, the more knowledge is likely to "rub off" on individuals. The idea that monopolistically competitive elements may account for increasing returns has been studied by many authors. My treatment draws on work by Kiyotaki [68] and Blanchard and Kiyotaki [21] and from papers by Benhabib and Farmer [17] and Farmer and Guo [49]. The idea that drives this chapter is closely related to Cooper and John's [36] concept of 'strategic complementarities'.

2. Strictly speaking, there needs to be a continuum of agents for the equilibrium concept to make sense, since I am going to think that agents think that their own actions cannot affect aggregate variables. Each agent is arbitrarily small, and you should think of each of these families as both a producer and a consumer.

3. The endogenous growth literature exploits the idea that externalities can push up the value of μ until it is equal to one. At this point the aggregate technology is linear in capital, and the model that comes from this assumption has a unit root even if it is driven by stationary productivity shocks. The magnitude of externalities that I will deal with in this book will always be smaller than the value that one requires for endogenous growth; that is, the aggregate technologies that I deal with will exhibit diminishing returns to capital. For an excellent survey that deals with endogenous growth, see the paper by King, Plosser, and Rebelo [67] in the *Journal of Monetary Economics*.

4. The division between the producer and the consumer is artificial, but it helps us to interpret the first-order conditions that come from this problem by introducing a real wage and a rental rate. The family producer will directly set the slope of its indifference curve to the slope of the production possibilities frontier. The wage and the rental rate represent the slopes of the supporting hyperplane at the point of tangency, and they also represent the prices that would support a decentralized allocation.

5. Recall that the final goods technology is linearly homogeneous in intermediate inputs. A producer who uses one unit of inputs, spread evenly over the continuum of intermediate commodities, will produce a single unit of output.

6. A variable that is positively correlated with the GNP is called pro-cyclical because it moves with the business cycle. Similarly a variable that is negatively correlated with the GNP is called countercyclical.

7. An alternative explanation of pro-cyclical productivity, favored by a number of authors, is referred to as *labor hoarding*. Argia Spordone [108] has argued that the labor hoarding explanation can be distinguished from the externalities explanation by examining the implications of these alternative theories for the effects of permanent and transitory disturbances to technologies. Spordone's interpretation of the data favors the labor hoarding account, although the jury is still out on this issue. For a discussion of theories of labor hoarding, see the paper by Burnside, Eichenbaum, and Rebelo [28] or Eichenbaum's survey [42] *Real Business Cycle Theory: Wisdom or Whimsy?*

8. Can you prove that the balanced growth path is unique?

9. In the early literature on this topic, the fact that rational expectations models often had steady states that were saddles was perceived to be a big problem because the perfect foresight steady state would be unstable for almost all initial conditions. The problem was "solved" by the introduction of the rational expectations hypothesis. See Sargent and Wallace [99] for an early application of rational expectations to Cagan's model of hyperinflation.

10. Benhabib and Farmer [17] use different notation. In particular, there definition of χ is the negative of the value that we use.

11. Make sure you understand what we are doing here. By assuming that the technology shock is a constant, we have reduced the dimension of the system from three to two. The matrix $\bar{J}$ is the two by two sub-block of J that remains after we make this reduction.

12. The results that I describe in this section are not very sensitive to the choice of $m + n$, and one may obtain similar results over a range of values. Jang Ting Guo and I [49] explored values from several alternative parameterizations in which we chose values of monopoly profits between 2% and 7%. We obtained similar results in all cases.

13. Recall that if $\lambda = 1$, then the model collapses back to the competitive case. Our choice of $\lambda = 0.58$ implies the values of v and μ reported in the table, since $n = \lambda v$ and $m = \lambda \mu$.

14. The assumption that $\chi = 0$ implies that the representative agent's utility function is linear in leisure, and it has become fairly standard in the real business cycle literature. See the discussion in chapter 5 and the paper by Gary Hansen [58] for an explanation.

15. It would be a good exercise to solve for these coefficients yourself. The simplest way is to write a computer program to do the algebra for you.

16. Since the covariance matrix in the data is close to being diagonal, the normalization issue is not significant.

17. Perhaps the leading advocate of the argument that formalism has gone too far is Larry Summers of Harvard University. His position is outlined in a *Scandinavian Journal* article [110] which I highly recommend.

Chapter 8

1. Published papers that study aggregate economic models with technologies that exhibit increasing returns to scale include Baxter and King [14], Benhabib and Farmer [17], Gali [53, 54], and Rotemberg and Woodford [95, 96].

2. See the paper by King, Plosser, and Rebelo [66] where this restriction is derived.

3. Consider the function $U(\sigma) \equiv f(\sigma)/h(\sigma)$. Consider a value of σ^* such that either $f(\sigma^*) = 0$ and $h(\sigma^*) = 0$, or $f(\sigma^*) = \infty$ and $h(\sigma^*) = \infty$. L'Hospital's rule says that as $\sigma \to \sigma^*$, $U(\sigma) \to f'(\sigma)/h'(\sigma)|_{\sigma=\sigma^*}$, where f' and h' are the partial derivatives of f and h.

4. The term "Frisch" demand and supply functions follows Browning [25] and Browning, Deaton, and Irish [26] who introduce the definition of a Frisch demand to refer to demands in which preferences are intertemporally separable, and the demand functions for contemporaneous commodities are expressed as a function of current prices and of the Lagrange multiplier associated with an intertemporal budget constraint. Browning, Deaton, and Irish cite Frisch [51] as their source for the term.

5. More generally in the two-sector model, when factor intensities are different, this frontier will be concave.

Chapter 9

1. One typically assumes that u is strictly concave, which may be shown to imply that the individual is risk averse. This assumption may be shown to be equivalent to the assumption that U is strictly quasi-concave. Strict quasi-concavity of U guarantees that demand functions are continuous and is used in the proof of existence of an equilibrium.

2. Epstein and Zin [44] have extended Kreps Porteus preferences in a number of directions. Specifically they consider the case of infinite-dimensional commodity spaces, and they allow for additional violations of the von Neumann-Morgenstern axioms.

3. An alternative approach is to allow securities to pay off in units of commodities. This avenue was followed by Hart [59] in his early work on incomplete markets. Hart's approach leads to problems when one wishes to model economies in which there are fewer securities than states of nature, since the payoff vector depends on relative commodity prices. This dependence may lead to the nonexistence of an equilibrium.

4. See Cass [32] for a simple example.

Chapter 10

1. It is important to note that Cass and Shell use the sunspots to refer to a random variable that has no direct influence on fundamentals. This is an entirely different usage from that of Jevons [63] who developed a sunspot theory of the business cycle based on the idea that the level of sunspot activity directly influenced agriculture through its impact on the weather.

2. It is important to keep in mind the fact that incomplete participation is different from incomplete markets, which refers to the idea that there may not be enough securities to trade across all future uncertainty. In the Cass-Shell world there is a complete set of markets, but some agents are unable to trade in those markets because they are born after the trades have occurred.

3. This amounts to the assumption that there are two conceptually different people, Mr. α and Mr. β.

4. Alternatively, g may be thought of as a public good that enters utility in a form that is additively separable from consumption so that variations in g do not affect the agent's marginal decisions about how to allocate time between leisure and consumption.

5. The proof of this result requires some additional assumptions on the distribution of u and is beyond the scope of this book. Stokey, Lucas, and Prescott [109] provide an excellent discussion of the techniques that are required to derive it rigorously.

6. This approach has been advocated by Sargent and Wallace [100] in the case of models of hyperinflation. Following Sargent and Wallace's suggestion, İmrohoroğlu [62] estimates the belief parameter in the case of a model of the German hyperinflation in the 1920s. His work suggests that this episode can be modeled as a movement from a low- to a high-inflation steady state but that extraneous uncertainty does not seem to have played a significant role in the episode; that is, sunspots did not matter. Although this research agenda is in its infancy, the idea that one can test for the presence of sunspots is an important one that deserves to be exploited more systematically.

7. Much of this section is taken from my paper "The Lucas critique, policy invariance and multiple equilibria," [46].

8. To verify that this is indeed a solution, substitute it back into the functional equation 10.31. Verifying that it is the only solution requires a little more work. The basic idea is to define a space of probability distributions and to write the functional equation as an operator equation on this space. The operator equation is then shown to be a contraction. Roughly speaking, this means that each time that the operator is applied to a probability distribution the result is a new probability distribution that differs from the old one by an amount that shrinks with each application of the operator. The reason that this argument is difficult to formalize is that one needs to say precisely what is meant by closer, operator, space, and so on.

9. A notable exception is the paper by Woodford [115] who demonstrates that two-period overlapping generations economies can be reinterpreted as infinite-life agent economies in which agents face borrowing constraints.

Chapter 11

1. This is where the frictionless world assumption comes in. You might think that Roger Farmer is less trustworthy than the United States government, and we could argue about that, but it is hard to find relevant properties of the government that cannot be duplicated by a large private institution.

2. The infinite horizon model relies on the assumption of money in the utility function or of cash in advance to explain *both* a positive exchange value of money *and* why money interest rates are different from zero. The overlapping generations model can explain positive valued fiat money, but it too needs an additional assumption like cash in advance to explain rate of return dominance.

3. Notice that there is a term $m_0 r_0$ in equation 11.3 which is canceled out by $-m_0 r_0$ in the first term of the summation (when $s = 1$).

4. Without the assumption of additively separable utility, it wouldn't make any difference which approach one used. When utility is separable through time, however, one would like the definition of cash balances to reflect the complementarities with consumption that arise from the exchange process.

5. The same comment that I made in the case of the family's constraint also applies here. The term $m_0 r_0$ is canceled out by an equivalent term inside the summation sign when s takes the value 1.

6. This section is adapted from the paper by Wilson [114].

Chapter 12

1. This chapter draws on a number of papers that present the argument that sticky prices should be regarded as an equilibrium phenomenon. See [47], [48], and [16] for further details.

2. There are a number of formal tests that one can perform to find out if a time series is stationary. The most common of these, due to Dickey and Fuller [40], is designed to try to discover whether the level of a time series has any influence on the differences of that series. The idea is that if a series is stationary, then it will display a tendency to return to trend. Velocity shows no such tendency and it fails a Dickey Fuller test for stationarity. This fact must be taken into account by any model that purports to understand the importance of money.

3. The existence of this function requires a restriction on the derivative of ϕ with respect to its second argument.

4. Notice that we are allowing the transfer x_t to be used in the exchange process in the period in which it is received.

5. The easiest way to solve this problem is to assume that the budget constraints hold with equality and to use these constraints to eliminate c_t from the objective function. Then take the first derivative of the objective function with respect to m_t.

6. Some studies have placed even higher values on this parameter, although it is often argued that very high values of ρ are unrealistic because they imply a much higher degree of risk aversion than many economists find plausible.

7. In the case where there are no exchange externalities, this parameter is negative if the technology is concave in z. When there are externalities, it no longer *necessarily* follows that $h(z)$ must be decreasing in z.

8. Cooley and Hansen [35] have calibrated a model in this way. Their work uses a cash-in-advance technology to model exchange, but it is easily translated to the framework in this chapter.

Bibliography

[1] Abel, Andrew, N. Gregory Mankiw, Lawrence H. Summers, and Richard Zeckhauser. 1989. Assessing dynamic efficiency. *Review of Economic Studies* 56: 1–19.

[2] Allais, Maurice. 1947. *Economie et intérêt*. Paris: Imprimerie Nationale.

[3] Arrow, Kenneth J. 1962. The economic implications of learning by doing. *Review of Economic Studies* 29: 155–73.

[4] Arrow, Kenneth J. 1964. The role of securities in the optimal allocation of risk bearing. *Review of Economic Studies* 31: 91–96.

[5] Arrow, Kenneth J., and Gerard Debreu. 1954. Existence of equilibrium for a competitive economy. *Econometrica* 22: 265–90.

[6] Auerbach, Alan J., and Laurence J. Kotlikoff. 1987. *Dynamic Fiscal Policy*. Cambridge: Cambridge University Press.

[7] Azariadis, Costas. 1981. Self-fulfilling prophecies. *Journal of Economic Theory* 25: 380–96.

[8] Azariadis, Costas, and Roger Guesnerie. 1986. Sunspots and cycles. *Review of Economic Studies* 53: 725–36.

[9] Azariadis, Costas. 1993. *Intertemporal Macroeconomics*. Oxford: Blackwell.

[10] Balasko, Yves, David Cass, and Karl Shell. 1980. Existence of competitive equilibrium in a general overlapping generations model. *Journal of Economic Theory* 23: 307–22.

[11] Bartlesman, E. J., Caballero, R., and R. K. Lyons. 1994. Customer- and supplier-driven externalities. *American Economic Review* 84: 1075–84.

[12] Basu, Susanto, and John G. Fernald. 1995. Are apparent productive spillovers a figment of specification error? *Journal of Monetary Economics* 36(1): 165–88.

[13] Basu, Susanto, and John G. Fernald. 1994b. Constant returns and small markups in US manufacturing. International Finance Discussion Paper 483. Board of Governors of the Federal Reserve System.

[14] Baxter, Marianne, and Robert King. 1991. Productive externalities and business cycles. Discussion Paper 53. Institute for Empirical Macroeconomics. Federal Reserve Bank of Minneapolis.

[15] Bennett, Rosalind L., and Roger E. A. Farmer. 1998. Indeterminacy with non-separable utility. UCLA Discussion Paper.

[16] Benhabib, Jess, and Roger E. A. Farmer. 1991. The aggregate effects of monetary externalities. Mimeo. UCLA.

[17] Benhabib, Jess, and Roger E. A. Farmer. 1994. Indeterminacy and increasing returns. *Journal of Economic Theory* 63: 19–46.

[18] Benhabib, Jess, and Roger E. A. Farmer. 1996. Indeterminacy and sector-specific externalities. *Journal of Monetary Economics* 37: 421–43.

[19] Benhabib, Jess, and K. Nishimura. 1996. Indeterminacy and sunspots with constant returns. Economic Research Report 96-44. C. V. Starr Center for Applied Economics. New York University.

[20] Blanchard, Olivier J., and Charles M. Kahn. 1980. The Solution of linear difference models under rational expectations. *Econometrica* 48: 1305–11.

[21] Blanchard, Olivier J., and Nobu Kiyotaki. 1987. Monopolistic competition and the effects of aggregate demand. *American Economic Review* 77: 647–66.

[22] Boldrin, Michele, and Luigi Montrucchio. 1986. On the indeterminacy of capital accumulation paths. *Journal of Economic Theory* 40: 26–39.

[23] Boldrin, Michele, and Michael Woodford. 1990. Equilibrium models displaying endogenous fluctuations and chaos: A survey. *Journal of Monetary Economics* 1: 133–50.

[24] Brock, William A. 1974. Money and growth: The case of long run perfect foresight. *International Economic Review* 15: 750–77.

[25] Browning, Martin J. 1982. Profit function representations for consumer preferences. Discussion Paper 82/125. Bristol University.

[26] Browning, Martin J., Angus Deaton, and Margaret Irish. 1985. A profitable approach to labor supply and commoditiy demands over the life-cycle. *Econometrica* 53: 503–43.

[27] Bryant, John, and Neil Wallace. 1984. The inefficiency of interest-bearing debt. *Journal of Political Economy* 87: 365–81.

[28] Burnside, Craig, Martin Eichenbaum, and Sergio Rebelo. 1993. Labor hoarding and the business cycle. *Journal of Political Economy* 101: 245–73.

[29] Caballero, Ricardo J., and Richard K. Lyons. 1992. External effects in U.S. procyclical productivity. *Journal of Monetary Economics* 29: 209–26.

[30] Cagan, Philip. 1956. The monetary dynamics of hyperinflation. In Milton Friedman, ed., *Studies in the Quantity Theory of Money*. Chicago, University of Chicago Press.

[31] Cass, David. 1966. On capital overaccumulation in the aggregate, neoclassical model of economic growth: A complete characterization. *Journal of Economic Theory* 4: 200–23.

[32] Cass, David. 1984. Sunspots and financial markets: The leading example. CARESS Working Paper 84-06. University of Pennsylvania.

[33] Cass, David, and Karl Shell. 1983. Do sunspots matter? *Journal of Political Economy* 91: 193–227.

[34] Chiappori, P. A., and Roger Guesnerie. 1991. Sunspot equilibria in sequential market models. In Werner Hildenbrand and Hugo Sonnenschein, eds., *Handbook of Mathematical Economics*, vol. 4. Amsterdam: North Holland.

[35] Cooley, Thomas F., and Gary D. Hansen. 1989. The inflation tax in a real business cycle model. *American Economic Review* 79: 733–48.

[36] Cooper, Russell, and Andrew John. 1988. Coordinating coordination failures in Keynesian models. *Quarterly Journal of Economics* 103: 441–63.

[37] Debreu, Gerard. 1959. *Theory of Value*. Cowles Foundation Monograph 17. New Haven: Yale University Press.

[38] Debreu, Gerard. 1982. Existence of competitive equilibrium. In K. J. Arrow and M. D. Intrilligator, eds., *Handbook of Mathematical Economics*, vol. 2, 697–730. Amsterdam: North Holland.

[39] Debreu, Gerard. 1983. Valuation equilibrium and Pareto optimum. In *Mathematical Economics: Twenty Papers of Gerard Debreu*, 98–104. Cambridge: Cambridge University Press.

[40] Dickey, D. A., and W. A. Fuller. 1979. Distribution of the estimators for autoregressive time series with a unit root. *Journal of the American Statistical Society* 74: 427–31.

[41] Domowitz, Ian R., Glenn Hubbard, and Bruce C. Peterson. 1988. Market structure and cyclical fluctuations in U. S. manufacturing. *Review of Economics and Statistics* 70: 55–66.

[42] Eichenbaum, Martin. 1990. Real business cycle theory: Wisdom or whimsy? *Journal of Economic Dynamics and Control* 15: 607–26.

[43] Epstein, Larry G., and J. Alan Hynes. 1983. The rate of time preference and dynamic economic analysis. *Journal of Political Economy* 91: 611–25.

[44] Epstein, Larry G., and Stanley Zin. 1989. Substitution, risk aversion and the temporal behavior of consumption and asset returns I: A theoretical framework. *Econometrica* 42: 937–69.

[45] Farmer, Roger E. A. 1990. RINCE preferences. *Quarterly Journal of Economics* 420: 43–60.

[46] Farmer, Roger E. A. 1991a. The Lucas critique, policy invariance and multiple equilibria. *Review of Economic Studies* 58: 321–32.

[47] Farmer, Roger E. A. 1991b. Sticky prices. *Economic Journal* 101: 1369–79.

[48] Farmer, Roger E. A. 1992b. Nominal price stickiness as a rational expectations equilibrium. *Journal of Economic Dynamics and Control* 16: 317–37.

[49] Farmer, Roger E. A., and Jang Ting Guo 1994. Real business cycles and the animal spirits hypothesis. *Journal of Economic Theory* 63: 42–73.

[50] Farmer, Roger E. A., and Michael Woodford. 1997. Self-fulfilling prophecies and the business cycle. *Macroeconomic Dynamics* 1: 740–69.

[51] Frisch, Ragnar. 1932. *New Methods of Measuring Marginal Utility*. Tubige: J.C.B. Mohr.

[52] Gale, David. 1973. Pure exchange equilibrium of dynamic economic models. *Journal of Economic Theory* 5: 12–36.

[53] Gali, Jordi. 1994a. Monopolistic competition, business cycles, and the composition of aggregate demand. *Journal of Economic Theory* 63: 73–96.

[54] Galí, Jordi. 1994b. Monopolistic competition, endogenous markups and growth. *European Economic Review* 38: 748–56.

[55] Grandmont, Jean Michel. 1985. On endogenous competitive business cycles. *Econometrica* 53: 995–1046.

[56] Hall, Robert E. 1988. The relation between price and marginal cost in US industry. *Journal of Political Economy* 96: 921–48.

[57] Hall, Robert E. 1990. Invariance properties of Solow's productivity residual. In Peter Diamond, ed., *Growth, Productivity, Unemployment*, 71–112. Cambridge: MIT Press.

[58] Hansen, Gary D. 1985. Indivisible labor and the business cycle. *Journal of Monetary Economics* 16: 309–28.

[59] Hart, Oliver. 1975. On the optimality of equilibrium when the market structure is incomplete. *Journal of Economic Theory* 11: 418–43.

[60] Hicks, John. 1939. *Value and Capital*. Oxford: Clarendon Press.

[61] Hodrick, Robert J., and Edward C. Prescott. 1997. Post-war U.S. business cycles: A descriptive empirical investigation. *Journal of Money Credit and Banking* 29: 1–16.

[62] İmrohoroğlu, S. 1993. Testing for sunspot equilibria in the German hyperinflation. *Journal of Economic Dynamics and Control* 17: 289–317.

[63] Jevons, H. Stanley. 1875. The solar period and the price of corn. Reprinted in *Investigations in Currency and Finance*, 2nd ed. London, 1909.

[64] Kehoe, Timothy J., and David K. Levine. 1985. Comparative statics and perfect foresight in infinite horizon economies. *Econometrica* 53: 433–53.

[65] Keynes, John Maynard. 1936. *The General Theory of Employment, Interest and Money*. London: Macmillan.

[66] King, Robert, Charles Plosser, and Sergio Rebelo. 1988. Production growth and business cycles, I: The basic neo-classical model. *Journal of Monetary Economics* 21: 195–232.

[67] King, Robert, Charles Plosser, and Sergio Rebelo. 1988. Production growth and business cycles, II: New directions. *Journal of Monetary Economics* 21: 309–42.

[68] Kiyotaki, Nobu. 1985. *Macroeconomics of Imperfect Competition*. PhD dissertation. Harvard University.

[69] Koopmans, Tjalling J. 1960. Stationary ordinal utility and impatience. *Econometrica* 33: 287–309.

[70] Koopmans, Tjalling C. 1965. The concept of economic growth. In *The Econometric Approach to Development Planning*. Pontificae Academiae Scientiarum Scripta Varia, 28. Amsterdam: North Holland.

[71] Kreps, David M., and E. L. Porteus. 1978. Temporal resolution of uncertainty and dynamic choice theory. *Econometrica* 46: 185–200.

[72] Kydland, Fynn E., and Edward C. Prescott. 1982. Time to build and aggregate fluctuations. *Econometrica* 50: 1345–70.

[73] Lahiri, Amartya. 1998. Growth and equilibrium indeterminacy: The role of capital mobility. Working Paper. UCLA.

[74] Long, John B., Jr., and Charles I. Plosser. 1983. Real business cycles. *Journal of Political Economy* 91: 39–69.

[75] Lucas, Robert E., Jr. 1976. Econometric policy evaluation: A critique. In Karl Brunner, and Alan H. Meltzer, eds., *The Phillips Curve and Labor Markets*. Carnegie Rochester Conference Series on Public Policy, vol. 1. Amsterdam: North Holland.

[76] Lucas, Robert E., Jr. 1978. Asset prices in an exchange economy. *Econometrica* 46: 1429–45.

[77] Lucas, Robert E., Jr. 1988. On the mechanics of economic development. *Journal of Monetary Economics* 22: 3–42.

[78] Lucas, Robert E., Jr., and Nancy Stokey. 1984. Optimal growth with many consumers. *Journal of Economic Theory* 32: 139–71.

[79] Malinvaud, Edmund M. 1953. Capital accumulation and efficient allocation of resources. *Econometrica* 21: 233–68.

[80] Mankiw, N. Gregory, and David Romer. 1991. *New Keynesian Economics*. Cambridge: MIT Press.

[81] Manuelli, Rodi, and Larry E. Jones. 1990. A convex model of equilibrium growth: Theory and policy implications. *Journal of Political Economy* vol. 98: 1008–38.

[82] Mas-Colell, Andreu. 1985. *The Theory of General Equilibrium: A Differentiable Approach*. Cambridge: Cambridge University Press.

[83] Matheny, Kenneth J. 1992. *Essays on Beliefs and Business Cycles*. PhD thesis. UCLA.

[84] McKenzie, Lionel W. 1954. On equilibrium in Graham's model of world trade and other competitive systems. *Econometrica* 22: 147–61.

[85] Merton, Robert K. 1948. The self-fulfilling prophecy. *Antioch Review* 193–211.

[86] Negishi, Takashi. 1960. Welfare economics and existence of an equilibrium for a competitive economy. *Metroeconomica* 12: 92–97.

[87] Nelson, Charles, and Charles Plosser. 1982. Trends and random walks in macroeconomic time series. *Journal of Monetary Economics* 10: 139–62.

[88] Pareto, V. 1906. *Manuel d' économie politique.* Paris: Marcel Giard.

[89] Patinkin, Don 1956. *Money Income and Prices*. 2d ed. Cambridge: MIT Press 1989.

[89a] Pelloni, Alessandra, and Robert Waldmann. 1997. Indeterminacy in a growth model with elastic labour supply. *Rivista Internazionale di Scienze Sociali*, no. 3: 201–11.

[90] Pesaran, M. Hashem. 1987. *The Limits to Rational Expectations*. Oxford: Blackwell.

[91] Phelps, Edmund S. 1961. The golden rule of capital accumulation: A fable for growthmen. *American Economic Review* 51: 638–43.

[92] Ramsey, Frank P. 1927. A contribution to the theory of taxation. *Economic Journal* 37: 47–61.

[93] Rogerson, Richard. 1988. Indivisible labor, lotteries and equilibrium. *Journal of Monetary Economics* 21: 3–16.

[94] Romer, Paul M. 1986. Increasing returns and long-run growth. *Journal of Political Economy* 94: 1002–37.

[95] Rotemberg, J. J., and M. Woodford. 1991. Markups and the business cycle. In O. J Blanchard and S. Fischer, eds., *NBER Macroeconomics Annual* 1991, 63–129. Cambridge: MIT Press.

[96] Rotemberg, J. J., and M. Woodford. 1992. Oligopolistic pricing and the effects of aggregate demand on economic activity. *Journal of Political Economy* 100: 1153–1207.

[97] Samuelson, Paul A. 1958. An exact consumption-loan model of interest with or without the social contrivance of money. *Journal of Political Economy* 66: 467–82.

[98] Sargan, J. Dennis. 1984. Alternative models for rational expectations in some simple irregular cases. Unpublished manuscript. London School of Economics.

[99] Sargent, Thomas J., and Neil Wallace. 1973. Rational expectations and the dynamics of hyperinflation. *International Economic Review* 14: 328–50.

[100] Sargent Thomas J., and Neil Wallace. 1985. Identification and estimation of a model of hyperinflation with a continuum of sunspot equilibria. Discussion Paper 220. University of Minnesota.

[101] Schmitt-Grohé, Stephanie. 1997. Comparing four models of aggregate fluctautions due to self-fulfilling expectations. *Journal of Economic Theory* 72: 96–147.

[102] Shafer, Wayne, and Hugo Sonnenschein. 1982. Market demand and excess demand functions. In Kenneth J. Arrow and Michael D. Intrilligator, eds., *Handbook of Mathematical Economics*, vol. 2, 671–92. Amsterdam: North Holland.

[103] Shea, John. 1993. Do supply curves slope up? *Quarterly Journal Of Economics* 108: 1–32.

[104] Shell, Karl. 1971. Notes on the economics of infinity. *Journal of Political Economy* 79: 1002–11.

[105] Sims, Christopher. 1989. Models and their uses. *American Journal of Agricultural Economics* 71: 489–94.

[106] Sims, Christopher. 1980. Comparison of interwar and postwar business cycles: Monetarism reconsidered. *American Economic Review* 70: 250–57.

[107] Solow, Robert M. 1956. A contribution to the theory of economic growth. *Quarterly Journal of Economics* 70: 65–94.

[108] Spordone, Argia M. 1991. Procyclical productivity: External economies or labor hoarding? Working Paper. University of Chicago.

[109] Stokey, Nancy L., and Lucas, Robert E., Jr., with Edward C. Prescott. 1989. *Recursive Methods in Economic Dynamics*. Cambridge: Harvard University Press.

[110] Summers, Lawrence H. 1991. The scientific illusion in empirical macroeconomics. *Scandinavian Journal of Economics* 93: 129–48.

[111] Swan, T. W. 1956. Economic growth and capital accumulation. *Economic Record* 32: 334–61.

[112] Wallace, N. 1983. A legal restrictions theory of the demand for "money" and the role of monetary policy. *Federal Reserve Bank of Minneapolis Quarterly Review* (Winter): 1–7.

[113] Weil, Philippe. 1990. Nonexpected utility and macroeconomics. *Quarterly Journal of Economics* 420: 29–42.

[114] Wilson, Charles. 1979. A infinite horizon model with money. In Jerry R. Green and José A. Scheinkman, eds., *General Equilibrium, Growth, and Trade*. New York: Academic Press.

[115] Woodford, Michael. 1986. Stationary sunspot equilibria in a finance constrained economy. *Journal of Economic Theory* 40: 128–37.

Name Index

Subject Index